Name _____ Date _____

Breaking SSAT
Lower Level (Gr.4)

Amanda Yang

Name _____ Date _____

Published January 2017
All rights reserved. No part of this book maybe copied, reproduced, duplicated, stored in a retrieval system, or transmitted, in any form or by any means without the prior written permission of the author.
homathandchess@hotmail.com

© Amanda Yang

SSAT and SAT are registered trade mark of the College Examination Board which is not affiliated with this product.

Name _____   Date _____

Index

A. **Whole Number** 7
    A1. Whole number place value 7
    A2. Addition 18
    A3. Subtraction 34
    A4. Multiplication 43
    A5. Division 61
    A6. Order of operations 66

B. **Whole Number Problem Solving** 74
    B1. How many triangles are there? 74
    B2. How many figures are there? 75
    B3. Congruent figures 77
    B4. One stroke drawing 78
    B5. Tiling 79
    B6. Number puzzles 80
    B7. Counting principles 82
    B8. Digit and number problems 85
    B9. Guess and check 86
    B10. Drawing a picture 87
    B11. Making a table 88
    B12. Coin problems 89
    B13. Age problems 91
    B14. Balance puzzles 93
    B15. Chicken and rabbit problems 95
    B16. Digital clock pattern 97
    B17. Not so clock pattern 98
    B18. Drawer problems 99
    B19. Number series 101
    B20. Working problems 103
    B21. Venn diagrams 104
    B22. Working backwards 106
    B23. Sum and difference problems 107
    B24. Give and take problems 108
    B25. Sum, difference, and sum difference multiple 109

C. **Rounding and Estimating** 110
    C1. Rounding whole numbers 110
    C2. Whole number estimations 115
    C3. Problem solving 121

D. **Number Patterns** 122

Name _____   Date _____

    D1. Patterns 125
    D2. T-Tables 128

E.   Time 131

    E1. 12-hour clock and 24-hour clock 131
    E2. Seconds, minutes, and hours 135
    E3. Hours, days, weeks, months, and years 140
    E4. Regular year and leap year 146
    E5. Calendar 147

F.   Coins 148

    F1. Coin problems 149
    F2. Problem solving 153
    F3. Rounding decimals 155
    F4. Decimal estimations 156

G.   Decimals 159

    G1. Units and tenths 159
    G2. Equivalent decimals 161
    G3. Hundredths 162
    G4. Thousandths 167
    G5. Adding decimals 177
    G6. Subtracting decimals 183
    G7. Multiplying decimals 187
    G8. Multiplying decimals by 10s 195
    G9. Dividing decimals 197
    G10. Rounding when divide decimals 213
    G11. Decimal operations 221
    G12. Problem solving 223

H.   Number Sense 225

    H1. Factors 225
    H2. Multiples 226
    H3. Even and odd numbers 230
    H4. Divisibility rules 231
    H5. Prime and composite numbers 233

I.   Integers 237

    I1. Representing integers 237
    I2. Word problems 241

J.   Fractions 243

    J1. Representing fractions 243
    J2. Fractions to decimals 244

Name _____ Date _____

J3. Equivalent fractions 253
J4. Lowest term fractions 260
J5. Equivalent fractions 263
J6. Proper fraction, improper fractions, and mixed numbers 264
J7. Improper fraction to mixed number 266
J8. Mixed number to improper fraction 268
J9. Comparing fractions 270
J10. Addition with like denominators 276
J11. Subtraction with like denominators 281
J12. Multiplication of fractions...285
J13. Division of fractions 292
J14. Problem solving 296

K.   Percentages 307

K1. Percentages to decimals..310
K2. Decimals to percentages 311
K3. Fractions to percentages 312
K4. Fractions, decimals, ratios, and percentages 315
K5. Problem solving...319

L.   Ratio and proportion 322

L1. Ratios 322
L2. Proportion 327
L3. Unit Price 331
L4. Unit Rate 332

M.   Measurement 336

M1. Mass and weight 336
M2. Length 339
M3. Area 342
M4. Volume 344
M5. Capacity 345
M6. The Metric System 348
M7. Weight (British units) 351
M8. Length (British Units) 352

N.   Plane Figures 353

N1. Directions...353
N2. Lines 355
N3. Angles 358
N4. Shapes 361
N5. Triangle 362
N6. Quadrilaterals 363
N7. Slide 368

Name _____ Date _____

N8. Turn 369
N9. Reflection 370
N10. Symmetry lines 371
N11. Congruent figures 373
N12. Similar figures 376

O. Perimeter and Area 377

O1. Perimeter 377
O2. Area 382
O3. Area and perimeter 389

P. Solids 393

P1. Name of solids 393
P2. Pyramids or prisms 394
P3. Faces of solids 398
P4. Nets of boxes 399
P5. Skeletons 401

Q. Graphs 402

Q1. Tally table 402
Q2. Line plots 405
Q3. Stem-and-leaf plots 408
Q4. Mean and range 410
Q5. Pictographs 413
Q6. Bar graphs 415
Q7. Circle graphs 417
Q8. Venn diagrams 418

R. Probability 420

Test 1 429

Test 2 436

Test 3 443

Test 4 450

Test 5 457

Name _____   Date _____

A. Whole Number

A1. Whole number place value

Thousands

Thousands	Hundreds	Tens	Ones
4	3	2	1

Standard form	4 321
Expanded form	4 000 + 300 + 20 + 1
Words	four thousand three hundred twenty-one

Write each number as a numeral in standard form.

1. six thousand, three hundred seven   _____
2. eight thousand, four hundred thirty-five _____
3. nine thousand, one hundred seventy   _____
4. five thousand, nine hundred fifteen   _____
5. three thousand, forty-one   _____
6. four thousand, two hundred eighty-nine   _____
7. five thousand, six   _____
8. four thousand, seven hundred thirteen   _____
9. seven thousand, twenty-five   _____
10. six thousand, ninety-two   _____
11. four thousand, thirty-six   _____
12. two thousand, six hundred forty   _____

Write each number in words.

1. 4528 _____
2. 6291 _____
3. 3406 _____
4. 8003 _____
5. 5014 _____

Name _____   Date _____

Write each number in standard form.

1. $3\,000 + 100 + 40 + 2 =$
2. $5\,000 + 200 + 30 + 8 =$
3. $2\,000 + 600 + 30 + 1 =$
4. $4\,000 + 900 + 30 + 2 =$
5. $2\,000 + 40 + 6 =$
6. $5\,000 + 200 + 8 =$
7. $4\,000 + 900 + 30 + 7 =$
8. $6\,000 + 800 + 20 + 4 =$
9. $8\,000 + 700 + 6 =$
10. $3\,000 + 800 + 50 + 1 =$
11. $5\,000 + 300 + 20 + 9 =$
12. $6\,000 + 800 + 7 =$
13. $1\,000 + 500 + 60 + 4 =$
14. $9\,000 + 700 + 20 + 6 =$
15. $7\,000 + 50 + 4 =$
16. $4\,000 + 300 + 3 =$

Write the following numbers from greatest to least.

1. 3680 5680 3608 3086 _____
2. 5721 5021 5701 5720 _____
3. 7890 9012 6473 5842 _____
4. 2498 7821 2509 2056 _____

Count in 10s.

1. 2500, 2510, ____ ____ ____ ____
2. 1380, 1390, ____ ____ ____ ____

Count in 100s.

3. 1060, 1160, ____ ____ ____ ____
4. 6538, 6638, ____ ____ ____ ____

Name _____ Date _____

Ten Thousands

Ten Thousands	Thousands	Hundreds	Tens	Ones
8	3	5	2	6

Standard form   83 526
Expanded form   80 000 + 3 000 + 500 + 20 + 6
Words   eighty-three thousand five hundred twenty-six

Write in expanded form

1. 56 732 = 50 000 + _____ + 700 + _____ + 2

2. 81 574 = _____ + 1000 + 500 + _____ + _____

3. 29316 = _____ + _____ + _____ + _____ + _____

4. 93 516 = _____ + _____ + _____ + _____ + _____

5. 12 684 = _____ + _____ + _____ + _____ + _____

Write in standard form.

1. 30 000 + 6 000 + 100 + 50 + 9 = _____

2. 70 000 + 8 000 + 20 + 3 = _____

3. 20 000 + 200 + 5 = _____

4. 60 000 + 7 000 + 9 = _____

5. 50 000 + 3 000 + 10 + 9 = _____

6. 90 000 + 5 000 + 700 + 20 + 8 = _____

7. 10 000 + 1 = _____

8. 10 000 + 100 + 20 = _____

Name _____   Date _____

Write each number in words.

1. 58 643 _____

2. 50 089 _____

3. 20 430 _____

4. 45 007 _____

5. 96 000 _____

Write the following in numerals.

1. forty-three thousand two hundred ten   _____

2. ninety thousand three hundred seventeen   _____

3. eighteen thousand two hundred five   _____

4. thirty-seven thousand four hundred two   _____

5. seventy thousand eight   _____

6. twelve thousand six hundred seventy-four   _____

Find the largest number

1. 36 075   36 157   34 945   36 167   _____

2. 46 371   45 713   46 373   46 271   _____

3. 56 292   56 382   56 392   45 923   _____

4. 74 634   74 578   64 634   74 637   _____

5. 82 465   82 365   81465   82 460   _____

Name _____   Date _____

What is the value of the digit '6' in each number?

1. 24 683 _____
2. 46 712 _____
3. 62 185 _____
4. 32 836 _____
5. 34 568 _____
6. 92 651 _____

Compare by using an inequality sign > or < to make each statement true.

1. 36 793 ____ 41 634
2. 64 009 ____ 64 900
3. 75 395 ____ 75 299
4. 28 452 ____ 31 452
5. 53 852 ____ 48 001
6. 16 482 ____ 16 480

What is each number?

1. 400 greater than 60 000 _____
2. 3000 less than 40 000 _____
3. 2000 more than 60 000 _____
4. 500 less than 80 000 _____
5. 10 less than 40 000 _____
6. 20 000 more than 60 000 _____
7. 1 more than 99 999 _____
8. Between 99 999 and 100 001 _____
9. Between 99 998 and 100 000 _____

Name _____ Date _____

Numbers above 100 000

Millions			Thousands			Ones		
Hundreds	Tens	Ones	Hundreds	Tens	Ones	Hundreds	Tens	Ones
9	8	7	6	5	4	3	2	1

Standard form   987 654 321
Expanded form   900 000 000 + 80 000 000 + 7 000 000 + 600 000 + 50 000 + 4 000 + 300 + 20 + 1
Words: Nine hundred eighty-seven million six hundred fifty-four thousand three hundred twenty-one

Write each number as a numeral in standard form.

1. Four hundred thirty-two thousand, six hundred seventy-eight   _____

2. One million nine hundred fourteen thousand, three hundred sixty-eight   _____

3. Fourteen million, seven hundred sixty-one thousand, nine hundred fifty-two   _____

4. Two hundred thirteen million, ninety-three thousand, three hundred eighty-five   _____

5. Nine hundred six million, three hundred twelve thousand, four hundred two   _____

6. Six hundred sixty-one million, seven hundred nine thousand, nine hundred nine   _____

7. Thirty million, four hundred forty-four thousand, four hundred eighty-five   _____

8. Fifteen million, two hundred twenty-six thousand, five hundred eighty-seven   _____

9. One hundred million, one hundred two thousand, three hundred forty-five   _____

10. Two hundred three million, four hundred fifteen thousand, nine hundred one   _____

11. Eight million, two hundred twenty-one thousand, seven hundred sixty-nine   _____

12. Nine million, three thousand, one   _____

Name _____ Date _____

Give the value of the digit '5'

1. 35 288 100   Five millions
2. 52 309   _____
3. 3 452 996   _____
4. 12 500 318   _____
5. 386 377 235   _____
6. 407 685 120   _____
7. 300 214 253   _____
8. 566 322 178   _____
9. 315 663 794   _____
10. 281 336 756   _____

Write the following numbers in words.

	MILLIONS			THOUSANDS			ONES		
	Hundreds	Tens	ones	Hundreds	Tens	ones	Hundreds	Tens	Ones
1.			2	6	3	4	3	2	1
2.	3	5	1	7	8	0	0	0	9
3.	5	0	0	6	3	1	7	9	8
4.	4	5	0	0	7	9	2	5	3
5.	1	3	2	0	5	7	8	4	6

1. _____

2. _____

3. _____

4. _____

5. _____

Name _____ Date _____

Fill in the blanks.

	THOUSANDS			ONES		
	Millions	Hundreds	Tens	ones	Hundreds	Tens	Ones
4 875 241	4	8	7	5	2	4	1
5 670 230							
8 642 605							
6 007 842							
753 007							
2 660 974							
1 018 406							
9 709 615							
9 613 712							
3 088 099							

In 7 654 321, what is the place value of the following digits?

'7' stands for _____   '3' stands for _____

'6' stands for _____   '2' stands for _____

'5' stands for _____   '1' stands for _____

'4' stands for _____

Write each number in standard form.

1. 70 000 + 4 000 + 200 + 80 + 9 = _____

2. 50 000 000 + 3 000 000 + 10 000 + 7 000 + 9 = _____

3. 8 000 000 + 500 000 + 10 000 + 7000 + 6 = _____

4. 2 000 000 + 3 000 + 600 + 9 = _____

5. 10 000 000 + 9 000 000 + 60 000 + 3 000 + 20 = _____

6. 6 000 000 + 200 000 + 80 000 + 3 000 + 400 + 10 + 5 = _____

7. 9 000 000 + 500 000 + 30 000 + 8 000 + 6 = _____

Name _____ Date _____

For each of the numbers, find the digit in each indicated place.

1. 24 689   thousands' place   4

2. 46 782   tens' place   _____

3. 1 567 890   tens' place   _____

4. 123 568 804   ten millions' place _____

5. 349 563 126   hundred thousands' place _____

6. 576 873   ones' place   _____

7. 673 653 904   millions' place   _____

8. 2 660 974   hundreds' place   _____

9. 263 4321   millions' place   _____

10. 873 642   thousands' place   _____

11. 78 234 763   ten thousands' place _____

12. 6 643 302   hundred thousands' place _____

Find the pattern and fill in the blanks.

1. 35 600   35 700   35 800   _____ _____ _____

2. 23 250   23 500   23 750   _____ _____ _____

3. 463 542   464 542   465 542   _____ _____ _____

4. 670 200   675 200   680 200   _____ _____ _____

5. 720 333   740 332   760 331   _____ _____

Name _____ Date _____

Find the largest and smallest numbers that can be formed by the digits given.

1. 4, 5, 7, 8, 1, 0, 9 (7-digit number)

    largest: smallest:

2. 2, 6, 4, 5, 8, 3, 5 (7- digit number)

    largest: smallest:

3. 1, 8, 5, 3, 7, 3, 6 (7 -digit number)

    largest: smallest:

4. 7, 3, 5, 6, 0, 9, 4 (7 -digit number)

    largest: smallest:

What is this number?
- It is between 100 000 and 200 000
- Three of its digits are odd number.   The rest are zeros.
- The ten-thousand's digit is three times the hundred thousand's digit.
- The thousand's digit is nine times the hundred thousand's digit.

What is this number?
- It is greater than 400 000
- The sum of all its digits is 16.
- The hundred's digit is 8.
- It has no zeros.

Name _____   Date _____

Renaming Numbers

1. 4 600 is _____ hundreds.

2. 520 is _____ tens.

3. 3 000 is _____ thousands.

4. 5 000 is _____ hundreds.

5. 2 740 000 is _____ hundreds.

6. 63 000 000 is _____ millions.

7. 4 000 000 is _____ ten thousands.

8. 81 000 000 is _____ hundred thousands.

9. 610 000 is _____ hundreds.

10. 540 000 is _____ hundreds.

11. 210 000 000 is _____ millions.

12. 439 000 000 is _____ ten thousands.

13. 425 000 is _____ tens.

14. 890 000 is _____ thousands.

15. 120 000 000 is _____ millions.

16. 63 000 is _____ thousand.

17. 43 000 000 is _____ million.

18. 84 000 000 is _____ hundred thousand.

Name _____ Date _____

A2. Addition

Commutative property of addition

We can add numbers in any order, and the sum will stay the same.
$$a + b = b + a$$
Example: $35 + 67 = 67 + 35$

1. $45 + 560 = 560 +$ _____
2. $462 +$ _____ $= 575 + 462$
3. $270 + 460 = 460 +$ _____
4. $673 +$ _____ $= 427 + 673$
5. $347 +$ _____ $= 627 +$ _____
6. $451 +$ _____ $= 231 +$ _____
7. _____ $+ 509 =$ _____ $+ 258$
8. _____ $+ 731 =$ _____ $+ 426$

Evaluate with commutative property of addition.

1. $246 + 532 + 54$
   $= 246 + 54 + 532$
   $= 300 + 532$
   $= 832$
2. $225 + 463 + 75$

3. $468 + 309 + 32$
4. $521 + 462 + 79$

5. $263 + 157 + 37$
6. $572 + 367 + 28$

7. $538 + 357 + 162$
8. $572 + 637 + 228$

Name _____ Date _____

9. 462 + 79 + 538

10. 635 + 347 + 365

11. 426 + 557 + 574

12. 738 + 576 + 262

13. 367 + 338 + 133

14. 573 + 525 + 1427

15. 648 + 366 + 352

16. 758 + 355 + 242

17. 675 + 459 + 25

18. 648 + 67 + 52

19. 784 + 463 + 216

20. 668 + 566 + 332

21. 579 + 568 + 421

22. 684 + 565 + 316

Name _____ Date _____

Associative property of addition

We can we change the order of addition, and the sum will stay the same.
$$(a + b) + c = a + (b + c)$$
Example: $(57 + 34) + 66 = 57 + (4 + 66) = 57 + 100 = 157$

Evaluate with associative property of addition.

1. $(78 + 45) + 55$

    $= 78 + (45 + 55)$

    $= 78 + 100$

    $= 178$

2. $(84 + 57) + 43$

3. $(23 + 74) + 26$

4. $(48 + 89) + 11$

5. $(72 + 86) + 14$

6. $(68 + 77) + 23$

7. $(58 + 73) + 27$

8. $(69 + 36) + 64$

9. $(84 + 29) + 71$

10. $(64 + 53) + 47$

11. (456 + 28) + 72

12. (647 + 59) + 41

13. (683 + 32) + 68

14. (757 + 56) + 44

15. (547 + 216) + 784

16. (670 + 456) + 544

17. (649 + 434) + 566

18. (353 + 167) + 833

19. (768 + 351) + 649

20. (68 + 253) + 747

21. (57 + 564) + 436

22. (573 + 469) + 31

23. (262 + 509) + 191

24. (671 + 285) + 315

Name _____   Date _____

Shortcuts with communicative and associative property of addition

1. Regroup tens, hundreds, or thousands.
Example: 23 + 42 + 77 + 38 = (23 + 77) + (42 + 38) = 100 + 80 = 180

Evaluate with shortcuts where applicable.

1.   42 + 73 + 27 + 58

       = (42 + 58) + (73 + 27)

       = 100 + 100

       = 200

2.   26 + 39 + 44 + 61

3.   85 + 36 + 115 + 34

4.   51 + 23 + 49 + 57

5.   73 + 42 + 28 + 27

6.   49 + 36 + 51 + 74

7.   153 + 57 + 63 + 47

8.   535 + 58 + 52 + 65

9.   73 + 69 + 51 + 127

10.   56 + 368 + 32 + 84

11.   43 + 542 + 77 + 158

12.   62 + 59 + 61 + 438

Name _____   Date _____

13. 651 + 156 + 244 + 349

14. 758 + 47 + 2 + 53

15. 74 + 481 + 226 + 19

16. 562 + 83 + 217 + 338

17. 462 + 157 + 538 + 43

18. 677 + 462 + 123 + 358

19. 752 + 680 + 148 + 120

20. 365 + 609 + 81 + 235

21. 572 + 758 + 132 + 128

22. 363 + 169 + 537 + 121

23. 567 + 436 + 133 + 144

24. 574 + 253 + 347 + 106

25. 537 + 416 + 63 + 314

26. 609 + 354 + 246 + 211

Name _____   Date _____

2. Split one number, and then regroup.
Example: 75 + 36 = 75 + 25 + 11 = 100 + 11 = 111

Evaluate using shortcuts where applicable.

1. 68 + 76

   = 68 + 32 + 44

   = 100 + 44

   = 144

2. 76 + 47

3. 54 + 69

4. 79 + 33

5. 54 + 67

6. 29 + 87

7. 48 + 74

8. 45 + 87

9. 187 + 35

10. 368 + 53

11. 53 + 157

12. 376 + 57

13. 467 + 354

14. 359 + 563

15. 684 + 109

16. 658 + 267

17. 453 + 678

18. 756 + 465

19. 473 + 269

20. 568 + 175

21. 576 + 368

22. 378 + 357

23. 476 + 257

24. 369 + 434

25. 387 + 756

26. 489 + 346

Evaluate using shortcuts where applicable.

1. 48 + 56 + 71

    = 48 + 52 + 4 + 71

    = (48 + 52) + 4 + 71

    = 100 + 75

    = 175

2. 57 + 35 + 69

3. 86 + 45 + 57

4. 48 + 55 + 74

5. 64 + 71 + 88

6. 59 + 36 + 78

7. 73 + 46 + 58

8. 42 + 26 + 79

9. 53 + 16 + 95

10. 32 + 43 + 69

11. 76 + 56 + 87

12. 57 + 28 + 49

Name _____   Date _____

13. 435 + 317 + 87   14. 562 + 274 + 59

15. 543 + 169 + 76   16. 473 + 261 + 88

17. 567 + 352 + 177   18. 409 + 524 + 47

19. 462 + 460 + 139   20. 256 + 328 + 479

21. 536 + 153 + 275   22. 466 + 257 + 351

23. 286 + 351 + 123   24. 259 + 316 + 768

25. 734 + 189 + 365   26. 162 + 687 + 146

3. Change addition to subtraction.
Example: 32 + 59 = 32 + 60 − 1 = 92 − 1 = 91

Evaluate using shortcuts where applicable.

1.   45 + 78

      = 45 + 80 − 2

      = 125 − 2

      = 123

2.   68 + 47

3.   28 + 36

4.   77 + 26

5.   57 + 68

6.   59 + 18

7.   247 + 78

8.   317 + 18

9.   52 + 249

10.   318 + 55

11.   174 + 268

12.   365 + 179

Rapidly add by regrouping and reordering.

1.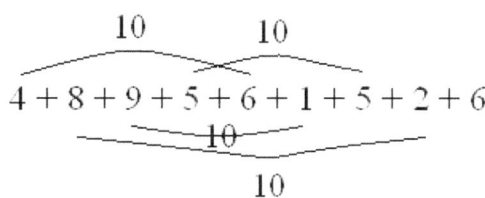

   = 40 + 6
   = 46

2. 7 + 5 + 8 + 3 + 9 + 2 + 5 + 7 + 1

3. 4 + 6 + 7 + 8 + 6 + 9 + 1 + 2 + 3

4. 5 + 4 + 7 + 4 + 8 + 6 + 3 + 2 + 5

5. 7 + 8 + 7 + 1 + 2 + 3 + 9 + 6 + 4

6. 6 + 8 + 4 + 7 + 9 + 3 + 5 + 2 + 1

7. 6 + 7 + 8 + 7 + 4 + 9 + 2 + 3 + 1

8. 7 + 4 + 5 + 6 + 5 + 8 + 9 + 3 + 2

9. 4 + 5 + 6 + 1 + 4 + 8 + 2 + 6 + 5

10. 2 + 8 + 9 + 1 + 6 + 3 + 3 + 4 + 5

11. 5 + 2 + 7 + 4 + 1 + 3 + 5 + 2 + 9

12. 3 + 6 + 2 + 2 + 7 + 3 + 1 + 8 + 3

Group tens to add more numbers.

1.
```
    4 2
  ┌ 2 7 ┐
  └ 8 5 ┘
    5 8
  ┌ 4 5 ┐
  │ 6 3 │
  └ 4 5 ┘
+   5 7
    4 2
+ 3 8
─────────
    4 2 2
```

2.
```
    5 8
    9 4
    5 2
    7 7
    3 3
    8 5
    3 7
+   2 6
```

3.
```
    4 1
    5 6
    2 3
    6 2
    8 7
    6 4
    2 8
+   5 3
```

4.
```
    9 5
    6 3
    4 2
    2 0
    5 7
    3 4
    6 5
+   2 3
```

5.
```
    1 7
    4 5
    2 3
    5 7
    3 4
    7 7
    2 8
+   4 6
```

6.
```
    2 4
    6 7
    4 5
    3 3
    7 6
    3 7
    3 3
+   6 8
```

7.
```
    6 1
    4 0
    2 6
    5 4
    7 6
    4 3
    6 2
+   3 7
```

8.
```
    3 6
    2 7
    5 4
    3 8
    6 2
    3 4
    4 6
+   1 3
```

9.
```
    5 7
    4 3
    8 6
    5 4
    3 2
    2 1
    5 5
+   4 9
```

10.
```
    3 4
    4 1
    6 7
    2 4
    8 3
    6 2
    5 1
+   2 8
```

11.
```
    4 1
    3 7
    6 8
    3 3
    6 4
    7 1
    2 6
+   1 9
```

12.
```
    2 2
    6 6
    4 4
    8 6
    5 1
    8 6
    2 1
+   6 8
```

30

Name _____   Date _____

13.
```
    3  4
    6  2
    9  4
    6  8
    4  6
    6  4
    3  3
+   1  6
```

14.
```
    3  3
    2  5
    4  2
    3  5
    1  7
    6  5
    8  2
+   5  8
```

15.
```
    4  0
    2  7
    6  8
    3  3
    7  5
    4  2
    3  6
+   6  5
```

16.
```
    7  3
    4  6
    2  7
    1  3
    4  1
    2  7
    5  4
+   6  2
```

17.
```
    5  7
    3  5
    3  3
    6  5
    7  3
    3  8
    5  7
+   1  6
```

18.
```
    2  7
    5  5
    7  8
    3  6
    6  4
    2  3
    1  1
+   4  8
```

19.
```
    3  6
    5  4
    1  2
    8  8
    3  1
    5  7
    2  4
+   5  3
```

20.
```
    3  5
    6  2
    4  4
    2  6
    1  3
    6  3
    8  5
+   7  7
```

21.
```
    2  7
    6  5
    5  3
    3  1
    6  6
    7  2
    3  5
+   1  4
```

22.
```
    3  5
    5  7
    1  5
    5  8
    6  4
    7  2
    3  6
+   2  1
```

23.
```
    3  1
    6  4
    4  6
    7  3
    3  6
    6  3
    1  2
+   7  7
```

24.
```
    3  6
    1  3
    6  1
    7  6
    4  4
    7  2
    3  6
+   5  3
```

25.	26.	27.	28.
1 2 3	4 0 2	3 6 3	3 5 4
5 5 5	3 4 5	4 7 2	6 7 2
3 3 0	7 6 3	1 0 6	4 0 6
1 6 7	3 3 6	3 4 3	6 5 0
2 3 2	7 6 2	6 6 6	3 2 6
4 5 4	4 1 5	4 3 1	2 7 3
5 7 1	2 2 3	7 2 5	7 9 1
+ 3 5 6	+ 1 5 8	+ 3 5 9	+ 5 3 5

29.	30.	31.	32.
4 4 4	2 4 4	4 0 2	3 0 2
3 6 6	5 6 6	6 4 6	6 6 5
2 7 3	6 7 4	8 6 7	4 2 1
5 0 0	1 2 3	3 8 6	5 6 7
3 3 7	2 6 1	2 3 4	4 4 4
6 4 0	2 6 5	7 0 1	3 7 6
3 8 3	6 8 9	4 2 3	8 5 0
+ 1 1 9	+ 8 3 7	+ 2 4 3	+ 2 8 5

33.	34.	35.	36.
4 4 9	5 2 6	5 5 1	3 5 5
6 4 6	3 6 4	2 3 3	6 7 3
2 6 4	7 3 2	4 7 7	4 5 6
7 2 7	4 5 3	6 7 4	7 2 6
8 6 0	7 1 2	8 3 3	4 3 8
2 0 3	2 3 6	3 5 7	7 6 3
7 0 3	9 6 7	6 3 5	4 6 2
+ 3 3 0	+ 8 4 8	+ 4 6 3	+ 2 4 4

37.	38.	39.	40.
434	442	255	542
653	327	583	365
446	567	707	763
743	782	383	286
260	453	756	202
388	638	703	637
620	364	545	404
+ 597	+ 853	+ 922	+ 240

41.	42.	43.	44.
532	463	663	403
300	376	807	566
266	602	254	583
575	675	326	737
250	407	166	202
836	765	602	648
374	433	848	970
+ 458	+ 353	+ 980	+ 129

45.	46.	47.	48.
523	551	685	164
366	370	403	642
534	587	877	904
167	736	342	650
582	883	227	335
721	359	772	567
237	774	986	350
+ 870	+ 445	+ 434	+ 475

A3. Subtraction

1. 21474 − 5726 = 15748   15748 + 5726 = 21474
2. 57390 − 3682 = +
3. 52681 − 4729 = +
4. 58203 − 14838 = +
5. 16839 − 2572 = +
6. 46829 − 36104 = +
7. 47294 − 3748 = +
8. 18316 − 17059 = +
9. 26281 − 6370 = +
10. 10472 − 8629 = +
11. 35016 − 16387 = +
12. 37085 − 6896 = +
13. 47142 − 7329 = +
14. 30018 − 16389 = +

Name _____   Date _____

Complimentary Subtraction

1. 10 – 4 =
2. 10 – 8 =
3. 10 – 9 =
4. 10 – 7 =
5. 100 – 7 =
6. 100 – 5 =
7. 100 – 55 =
8. 100 – 22 =
9. 100 – 72 =
10. 100 – 39 =
11. 100 – 45 =
12. 100 – 56 =
13. 1000 – 1 =
14. 1000 – 7 =
15. 1000 – 3 =
16. 1000 – 8 =
17. 1000 – 33 =
18. 1000 – 66 =
19. 1000 – 47 =
20. 1000 – 73 =
21. 1000 – 555 =
22. 1000 – 777 =
23. 1000 – 265 =
24. 1000 – 352 =
25. 10000 – 1 =
26. 10000 – 3 =
27. 10000 – 44 =
28. 10000 – 67 =
29. 10000 – 8888 =
30. 10000 – 3465 =
31. 10000 – 5326 =
32. 10000 – 9652 =

Name _____   Date _____

Subtract more numbers

1. 542 − 45 − 128 =

```
    5 4 2
  −   4 5
  -------
    4 9 7
  − 1 2 8
  -------
    3 6 9
```

2. 572 − 56 − 77 =

3. 654 − 105 − 63 =

4. 351 − 88 − 135 =

5. 537 − 264 − 106 =

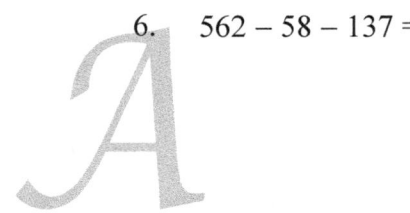

6. 562 − 58 − 137 =

7. 473 − 164 − 157 =

8. 607 − 174 − 338 =

9. 562 − 243 − 155 =

10. 506 − 134 − 177 =

11. 643 − 231 − 78 =

12. 752 − 365 − 124 =

13. 605 − 354 − 127 =

14. 562 − 168 − 143 =

15. 574 − 431 − 65 =

16. 345 − 79 − 106 =

17. 865 − 265 − 357 =

18. 672 − 243 − 367 =

19. 789 − 431 − 109 =

20. 815 − 109 − 454 =

Name _____   Date _____

Shortcuts with subtraction

1. A number subtracted by itself but in reverse order.

Example: $73 - 37 = (7 - 3) \times 9 = 4 \times 9 = 36$

Evaluate using shortcuts where applicable.

1. $75 - 57 =$
2. $51 - 15 =$
3. $63 - 36 =$
4. $72 - 27 =$
5. $85 - 58 =$
6. $93 - 39 =$
7. $65 - 56 =$
8. $81 - 18 =$
9. $73 - 37 =$
10. $42 - 24 =$
11. $31 - 13 =$
12. $62 - 26 =$
13. $91 - 19 =$
14. $84 - 48 =$
15. $62 - 26 =$
16. $76 - 67 =$
17. $94 - 49 =$
18. $86 - 68 =$
19. $74 - 47 =$
20. $96 - 69 =$

Example: $321 - 123 = (3 - 1) \times 99 = 2 \times 99 = 198$

Evaluate using shortcuts where applicable.

1. $341 - 143 =$
2. $523 - 325 =$
3. $664 - 466 =$
4. $572 - 275 =$
5. $744 - 447 =$
6. $805 - 508 =$
7. $653 - 356 =$
8. $785 - 587 =$

2. Shortcuts with adding

Example: 65 − 28 = 65 − 30 + 2 = 35 + 2 = 37

Evaluate using shortcuts where applicable.

1. 71 − 19

2. 85 − 57

3. 63 − 29

4. 75 − 38

5. 61 − 27

6. 83 − 48

7. 73 − 59

8. 82 − 37

9. 85 − 49

10. 72 − 28

11. 85 − 19

12. 74 − 27

13. 562 − 197

= 562 − 200 + 3

= 362 + 3

= 365

14. 576 − 88

15. 713 − 96

16. 642 − 98

17. 670 − 193

18. 462 − 194

19. 703 − 293

20. 561 − 289

21. 462 − 195

22. 624 − 396

23. 531 − 187

24. 462 − 91

25. 761 − 189

26. 561 − 197

3. Shortcuts with alternating numbers

Example: 73 − 36 = (73 + 4) − (36 + 4) = 77 − 40 = 37

Evaluate using shortcuts where applicable.

1. 67 − 39

2. 74 − 36

3. 83 − 57

4. 81 − 46

5. 73 − 56

6. 61 − 26

7. 83 − 29

8. 61 − 37

9. 73 − 47

10. 72 − 58

11. 45 − 16

12. 74 − 29

13. 642 − 389

 = (642 + 11) − (389 + 11)

 = 653 − 400

 = 253

14. 525 − 78

15. 642 − 95

16. 641 − 98

17. 575 − 293

18. 741 − 496

19. 713 − 188

20. 624 − 166

21. 562 − 187

22. 372 − 190

23. 309 − 78

24. 523 − 386

25. 752 − 197

26. 702 − 192

A4. Multiplication

1. 208 × 47	2. 319 × 25	3. 417 × 38	4. 158 × 27 = **4266**
5. 703 × 19	6. 528 × 61	7. 462 × 52	8. 481 × 13
9. 372 × 29	10. 461 × 48	11. 275 × 36	12. 308 × 54
13. 364 × 25	14. 392 × 55	15. 473 × 26	16. 375 × 62
17. 418 × 67	18. 738 × 26	19. 537 × 28	20. 809 × 78

Name _____ Date _____

Commutative property of multiplication

$$A \times B = B \times A$$

Example: $\quad 7 \times 15 = 15 \times 7 = 105$

Fill in the following blanks and evaluate.

1. $8 \times 17 = 17 \times$ _____ =
2. $5 \times 29 = 29 \times$ _____ =
3. $7 \times 45 = 45 \times$ _____ =
4. $5 \times 72 = 72 \times$ _____ =
5. $3 \times 37 = 37 \times$ _____ =
6. $8 \times 43 = 43 \times$ _____ =
7. $9 \times 83 = 83 \times$ _____ =
8. $2 \times 64 = 64 \times$ _____ =
9. $4 \times 539 = 539 \times$ _____ =
10. $6 \times 152 = 152 \times$ _____ =
11. $6 \times 607 = 607 \times$ _____ =
12. $7 \times 208 = 208 \times$ _____ =
13. $0 \times 3808 = 3808 \times$ _____ =
14. $6 \times 317 =$
15. $4 \times 165 =$
16. $3 \times 758 =$
17. $9 \times 106 =$
18. $6 \times 509 =$
19. $7 \times 273 =$
20. $7 \times 428 =$
21. $6 \times 218 =$
22. $8 \times 436 =$
23. $3 \times 768 =$
24. $5 \times 834 =$
25. $5 \times 382 =$
26. $9 \times 638 =$
27. $7 \times 251 =$
28. $4 \times 725 =$
29. $9 \times 418 =$
30. $5 \times 518 =$
31. $6 \times 327 =$
32. $7 \times 459 =$

Name _____ Date _____

Associative property of multiplication

$$(A \times B) \times C = A \times (B \times C)$$

Evaluate.

1. $8 \times 7 \times 5$

   $= 8 \times 5 \times 7$

   $= 40 \times 7$

   $= 280$

2. $5 \times 9 \times 6$

3. $25 \times 9 \times 4$

4. $8 \times 7 \times 35$

5. $13 \times 25 \times 4$

6. $11 \times 25 \times 4$

7. $8 \times 19 \times 125$

8. $125 \times 7 \times 8$

Name _____ Date _____

9. 5 × 9 × 16

10. 17 × 4 × 25

11. 15 × 13 × 2

12. 35 × 7 × 2

13. 45 × 17 × 2

14. 15 × 45 × 4

15. 125 × 27 × 8

16. 4 × 39 × 25

17. 75 × 57 × 4

18. 45 × 31 × 2

Evaluate.

62×15

$= 31 \times 2 \times 15$

$= 31 \times 30$

$= 930$

96×125

$= 12 \times 8 \times 125$

$= 12 \times 1000$

$= 12000$

44×58

$= 11 \times 4 \times 58$

$= 11 \times 232$

$= 2552$

$64 \times 25 \times 5 \times 125$

$= 4 \times 25 \times 2 \times 5 \times 8 \times 125$

$= 100 \times 10 \times 1000$

$= 1000000$

1. $56 \times 5 \times 25$

2. $72 \times 25 \times 5$

3. 66×17

4. 18×45

Name _____   Date _____

5. 125 × 16 × 5

6. 25 × 125 × 96

7. 78 × 22

8. 33 × 41

9. 145 × 36

10. 15 × 45

11. 606 × 65

12. 25 × 75

13. 105 × 35

14. 85 × 77

Distributive property of multiplication

$$(A + B) \times C = A \times C + B \times C$$

Evaluate.

7×38

$= 7 \times (30 + 8)$

$= 210 + 56$

$= 266$

36×21

$= 36 \times (20 + 1)$

$= 36 \times 20 + 36 \times 1$

$= 720 + 36$

$= 756$

1. 5×79

2. 4×72

3. 9×47

4. 7×52

5. 6×75

6. 4×93

7. 17 × 31

8. 35 × 22

9. 36 × 21

10. 45 × 31

11. 48 × 41

12. 34 × 32

13. 47 × 42

14. 25 × 14

15. 125 × 18

16. 125 × 28

Name _____   Date _____

Evaluate using distributive property.

$36 \times 8 + 36 \times 12$ $56 \times 48 + 56 \times 52$

$= 36 \times (8 + 12)$ $= 56 \times (48 + 52)$

$= 36 \times 20$ $= 56 \times 100$

$= 720$ $= 5600$

1. $73 \times 7 + 73 \times 3$ 2. $81 \times 4 + 81 \times 6$

3. $693 \times 2 + 693 \times 8$ 4. $239 \times 8 + 239 \times 2$

5. $421 \times 9 + 421 \times 1$ 6. $326 \times 5 + 326 \times 5$

7. 43 × 26 + 43 × 74

8. 61 × 45 + 61 × 55

9. 48 × 36 + 48 × 64

10. 68 × 28 + 28 × 32

11. 57 × 35 + 43 × 35

12. 69 × 41 + 41 × 31

13. 58 × 31 + 58 × 69

14. 29 × 47 + 71 × 47

15. 57 × 58 + 43 × 58

16. 19 × 76 + 76 × 81

Name _____ Date _____

Evaluate using distributive property.

$45 \times 13 - 45 \times 3$ $129 \times 147 - 129 \times 47$

$= 45 \times (13 - 3)$ $= 129 \times (147 - 47)$

$= 45 \times 10$ $= 129 \times 100$

$= 450$ $= 12900$

1. $61 \times 17 - 61 \times 7$ 2. $87 \times 16 - 87 \times 6$

3. $52 \times 15 - 52 \times 5$ 4. $43 \times 27 - 43 \times 7$

5. $67 \times 25 - 67 \times 5$ 6. $66 \times 74 - 66 \times 4$

7. 48 × 132 − 48 × 32

8. 63 × 143 − 63 × 43

9. 77 × 124 − 77 × 24

10. 57 × 119 − 57 × 19

11. 48 × 265 − 48 × 65

12. 71 × 335 − 71 × 35

13. 63 × 47 − 47 × 13

14. 78 × 32 − 32 × 38

15. 53 × 26 − 33 × 26

16. 27 × 59 − 59 × 17

Name _____ Date _____

Evaluate using distributive property.

43×19

$= 43 \times (20 - 1)$

$= 43 \times 20 - 43 \times 1$

$= 860 - 43$

$= 817$

67×98

$= 67 \times (100 - 2)$

$= 67 \times 100 - 67 \times 2$

$= 6700 - 134$

$= 6566$

1. 28×19

2. 72×19

3. 82×49

4. 76×49

5. 69×47

6. 59×77

7. 67 × 99

8. 34 × 99

9. 62 × 98

10. 35 × 98

11. 64 × 95

12. 95 × 42

13. 99 × 58

14. 99 × 26

15. 57 × 199

16. 199 × 47

Evaluate using the commutative, associative, and distributive property of multiplication.

1. 98×67

2. $25 \times 37 + 25 \times 63$

3. 66×99

4. $32 \times 102 - 32 \times 2$

5. 43×102

6. $57 \times 81 + 19 \times 57$

7. 105×28

8. $26 \times 117 - 17 \times 26$

9. 24×25

10. 68×25

Name _____ Date _____

11. $51 \times 4 \times 75$

12. $125 \times 17 \times 8$

13. $53 \times 138 - 38 \times 53$

14. 69×102

15. 88×125

16. 404×25

17. $46 \times 149 + 46 \times 51$

18. $73 \times 157 - 56 \times 73$

19. $35 \times 57 \times 8$

20. 96×125

21. $25 \times 5 \times 24$

22. $71 \times 99 + 71$

23. 606×25

24. $27 \times 25 + 25 \times 23$

25. 98×46

26. 63×102

27. 96×125

28. $48 \times 67 + 33 \times 48$

29. 201×57

30. $64 \times 125 \times 5$

31. $64 \times 125 \times 5$

32. 61×401

33. 44×79

34. $48 \times 67 + 33 \times 48$

35. 505×56

36. $25 \times 5 \times 48$

37. $79 \times 209 - 9 \times 79$

38. $83 \times 25 + 25 \times 17$

39. $53 \times 96 + 53 \times 5$

40. $175 \times 28 - 74 \times 28$

A5. Division

1. $12 \overline{)3627}$

2. $17 \overline{)3672}$

3. $24 \overline{)4681}$

4. $23 \overline{)7480}$

5. $15 \overline{)8573}$

6. $26 \overline{)3759}$

7. $33 \overline{)9361}$

8. $18 \overline{)5738}$

9. $24 \overline{)6429}$

10. $26 \overline{)7385}$

11. $19 \overline{)5832}$

12. $28 \overline{)5904}$

Division with zeros

$$\,12\,R\,1\,0\,0$$
$$300\overline{)3\,7\,0\,0}$$
(zeros crossed out on 300 → 3, and last two zeros of 3700 → 37)
$$\underline{3}$$
$$\,7$$
$$\underline{6}$$
$$\,1$$

Because before we do division, we cross out the zeros with a reminder 1, when we finish division, we must add the same number of zeros after 1.

1. $40\overline{)270}$

2. $200\overline{)1500}$

3. $400\overline{)6700}$

4. $300\overline{)860}$

5. $50\overline{)3100}$

6. $70\overline{)2000}$

7. $900\overline{)12700}$

8. $400\overline{)78100}$

9. $6000\overline{)467000}$

Name _____   Date _____

1.   4370 ÷ 40 =

2.   2600 ÷ 400 =

3.   1700 ÷ 40 =

4.   36300 ÷ 500 =

5.   6140 ÷ 60 =

6.   1460 ÷ 70 =

7.   5700 ÷ 800 =

8.   5040 ÷ 50 =

9.   5860 ÷ 80 =

10.   3000 ÷ 400 =

11.   5710 ÷ 60 =

12.   4800 ÷ 70 =

Divide

1. 27272727 ÷ 3

2. 27272727 ÷ 27

3. 48484848 ÷ 48

4. 11111111 ÷ 11

5. 333333 ÷ 333

6. 99999999 ÷ 99

7. 6666666666 ÷ 33

8. 132132132132 ÷ 66

Name _____ Date _____

Evaluate.

1. 5479 + 48

2. 6085 + 15

3. 4426 + 877

4. 7264 + 1756

5. 7139 − 5162

6. 5003 − 65

7. 4136 − 708

8. 5420 − 467

9. 52 × 41

10. 106 × 27

11. 45 × 36

12. 201 × 502

13. 1073 ÷ 29

14. 975 ÷ 13

15. 2884 ÷ 14

16. 3910 ÷ 23

17. 120 × 300

18. 250 × 120

19. 2300 × 7000

20. 3600 × 400

21. 1800 ÷ 20

22. 504000 ÷ 900

23. 42000 ÷ 6000

24. 4500 ÷ 15

A6. Order of operations

Do multiplication and division first, then do addition and subtraction in the order that they appear.

1. $5 + 3 \times 6$
   $= 5 + 18$
   $= 23$

2. $6 + 5 \times 2$

3. $9 + 18 \div 3$

4. $4 + 6 \div 2$

5. $5 + 7 \times 3$

6. $3 + 10 \div 2$

7. $7 + 7 \times 5$

8. $8 - 15 \div 3$

9. $10 + 28 \div 4$

10. $6 - 3 \div 3$

11. $8 + 28 \div 4$

12. $27 - 3 \times 2$

13. $6 + 2 \times 6$

14. $6 + 5 \times 4$

15. $32 - 7 \times 4$

16. $3 + 36 \div 6$

17. $9 - 10 \div 5$

18. $4 + 7 \times 3$

19. $6 - 15 \div 3$

20. $4 + 18 \div 6$

Name _____ Date _____

21. $3 \times 6 - 2 \times 5$

22. $8 \div 2 + 2 \times 4$

23. $5 \times 8 - 6 \times 5$

24. $9 \times 4 - 5 \times 3$

25. $8 \div 2 + 3 \times 7$

26. $7 \times 3 + 8 \times 4$

27. $3 \times 8 + 45 \div 5$

28. $5 \times 8 - 3 \times 6$

29. $10 \div 1 - 24 \div 4$

30. $5 \div 5 + 21 \div 3$

31. $51 \div 3 - 28 \div 28$

32. $24 \div 4 - 29 \div 29$

33. $7 \times 4 + 2 \times 3$

34. $4 \times 5 + 72 \div 8$

35. $63 \div 7 - 36 \div 9$

36. $3 \times 9 - 3 \times 2$

37. $18 \div 6 + 7 \times 2$

38. $77 \div 7 + 5 \times 1$

39. $6 \times 9 - 18 \div 6$

40. $30 \div 3 - 35 \div 7$

Name _____   Date _____

Brackets

Do all operations that are inside parentheses first. Secondly, do multiplication and division in the order that they appear. Then do addition and subtraction in the order that they appear.

1. $(3+7) \times (3+4)$
   $= 10 \times 7$
   $= 70$

2. $(6+2) + (7+4)$

3. $(1+6) + (4-1)$

4. $(7+9) \div (5-1)$

5. $(11+5) \div (2+6)$

6. $(9+5) + (5+3)$

7. $(7+9) \div (12-4)$

8. $(6-2) - (6-4)$

9. $(9+2) - (4+1)$

10. $(6-2) \times (7-1)$

11. $(3+5) \div (7-3)$

12. $(9-2) - (2+3)$

13. $(4+7) - (3+2)$

14. $(7+8) \div (2+3)$

15. $(7-3) \times (10-9)$

16. $(6+7) + (8-5)$

17. $(7-2) \div (4-3)$

18. $(6+4) \div (3+2)$

19. $(7-3) + (6+9)$

20. $(6+6) - (9-2)$

Name _____ Date _____

21. $(8-1) - (9-6)$

22. $(8+2) \times (2+9)$

23. $(7-3) \div (7-5)$

24. $(5+7) + (7-2)$

25. $(8-3) \times (5+6)$

26. $(9+2) - (4+2)$

27. $(9+6) - (3+2)$

28. $(9+2) + (8-5)$

29. $(9+7) \div (7-3)$

30. $(8+7) \div (4+1)$

31. $(7+8) - (7-4)$

32. $(8+7) \div (5-2)$

33. $(7+1) \times (7+3)$

34. $(7+6) + (3+6)$

35. $(2+5) \times (7-3)$

36. $(7+8) - (6-3)$

37. $(6+7) - (2+2)$

38. $(7+9) \div (3+1)$

39. $(8+4) \div (3-1)$

40. $(6-1) + (6+7)$

Evaluate.

1. 4 × 6 + 9 × 3

2. 4 × (6 + 9) × 3

3. 4 × (6 + 9 × 3)

4. (4 × 6 + 9) × 3

5. 96 ÷ 6 + 24 ÷ 8

6. (48 ÷ 6) + (72 ÷ 8)

7. 96 ÷ (7 + 5) ÷ 8

8. 45 ÷ (5 + 32 ÷ 8)

9. (84 ÷ 6 + 7) ÷ 3

10. 1 + 2 + 8 ÷ 8 − 2 − 1

11. (16 + 12 + 8) ÷ (8 − 2) − 1

12. 1 + 2 + 18 ÷ (8 − 2) − 1

13. 1 + 2 + 40 ÷ 8 × 2 − 1

14. 10 + 2 + 40 ÷ 8 × (2 − 1)

Order of operations

1. $7 - 2 \times 3$
2. $7 - (2 \times 3)$
3. $(7 - 2) \times 3$
4. $7 \times 2 - 3$
5. $(2 \times 7) - 3$
6. $2 \times (7 - 3)$
7. $4 \times 5 + 6 \times 7$
8. $4 \times (5 + 6) \times 7$
9. $(4 \times 5 + 6) \times 7$
10. $4 \times (5 + 6 \times 7)$
11. $(45 \div 5) + (9 \div 3)$
12. $42 \div (5 + 9) \div 3$
13. $48 \div (5 + 9 \div 3)$
14. $(45 \div 5 + 9) \div 3$
15. $1 + 2 + 3 \div 3 - 2 - 1$
16. $(1 + 2 + 3) \div (3 - 2) - 1$
17. $1 + 2 + 3 \times (3 - 2) - 1$
18. $1 + 2 + 3 \div 3 \times 2 - 1$
19. $1 + 2 + 3 \div 3 \times (2 - 1)$
20. $24 - 12 \div 2 \div 1 + 2 \times 3 \times 1$
21. $12 \div (8 \div 2 \times 2 - 4 - 2)$
22. $25 \div 5 + 4 \div 2 - 2 \div 1$

Find the missing numbers.

1. $(28 + 36 + 10) \div 2 = 14 + 18 + \square$

2. $(26 + 18 + 40) \div 2 = 13 + \square + 20$

3. $(54 + 18 - 36) \div 6 = 9 + 3 - \square$

4. $100 \div 4 = 40 \div 4 + 40 \div 4 + \square \div 4$

5. $360 \div 8 = \square \div 8 + 40 \div 8$

6. $8109 \div 9 = \square \div 9 + 9 \div 9$

7. $4080 \div 8 = \square \div 8 + 80 \div 8$

8. $594 \div 6 = 600 \div 6 - \square \div 6$

9. $495 \div 5 = 500 \div 5 - \square \div 5$

10. $48024 \div 4 = 48000 \div \square + 24 \div 4$

11. $6024 \div 8 - \square \div 8 = 6000 \div 8$

12. $5035 \div 5 = 5000 \div 5 + \square \div 5 + 5 \div 5$

13. $594 \div 3 = \square \div 3 - 6 \div 3$

14. $2580 \div 20 = 2400 \div 20 + \square \div 20$

15. $4756 \div 4 = 4000 \div 4 + 400 \div 4 + \square \div 4$

Name _____ Date _____

Find the missing numbers.

1. $26 + 43 = 100 - \square$

2. $8 \times 5 = \square \times 10$

3. $9 \times 7 = 60 + \square$

4. $54 + 29 = 38 + \square$

5. $80 \div 4 = 80 - \square$

6. $50 - 15 = 5 \times \square$

7. $60 - 15 = 5 \times \square$

8. $27 + 81 = 9 \times \square$

9. $\square \times 3 = 6 \times 9$

10. $15 + 39 = 40 + \square$

11. $\square + 24 = 6 \times 12$

12. $100 \div 20 = 80 \div \square$

13. $16 + 64 = 10 \times \square$

14. $90 \div 6 = 3 \times \square$

15. $98 \times 6 = \square \times 6 - 12$

16. $59 \times 7 = 60 \times \square - 7$

17. $102 \div 6 = 60 \div 6 + \square \div 6$

18. $58 - 9 = 59 - \square$

19. $99 \times 5 = 500 - \square$

20. $101 \times 10 = 1000 + \square$

21. $70 + 7 = \square \times 7$

22. $21 + 63 = 12 \times \square$

23. $120 \times 8 = \square \times 2$

24. $96 \div 6 = \square \div 12$

73

Name _____   Date _____

B. Whole Number Problem Solving

B1. How many triangles are there?

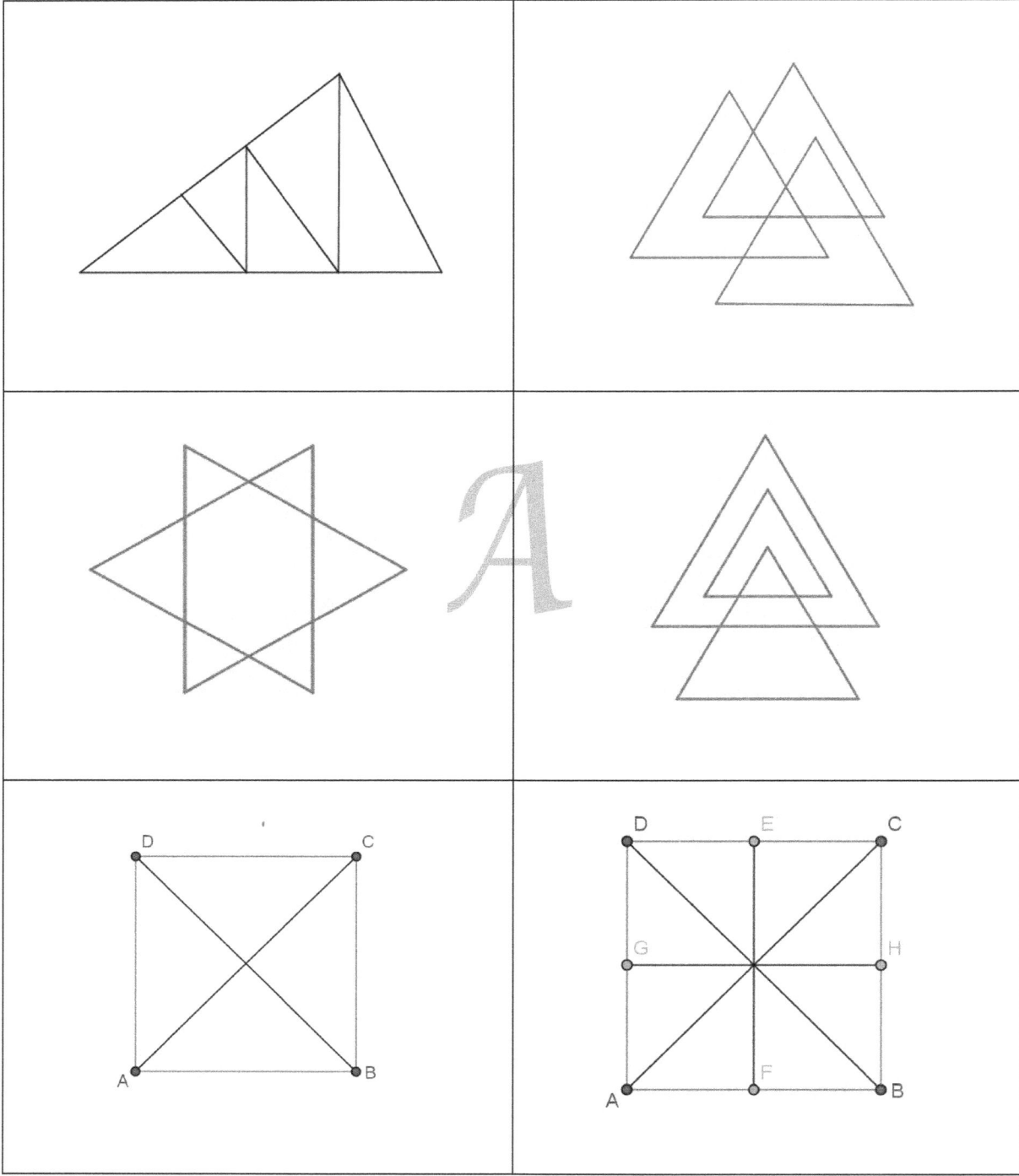

B2. How many figures are there?

How many squares are there?

How many squares are there?

How many rectangles are there?

How many rectangles are there?

How many rectangles are there?

How many rectangles are there?

Name _____ Date _____

Draw lines between dots,

• • •

• • •   1. How many squares can you make?

• • •   2. How many different sizes of squares can you get?

• • •

• • •   1. How many different triangles are there?
          2. How many different sizes of triangles are there?

• • • •

• • • •   1. How many squares can you get?

• • • •   2. How many different sizes of squares can you get?

• • • •

B3. Congruent figures

Divide each of the following figures into four congruent parts (the same shape and the same size).

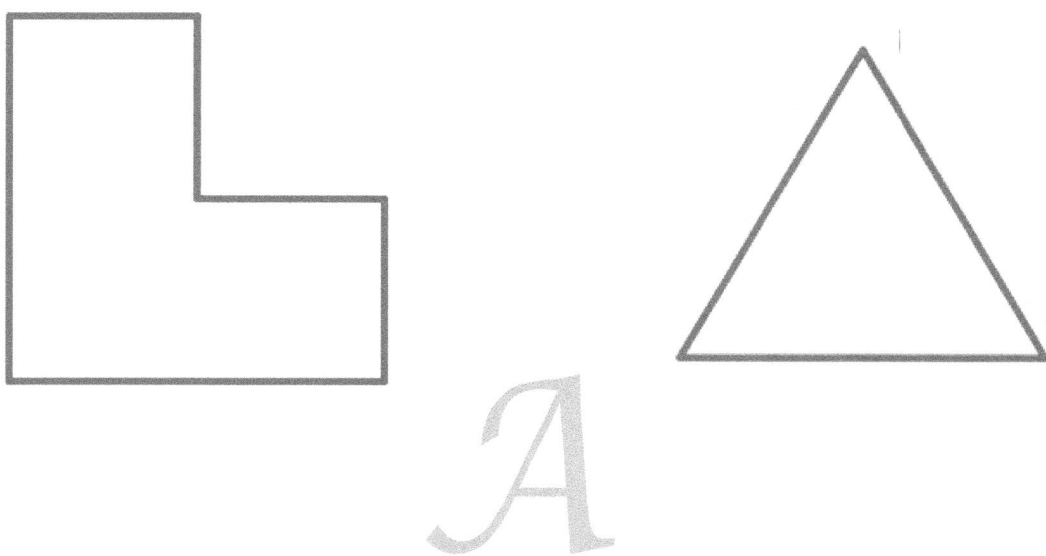

B4. One stroke drawing

Draw the following figures with one stroke without lifting your pencil from the page or going over any line twice.

B5. Tiling

1. Cover the board on the right with tiles shown below with no overlaps or gaps.

2. Cover the board on the right with tiles shown below with no overlaps or gaps.

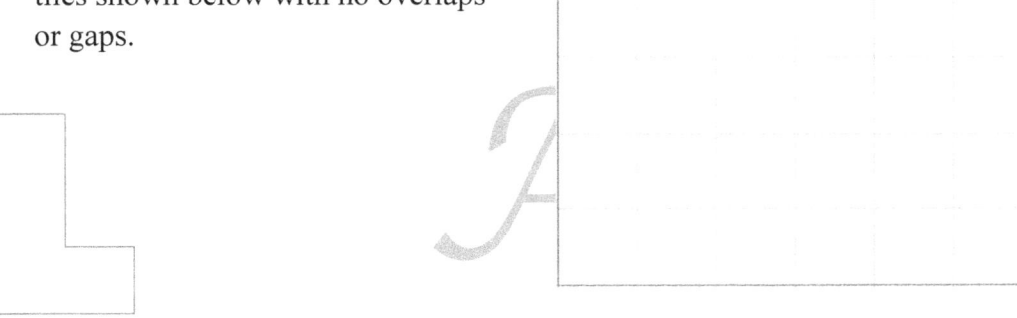

3. Cover the board on the right with tiles shown below with no overlaps or gaps.

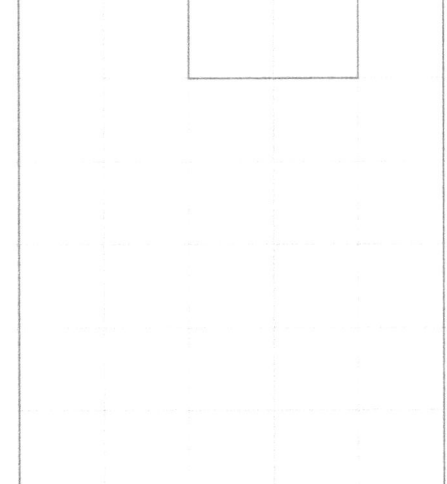

B6. Number puzzles

Enter numbers into the blank spaces so that each row and column contain the numbers 1 to 5.

1.

4		5		1
	5			
5		1		3
			3	
1		3		2

2.

1	2			5
			3	1
3		2		
				2
5	4	1		

3.

2	1			
			3	4
3			1	
	3	2		
	4	1	2	

4.

	3		2	
3		1		
	1		3	
				4
	2			

5.

1				4
		2		
4			3	
5	1			3

6.

				5
4		2		
			3	
	1			3
	2			

Place the numbers 1, 2, 3, 4, 5, 6 in the circles so that all three sides of the triangle have the same sum.

1. sum = 9

2. sum = 10

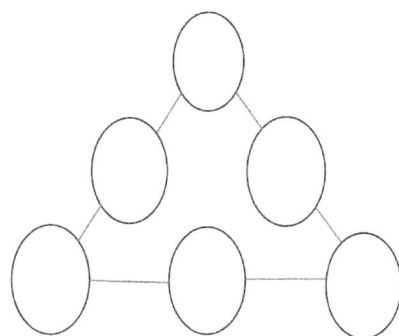
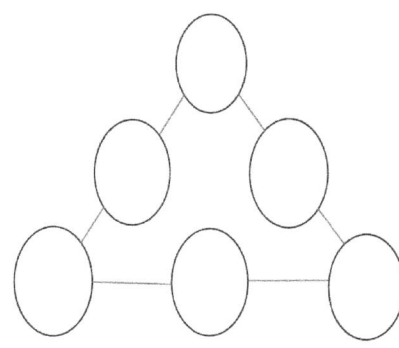

3. sum = 11

4. sum = 12

Place the numbers 1, 2, 3, 4, 5, 6 in the circles so that all three sides of the triangle have the same sum.

5. sum = 17

6. sum = 20

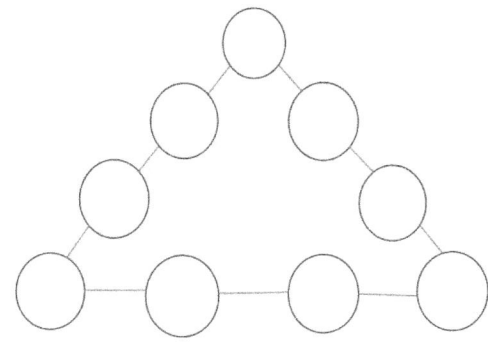
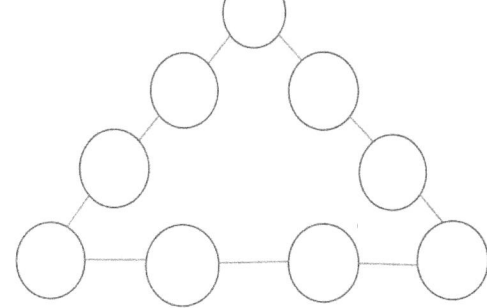

Name _____ Date _____

B7. Counting principles

1. How many numbers are there from 1 to 10?

2. How many numbers are there from 10 to 20?

3. How many numbers are there from 10 to 99?

4. How many numbers are there from 107 to 701?

5. How many digits are there from 1 to 10?

6. How many digits are there from 10 to 99?

7. How many digits are there from 1 to 100?

8. How many digits are there from 11 to 258?

Name _____   Date _____

9. How many multiples of 3 are there from 1 to 100?

10. How many multiples of 8 are there from 1 to 100?

11. If you wrote all the numbers from one to one-hundred. How many times would you write the digit 9?

12. One hundred tickets numbered from 1 to 100 are sold. Any ticket with a 6 on it wins a price. How many people win a prize?

13. Lisa has a story book. Some of the pages are missing. The number on the left page is 24. The number on the right page is 59. How many pages are missing?

14. Sam opened a story book. The sum of the numbers on both pages is 57. Which pages are they?

1. A group of children standing in a circle are numbered 1, 2, 3, 4...etc.

   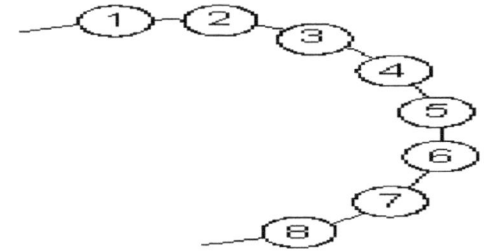

   If student 1 is standing opposite student 12, how many children are there in the circle?

2. A group of children standing in a circle are numbered 1, 2, 3, 4...etc. If number 5 is standing opposite number 14, how many children are there in the circle?

3. A group of children standing in a circle are numbered 1, 2, 3, 4...etc. If number 15 is standing opposite number 32, how many children are there in the circle?

4. There are 32 cabins in a Ferris wheel. Cabins in the Ferris wheel are numbered 1, 2, 3, 4...etc. When cabin 9 is on top, which cabin is on the bottom?

5. There are 40 seats in a merry-go-round. Seats in the merry-go-round are numbered 1, 2, 3, 4...etc. Which seat is opposite to seat 32?

B8. Digit and number problems

1. $82 - 28 = (8 - 2) \times 9 =$
2. $73 - 37 =$
3. $92 - 29 =$
4. $86 - 68 =$
5. $41 - 14 =$
6. $62 - 26 =$
7. $71 - 17 =$
8. $52 - 25 =$

1. The sum of the digits of a two-digit number is 10. If the digits are reversed, the new number is 18 greater than the original number. Find the original number.

2. The sum of the digits of a two-digit number is 12. If the digits are reversed, the new number is 36 less than the original number. Find the original number.

3. For each of the numbers: 53, 96, 74, the first digit is greater in value than the second digit. How many 2-digit numbers have this property?

4. The product of the digits in 36, $3 \times 6 = 18$, is even and the product of the digits in 57, $5 \times 7 = 35$, is odd. How many 2-digit numbers have an odd product?

5. There are exactly four different pairs of positive integers that add to make eight.
$$1 + 7 = 8$$
$$2 + 6 = 8$$
$$3 + 5 = 8$$
$$4 + 4 = 8$$
How many different pairs of numbers add to make 110?

B9. Guess and check

1. Of the 50 marbles in a jar, there are 6 more blue marbles than white marbles. How many blue marbles are there?

2. There is a 2-digit number. The digit in the tens place is greater than the digit in the ones place. The sum of its digits is 8. The product of its digits is 15. What is the number?

3. There is a 3-digit number. The sum of its digits is 7. The number is divisible by 4. It has no zeros. What is the number?

4. Carmen has 18 pencils and erasers altogether. Carmen has twice as many erasers than pencils. How many pencils does she have?

5. There are 26 chickens and rabbits altogether. There are 68 feet altogether. How many chickens and how many rabbits are there?

6. Marty bought two items from the menu. He paid $10.00, and got $3.75 change back. Which two items did Marty buy? (Hint: Make a guess. Then check your guess.)

Items	cost
tea	$2.50
juice	$4.00
cup cake	$3.50
muffin	$5.75

B10. Drawing a picture

1. Vanessa put up a 20 m colored string along the hallway. She put a bow at every 4 m of the string. How many bows did she use?

2. Points A, B, C, D, all of which lie on a straight line, are marked in the figure below. The distance between points A and C is 12 m, between B and D is 16 m, and between A and D is 25 m. What is the distance between points B and C?

   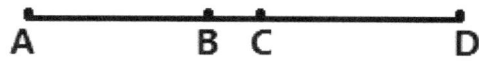

3. Mr. Porterfield put a fence around his square garden. Each side was 10 m. If the posts were placed 2 m apart, how many posts did he use?

4. John gets on an elevator at the ground floor. He goes up to the ninth floor then comes down 3 floors. He then goes up 1 floor and down 4 floors. What floor is John on now?

5. Steven sits in the third pew in a church if counted from the front and in the ninth pew if counted from the back. There is a center aisle. Each pew seats 6 people. What is the seating capacity in the church?

6. Wesley fenced a square piece of land. There are 9 posts on each side. How many posts did he use altogether?

7. You have a balance scale with three weights. With these three weights, you must balance any whole number load from 1kg all the way up to 13kg. How much should each of the three weights weigh?

Name _____   Date _____

B11. Making a table

1. Sam wrote out consecutive numbers starting with 5 until he had written 47 digits. What was the greatest number that Sam wrote?

	digit	# of digits
5 – 9	1	$5 \times 1 = 5$
10 – 19	2	$10 \times 2 = 20$
20 -- 29	2	$10 \times 2 = 20$
30	2	$1 \times 2 = 2$

2. It takes 288 digits to number the pages of a book consecutively. How many pages are there in the book?

3. Elise is 7 years old. Her mother is 35 years old. In how many years will the mother three times as old as Elise?

4. Alice, Bill, Clara, and Danny are in a race. In how many different orders can they come in 1st, 2nd, and 3rd?

5. Groups of friends joined in a party. Each person shook hands exactly once with each of the others. If there were a total of 15 handshakes, how many people were present at the party?

B12. Coin problems

1. Austin has 25 coins consisting of nickels, dimes, and quarters. There are two more nickels than dimes and three more quarters than nickels. What is the total number of quarters that Austin has?

Nickels	Dimes	Quarters	total
3	1	6	10
4	2	7	13

2. Austin has 40 coins consisting of nickels, dimes, and quarters. There are four more nickels than dimes and two more quarters than nickels. What is the total number of quarters that Austin has?

Nickels	Dimes	Quarters	total

3. Lawrence has 4 coins in his pocket. The coins have a value of 50 cents. What coins are in Lawrence's pocket? Use denominations of 1¢, 5¢, 10¢ and 25¢.

4. Mary has 6 coins with a total value of 67 cents. What combinations of coins could she have? Use denominations of 1¢, 5¢, 10¢ and 25¢.

5. A jar of dimes and quarters contains $4.15. There are 25 coins in all. How many of each are there?

6. We need to make change for 67¢. We can use pennies, nickels, dimes, and quarters. What is the fewest number of coins possible?

7. Jessica has exactly 87¢, comprising of six coins made up of pennies, dimes, and quarters. How many of each coin does Jessica have?

8. Jessica has exactly 91¢, comprising of six coins made up of pennies, nickels, dimes, and quarters. How many of each coin does Jessica have?

9. Jessica has exactly 51¢, comprising of seven coins made up of pennies, nickels, dimes, and quarters. How many of each coin does Jessica have?

10. How many ways can you pay for a 26¢ item using a combination of pennies, nickels, and dimes?

11. How many different combinations of pennies, nickels, dimes, and quarters could you use to make a change of 42¢?

B13. Age problems

1. The sum of Catherine and Isabella's age is 16. Catherine is two years older than Isabella. How old is Catherine?

2. The sum of Catherine and Isabella's age is 27. Catherine is three years older than Isabella. How old is Catherine?

3. The sum of Catherine and her mom's age is 42. Her mom is five times as old as Catherine. How old is Catherine?

4. The sum of Catherine and her mom's age is 45. Her mom is four times as old as Catherine. How old is Catherine?

5. The difference between Catherine and her mom's age is 28. Her mom is five times as old as Catherine. How old is Catherine?

6. In 18 years, Jimmy will be three times as old as he is now. How old is he now?

7. Isabella is 8 years old and her mom is 36 years old. How many years later will her mom be three times as old as she is?

8. Isabella is 6 years old and her mom is 33 years old. How many years later will her mom be four times as old as Isabella?

9. Kelly is 12 years old, and her mom is 36 years old. How many years ago was her mom four times as old as Kelly?

10. Kelly is 15 years old, and her mom is 43 years old. How many years ago was her mom five times as old as Kelly?

11. Two years ago, the sum of Jack's age and his dad was 36 two years ago. The dad is four times as old as Jack is now. How old is Jack?

B14. Balance puzzles

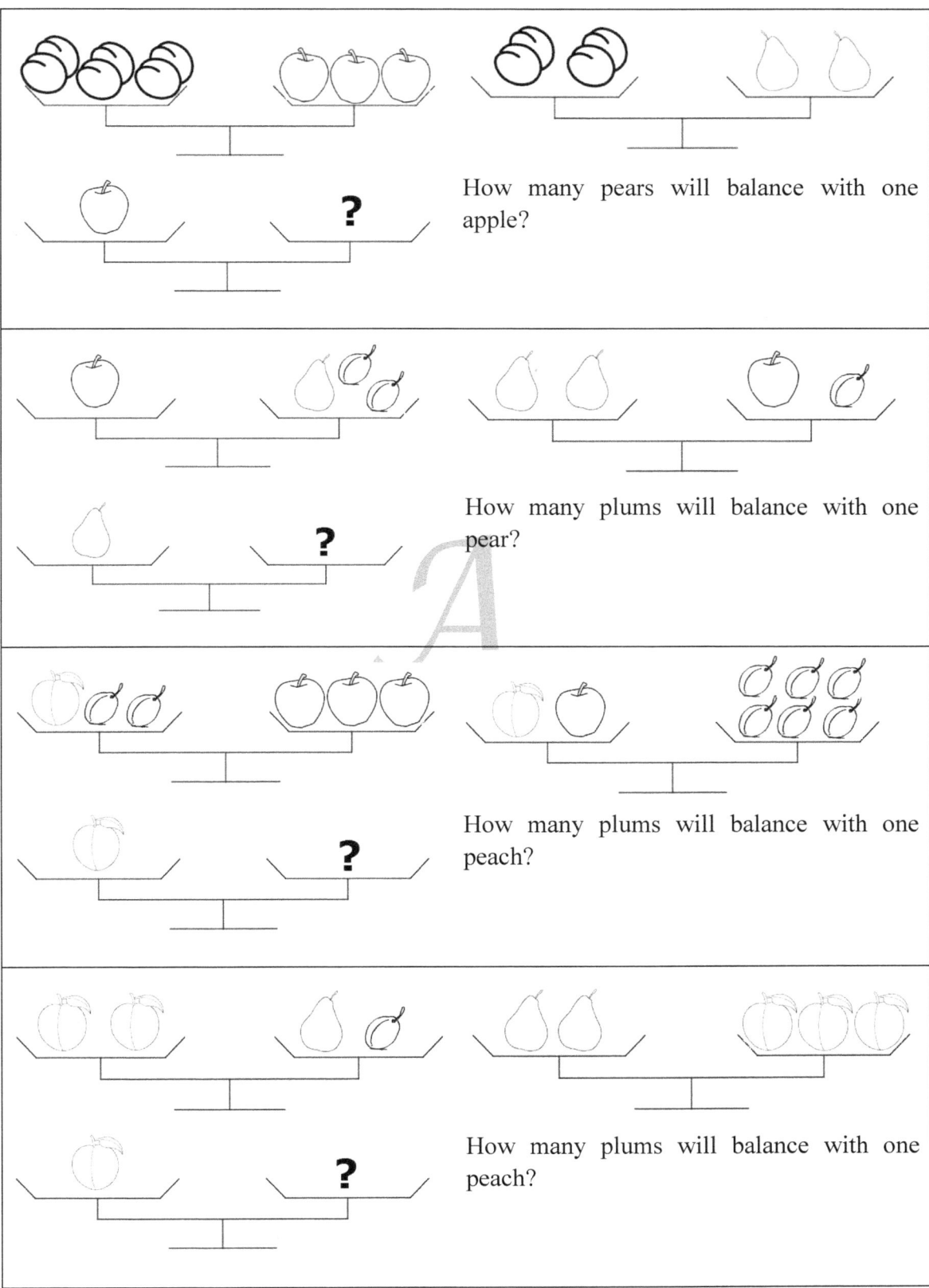

Name _____   Date _____

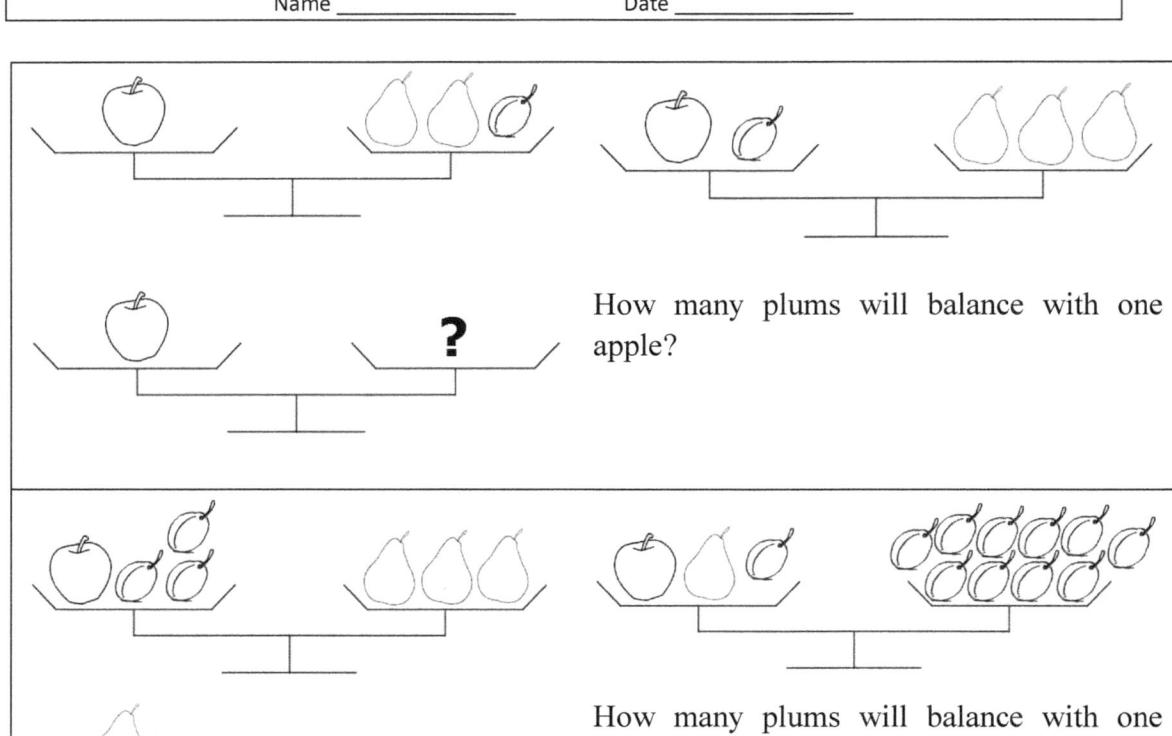

How many plums will balance with one apple?

How many plums will balance with one pear?

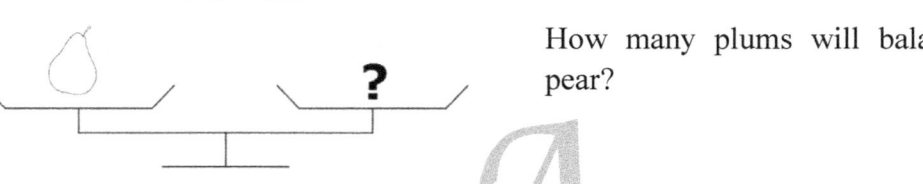

If each cherry weighs 20g, what is the total weight of the bananas?

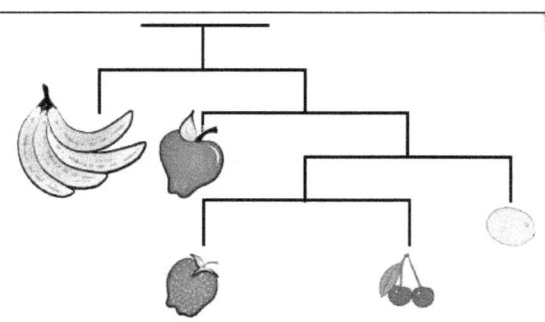

If each plum weighs 25g, what is the weight of each orange?

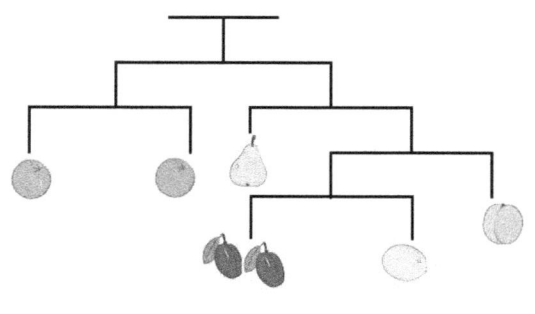

Name _____   Date _____

B15. Chicken and rabbit problems

1. Tony counts 15 heads and 48 legs among the chickens and rabbits on his farm. How many chickens and rabbits does he have?

2. There are 45 crabs (8 legs) and sea gulls and together they have 264 legs. How many crabs and sea gulls are there?

3. Will has 13 coins in nickels and dimes. He has $1 in total. How many nickels does he have?

4. There are 10 chickens and rabbits altogether. The total number of legs among the chickens is 2 more than the rabbits. How many chickens and how many rabbits are there?

5. There are 20 chickens and rabbits altogether. The chickens have 8 less legs than the rabbits. How many chickens and how many rabbits are there?

6. Angelina has 52 coins of nickels and quarters. Altogether she has $5. How many quarters does she have?

7. 55 people rent 8 cars and vans for camping. A car can hold 5 people, and a van can hold 8 people. A car costs $30 per day and a van costs $35 per day. The 55 people just fill all vehicles. What is the total cost of renting the 8 vehicles?

8. A ticket costs $10 for an adult and $6 for a student. A theater sold 50 tickets and got $108 more from students than adults. How many adult tickets were sold?

9. A big rabbit eats two carrots each time. Two little rabbit eat one carrot each time. There are 15 more little rabbits than big rabbits. The number of carrots eaten by the little rabbits is 3 more than big rabbits. How many little rabbits are there?

10. A big rabbit eats two carrots each time. Two little rabbits eat one carrot each time. There are 7 more little rabbits than big rabbits. The total number of carrots eaten by little rabbits is 4 less than by big rabbits. How many little rabbits are there?

Name _____ Date _____

B16. Digital clock pattern

1.

2.

3.

4.

5.
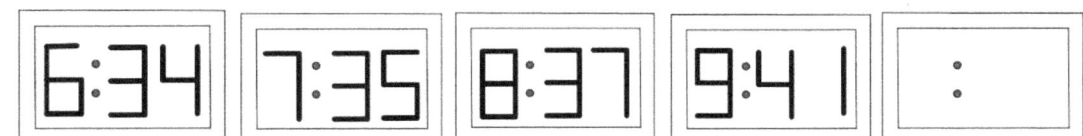

B17. Not so clock pattern

1. Where should the hour hand point to?

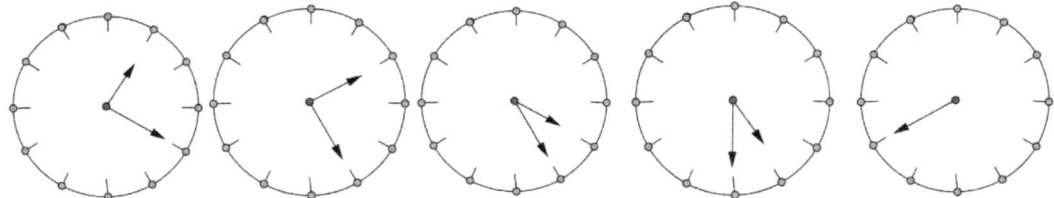

2. Where should the hour hand point to?

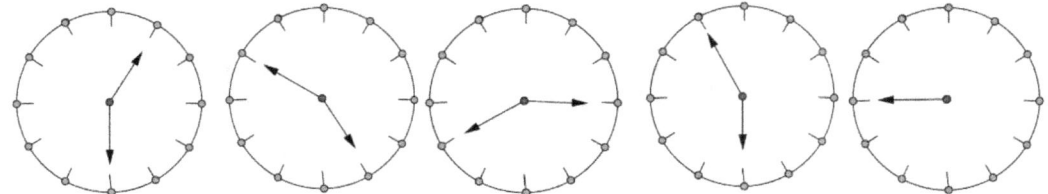

3. Where should the hour hand point to?

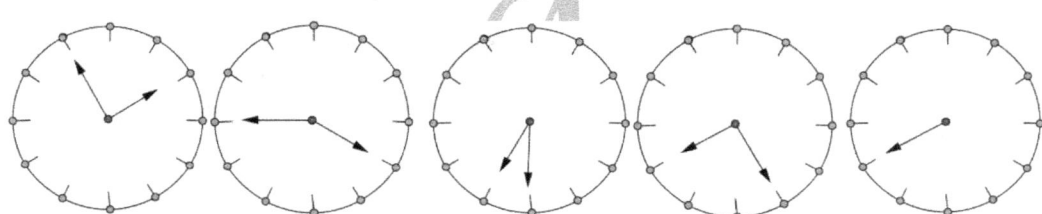

4. Where should the hour hand point to?

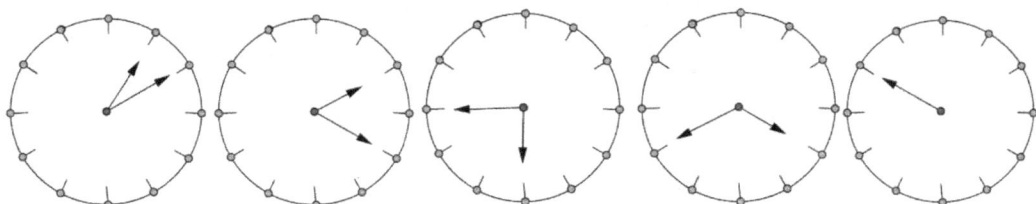

5. Where should the hour hand point to?

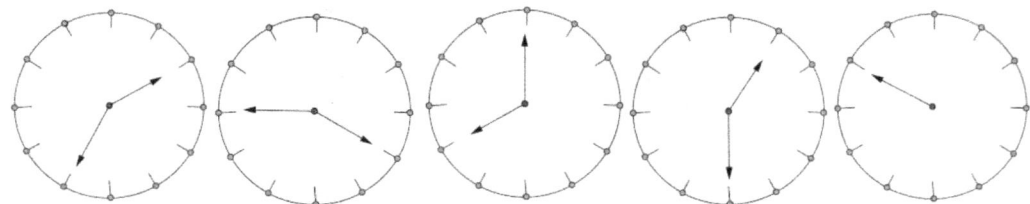

B18. Drawer problems

1. My drawer contains 3 blue socks, 6 red socks, and 5 yellow socks. At least how many socks should I take without looking to make sure I have at least one matching pair?

2. A drawer contains 3 red marbles, 2 yellow marbles, and 5 purple marbles. At least how many marbles should I take without looking to make sure I have at least one red marble?

3. A drawer contains 3 red marbles, 2 yellow marbles, and 5 purple marbles. At least how many marbles should I take without looking to make sure I have at least one marble of each color?

4. A box contains 5 red marbles, 4 yellow marbles, and 3 purple marbles. At least how many marbles should I take without looking to make sure I have at least one red marble and one yellow marble?

5. A box contains 5 red marbles, 4 yellow marbles, and 3 purple marbles. At least how many marbles should I take without looking to make sure I have at least one red, one yellow and one purple marble?

6. There are 8 marbles and 11 stones. Five of the items are red, and the rest are blue. At least how many blue stones are there?

7. There are 15 cubes and 23 balls. Seventeen of them are red, and the rest are blue. At least how many red balls are there?

8. There are four pairs of socks in each color: red, black, and white. At least how many socks should you take to make sure there are two pairs of sock in the same color?

9. There are four kinds in a deck of 52 playing cards: heart, diamond, spade, and club. How many cards should you take to make sure you have all kinds?

10. There are 13 ranks in a deck of 52 cards. Each suit includes an Ace, a King, Queen, and Jack, and ranks two through ten. At least how many cards should you take to make sure you have a pair? (A pair means two cards of the same rank - such as ♣8-♦8 or ♦J-♠J.)

11. There are 13 ranks in a deck of 52 cards. Each suit includes an Ace, a King, Queen, and Jack, and ranks two through ten. At least how many cards should you take to make sure you have a triple? (A triple means three cards of the same rank - such as ♦4-♥4-♣4)

12. In a deck of 40 cards, there are four kinds and 10 cards for each kind from Ace through ten. At least how many cards should you take to make sure you have three cards of a sequence? (A sequence means three or more cards of consecutive rank, the suits can be mixed, - such as ♦6-♠7-♥8)

B19. Number series

Evaluate.

1. $1 + 2 + 3 + 4 + 5 =$

2. $1 + 2 + 3 + 4 + 5 + 6 + 7 + 8 + 9 + 10 =$

3. $11 + 12 + 13 + 14 + 15 + 16 + 17 + 18 + 19 + 20 =$

4. $2 + 4 + 6 + 8 + 10 =$

$$Sum = \frac{(first\ number + last\ number) \times how\ many\ numbers}{2}$$

Redo the above questions using this new method.

1. $1 + 2 + 3 + 4 + 5 =$

2. $1 + 2 + 3 + 4 + 5 + 6 + 7 + 8 + 9 + 10 =$

3. $11 + 12 + 13 + 14 + 15 + 16 + 17 + 18 + 19 + 20 =$

4. $2 + 4 + 6 + 8 + 10 =$

Name _____ Date _____

Number series application

1. There are ten points around a circle. How many lines can be drawn through these points?

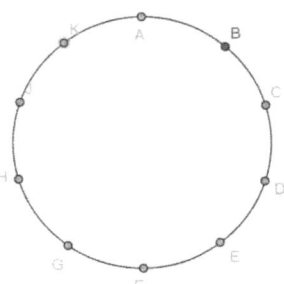

2. Each domino is a rectangular tile with a line dividing its face into two square ends. Each end is marked with several spots. The number of spots varies from 0 to 6. Following are some examples. Every domino is identical. How many dominoes are there in a domino set?

 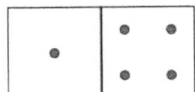 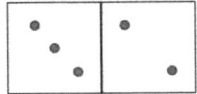

3. There are 15 players for a chess tournament. If two games are played between each other, how many games will be played in total?

4. How many Two-digit numbers are there in which the digit at ten's place is less than the one's place?

5. There is one hexagon in the first figure, seven hexagons in the second figure, and nineteen hexagons in the third figure. If this pattern continues, how many figures will there be in the eighth figure?

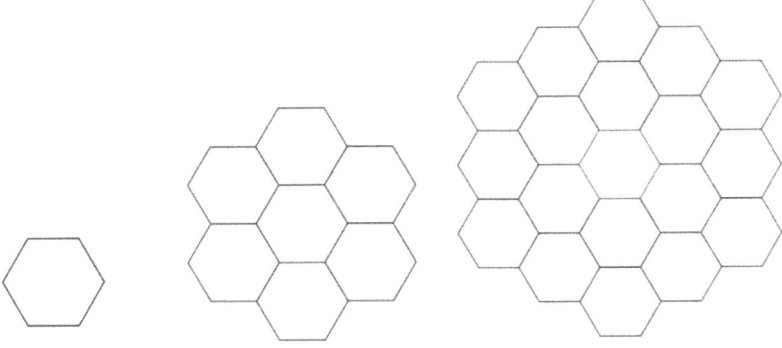

B20. Working problems

1. Jack walks 300 m in 5 minutes. How long will it take him to walk 2400 m?

2. Four rabbits eat 20 carrots in three days. How many carrots will six rabbits eat in three days?

3. Ten rabbits eat 150 carrots in six days. How many carrots will 8 rabbits eat in four days?

4. Isabella can paint a square board with side length of 1 yard in 15 minutes. How long will it take her to paint a square board with side length of 2 yards?

5. Six people went camping. They bought supplies for 12 days. Later, two more people joined in without buying any more supplies. How many days would they stay at the camp before all the supplies were used up?

6. Six people can carpet a house in 5 hours. How long will it take eight people to carpet two houses?

B21. Venn diagrams

1. Put the following numbers in their appropriate place:

   4, 5, 6, 10, 15, 18, 20, 25

   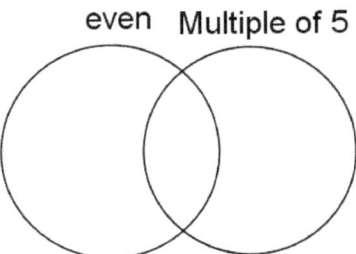

2. Put the following numbers in their appropriate place:

   2, 4, 6, 8, 12, 20, 22, 32

   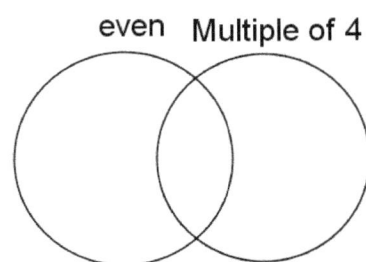

3. In a class of 20 students, everyone likes singing or drawing. 15 students like singing and 12 students like drawing. How many students like both?

   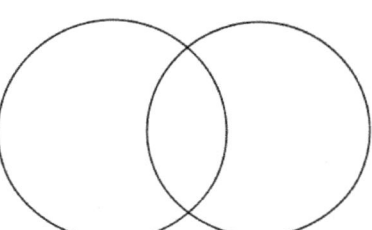

4. In a class of 18 students, everyone likes hockey or drama. 10 students like hockey and 11 students like drama. How many students like both?

   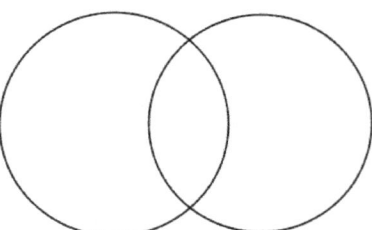

5. In a class of 24 students, everyone likes candy or chocolate. 13 students like candy and 5 students like both. How many students like only chocolate?

   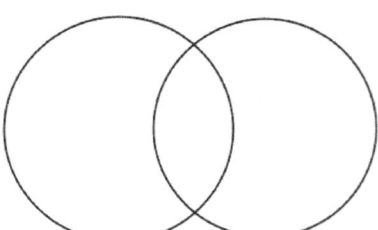

Name _____ Date _____

6. Put the following numbers in their appropriate place:

   4, 7, 8, 12, 15, 21, 25, 30

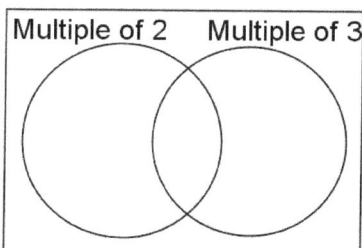

7. In a class of 21 students, 13 like swimming and 9 like skiing. There are 3 students who do not like either. How many students like both?

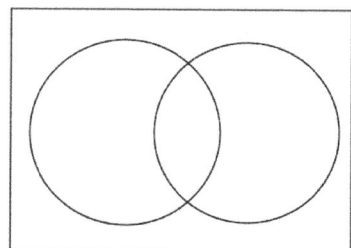

8. In a class of 28 students, 11 take drama, 16 take Band, and 4 take both drama and band. How many students in the class are not enrolled in either drama or band?

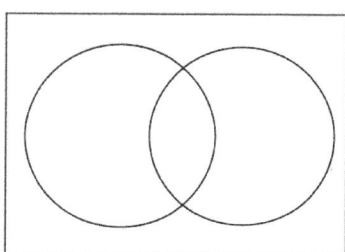

9. In a class of 50 students, 8 students like both dancing and swimming. 21 students like dancing only and 5 students like neither. How many students like swimming only?

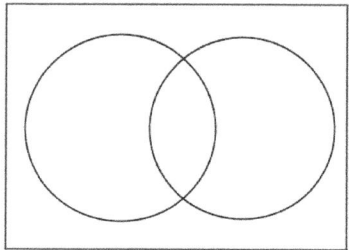

10. In a class of 35 students, 20 students like both red and blue. 24 students like red and 6 students like neither. How many students like blue?

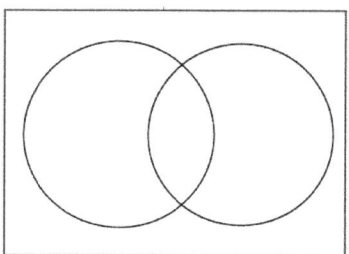

B22. Working backwards

1. $\square \xrightarrow{\times 2} \square \xrightarrow{-5} \square \xrightarrow{\div 3} \square \xrightarrow{+3} 12$

2. $\square \xrightarrow{-9} \square \xrightarrow{\times 4} \square \xrightarrow{+5} \square \xrightarrow{-1} 148$

3. Kylie went shopping. She paid $10 for an ice cream and got $6.50 back. Then she bought a calculator for $15.20. She went home with $4.25. How much did she have originally?

4. Emily bought some stickers. She kept half of the stickers to herself, and gave the rest evenly to her four friends. If each person got 16 stickers, how many stickers did Emily buy?

5. Leo wanted to know the age of his grandpa's dog. Grandpa told him that if he added 5 years to the age of the dog and then doubled it, the dog would be 28 years. How old was the dog?

6. The rabbit population doubles every year. The forest is crowded in year six when there are 4800 rabbits. How many rabbits were there in year one?

7. I bought a bag of apples. I kept 15 apples for myself. I gave the rest to three friends. Each friend got 4 apples. How many apples did I buy?

Name _____   Date _____

B23. Sum and difference problems

1. Tom has 6 more cards than Jerry. They have 120 cards together. How many cards does each have?

2. There are 156 students in Steven's grade 6 class. There are 16 more boys than girls. How many boys and girls are there?

3. Adam and Bob have 493 apples altogether. If Adam gives 7 apples to Bob, then Adam still has 17 apples more than Bob. How many apples does each one of them have at the beginning?

4. The perimeter of a garden is 92 m. The length is 12 m longer than the width. What is the length and width?

5. The sum of Adam's age and Bob's age is 36. Five years ago Adam was 6 years older than Bob. How old is Adam and Bob?

B24. Give and take problems

1. Adam has 14 apples and Bob has 6 apples. How many apples does Adam have to give to Bob so that they each have an equal number of apples?

2. David has 128 marbles and Amanda has 96 marbles. How many marbles should David give to Amanda so that both have the same number of marbles?

3. After Frank gave 8 pencils to Kirsten, they both have the same number of pencils. If they have 32 pencils in total, how many pencils did Frank have at the beginning?

4. After Aiden took 5 candies from Kirsten, they both had the same numbers of candies. If there were 40 candies among them, how many candies did Aiden have originally?

5. Aden gave half of his books to Benjamin and Carmen evenly. Then Benjamin gave half of his books to Carmen and Aden evenly. Then Carmen gave half of her books to Aden and Benjamin evenly. The three friends have the same number of books now. If they have 96 books in total, how many books did each start with?

B25. Sum, difference, and sum difference multiple

1. There are three angles in a triangle. The second angle is four times as big as the first angle. The third angle is 60^0 greater than the first one. How large are the three angles?

2. Jim is 28 years younger than his father and his father is five times as old as Jim. How old are Jim and his father now?

3. The perimeter of a rectangular garden is 72 m. The length is 2 m less than three times of width. What is the area of the garden?

4. Adam has 200 more apples than Bob. Adam has three times as many apples as Bob does. How many apples does each one of them have?

5. Adam has 90 more apples than Bob. Adam has three times as many apples as Bob. How many apples does each of them have originally?

6. After Adam gives 200 apples to Bob, Bob has 3 times as many apples as Adam. Together they have 2000 apples. How many apples did Adam have originally?
    2000

C. Rounding and Estimating

C1. Rounding whole numbers

Example: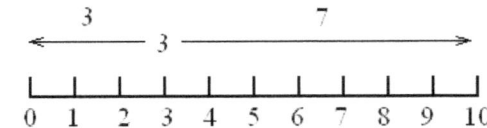

From 3 to 0 is 3, from 3 to 10 is 7, so 3 is closer to 0.

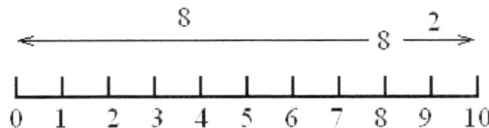

From 8 to 0 is 8, from 8 to 10 is 2, so 8 is closer to 10.

> The number 1, 2, 3, 4 are rounded down to 0.
> The umber 5, 6, 7, 8, 9 are rounded up to 10.

Round the following numbers to either 0 or 10

1. 2 —rounded→
2. 8 —rounded→
3. 4 —rounded→
4. 3 —rounded→
5. 9 —rounded→
6. 7 —rounded→
7. 6 —rounded→
8. 5 —rounded→

Round the following numbers to the nearest ten

We look at the tens place digit, if it is less than five, then round it up; otherwise, round it down.

5<u>4</u> is rounded down to 50; 6<u>7</u> is rounded up to 70.

1. 32 —rounded→
2. 47 —rounded→
3. 38 —rounded→
4. 24 —rounded→
5. 19 —rounded→
6. 76 —rounded→
7. 52 —rounded→
8. 65 —rounded→

Name _____ Date _____

Round each of the following numbers to the nearest hundred

We look at the tens place digit, if it is greater than five, then round it up; otherwise, round it down.

    6<u>8</u>3 is rounded up to 700; 2<u>3</u>9 is rounded down to 200.

1. 256 —rounded→

2. 218 —rounded→

3. 363 —rounded→

4. 649 —rounded→

5. 409 —rounded→

6. 832 —rounded→

7. 271 —rounded→

8. 551 —rounded→

9. 759 —rounded→

10. 725 —rounded→

11. 647 —rounded→

12. 527 —rounded→

Rounding the following numbers to the nearest thousand

We look at the hundreds place digit, if it is less than five, then round it up; otherwise, round it down.

    2<u>4</u>64 is rounded down to 2000; 6<u>8</u>37 is rounded up to 7000.

1. 4680 —rounded→

2. 1843 —rounded→

3. 3279 —rounded→

4. 8419 —rounded→

5. 1862 —rounded→

6. 6708 —rounded→

7. 7498 —rounded→

8. 5275 —rounded→

9. 2673 —rounded→

10. 2751 —rounded→

11. 4501 —rounded→

12. 9999 —rounded→

Round each of the following numbers to the indicated place.

1) 10 649 to the nearest ten _____

2) 7 548 to the nearest hundred _____

3) 5 879 to the nearest ten _____

4) 139 403 to the nearest thousand _____

5) 592 271 to the nearest ten thousand _____

6) 98 879 to the nearest thousand _____

7) 95 423 468 to the nearest million _____

8) 2 859 607 to the nearest million _____

9) 4 152 to the nearest hundred _____

10) 774, 139 to the nearest ten thousand _____

11) 206 837 to the nearest ten _____

12) 6 779 to the nearest hundred _____

13) 807 486 to the nearest ten thousand _____

14) 5 403 to the nearest hundred _____

15) 7 495 to the nearest ten thousand _____

16) 64 076 to the nearest hundred _____

17) 17 589 to the nearest thousand _____

18) 2 469 745 to the nearest million _____

19) 25 173 to the nearest thousand _____

20) 1 974 to the nearest ten _____

Name _____ Date _____

Round each of the following numbers to the indicated place.

1) 60 852 to the nearest ten _____

2) 9 754 to the nearest hundred _____

3) 7 492 to the nearest ten _____

4) 612 501 to the nearest thousand _____

5) 723 396 to the nearest ten thousand _____

6) 24 492 to the nearest thousand _____

7) 27 531 584 to the nearest million _____

8) 3 472 809 to the nearest million _____

9) 5 673 to the nearest hundred _____

10) 995, 612 to the nearest ten thousand _____

11) 308 419 to the nearest ten _____

12) 8 992 to the nearest hundred _____

13) 409 548 to the nearest ten thousand _____

14) 7 501 to the nearest hundred _____

15) 9 527 to the nearest ten thousand _____

16) 85 098 to the nearest hundred _____

17) 69 742 to the nearest thousand _____

18) 3 582 957 to the nearest million _____

19) 37 691 to the nearest thousand _____

20) 6 295 to the nearest ten _____

Name _____ Date _____

Write the place value to which each number has been rounded.

1. 3590 ⇒ 3600   hundreds
2. 3590 ⇒ 4000   _____
3. 3590 ⇒ 4000   _____
4. 135910 ⇒ 135900   _____
5. 43995 ⇒ 44000   _____
6. 135910 ⇒ 136000   _____
7. 43995 ⇒ 40000   _____
8. 135910 ⇒ 100000   _____

Round off 123,456,789 to the indicated degree of precision

1) to the nearest hundred million   _____
2) to the nearest ten million   _____
3) to the nearest million   _____
4) to the nearest hundred thousand   _____
5) to the nearest ten thousand   _____
6) to the nearest thousand   _____
7) to the nearest hundred   _____
8) to the nearest ten   _____

Insert suitable digit in each blank so that the rounding would make sense. (Answers may vary)

1) 6 5 ☐ 8 rounds to 6 600
2) 7 ☐ 84 rounds to 7 500
3) 5 ☐ 8 rounds to 500
4) 7 8 ☐ 8 rounds to 7 800
5) 4 48 ☐ rounds to 4 490
6) 2 ☐ 38 rounds to 3 000
7) ☐ 524 rounds to 5 000
8) ☐ 496 rounds to 6 000

Complete the chart.

	Round to the nearest		
	hundred	thousand	million
8 485 386			
9 581 653			
4 735 619			
7 095 498			7

C2. Whole number estimations

Rounding Method
Estimating Sums

```
    3 5 1  →      4 0 0        351 is close to 400
  + 1 6 8  →    + 2 0 0        168 is close to 200
                  6 0 0        400 + 200 = 600.
                               So 351 + 168 is about 600.
```

1.   2 5 2 →   2.   3 3 7 →
    + 4 7 6 →   + _____   + 5 7 5 →   + _____

3.   5 3 7 →   4.   3 7 9 →
    + 1 5 9 →   + _____   + 5 8 2 →   + _____

5.   3 7 3 →   6.   3 6 8 →
    + 7 2 7 →   + _____   + 2 0 8 →   + _____

7.   3 4 7 →   8.   3 5 8 →
    + 5 6 3 →   + _____   + 5 3 7 →   + _____

9.   3 0 6 →   10.   3 6 9 →
    + 2 4 7 →   + _____   + 2 7 4 →   + _____

11.   2 8 1 →   12.   6 2 8 →
    + 4 3 5 →   + _____   + 2 4 1 →   + _____

Estimate Sums

```
    3 5 2  →      3 5 0     352 is close to 350
  +   7 9  →    +   8 0     79 is close to 80
  ─────────    ─────────    350 + 80 = 430.
                 4 3 0     So, 352 + 79 is about 430.
```

13. 4 6 9 →   14. 4 7 9 →
   +   2 6 →   +   +   4 7 →   +

15. 3 6 1 →   16. 3 6 2 →
   +   5 7 →   +   +   3 4 →   +

17. 6 3 7 →   18. 3 0 9 →
   +   6 8 →   +   +   3 1 →   +

19.   8 1 →   20.   1 8 →
   + 3 5 2 →   +   + 3 7 6 →   +

21. 3 7 2 →   22. 4 0 8 →
   +   9 →   +   +   3 →   +

23. 4 8 1 →   24. 3 7 2 →
   +   1 6 →   +   +   4 4 →   +

116

Estimating Differences

```
    5 7 9  →    6 0 0         5 4 2  →    5 4 0
  - 3 1 2  →  - 3 0 0       -   7 5  →  -   8 0
               3 0 0                      4 6 0
```

1.   4 8 1 → _____
     − 2 2 6 → − _____

2.   7 3 1 → _____
     − 4 7 2 → − _____

3.   4 8 2 → _____
     − 3 6 9 → − _____

4.   4 6 5 → _____
     − 2 7 3 → − _____

5.   5 3 8 → _____
     − 4 0 7 → − _____

6.   6 2 9 → _____
     − 1 2 4 → − _____

7.   6 2 4 → _____
     − 6 4 → − _____

8.   3 8 3 → _____
     − 5 8 → − _____

9.   5 3 9 → _____
     − 2 7 → − _____

10.   7 4 1 → _____
     − 7 3 → − _____

11.   5 8 2 → _____
     − 1 0 5 → − _____

12.   5 3 7 → _____
     − 3 6 2 → − _____

Name _____ Date _____

Estimating Products

```
    3 2 5  →        3 0 0
  ×   2 4  →      ×   2 0
  ─────────      ─────────
                   6 0 0 0
```

325 is close to 300
24 is close to 20
325 × 20 = 6000.
So, 325 × 20 is about 6000.

1. 460 →   ×_____
  × 29 →

2. 391 →   ×_____
  × 32 →

3. 417 →   ×_____
  × 53 →

4. 716 →   ×_____
  × 61 →

5. 826 →   ×_____
  × 209 →

6. 431 →   ×_____
  × 572 →

7. 280 →   ×_____
  × 72 →

8. 328 →   ×_____
  × 183 →

9. 631 →   ×_____
  × 826 →

10. 495 →   ×_____
  × 52 →

11. 274 →   ×_____
  × 33 →

12. 472 →   ×_____
  × 83 →

118

Name _____ Date _____

Estimating Quotients with 1-digit divisors

Example:
3747 ÷ 6   Round the front-end of the dividend to the nearest multiple of the divisor.   Round the front-end 37 hundred to the nearest multiple of 6. 3747 → 3600,
and 3600 ÷ 6 = 600

1. 372 ÷ 5

    → 350 ÷ 5

    = 70

2. 572 ÷ 7

    →

3. 4726 ÷ 6

    →

4. 3729 ÷ 9

    →

5. 4371 ÷ 5

    →

6. 5231 ÷ 9

    →

7. 6217 ÷ 8

    →

8. 2416 ÷ 5

    →

9. 4642 ÷ 3

    →

10. 5725 ÷ 2

    →

11. 6438 ÷ 7

    →

12. 5373 ÷ 9

    →

Name _____   Date _____

Estimating Quotients with 2-digit divisors

Example:
6429 ÷ 28   Round the divisor first. Then round the front-end of the dividend to the nearest multiple of the divisor.

28 is rounded to 30. Round the front-end 64 hundred to the nearest multiple of 30. 6429 → 6300, and 6300 ÷ 30 = 210

1. 2351 ÷ 32
    →

2. 4725 ÷ 73
    →

3. 3825 ÷ 93
    →

4. 7925 ÷ 87
    →

5. 5330 ÷ 62
    →

6. 6528 ÷ 78
    →

7. 3709 ÷ 59
    →

8. 3642 ÷ 51
    →

9. 3178 ÷ 38
    →

10. 5189 ÷ 42
    →

11. 6235 ÷ 73
    →

12. 4627 ÷ 19
    →

Name _____   Date _____

C3. Problem solving

1. I'm a 3-digit number. The sum of my digits is 10. When rounded to the nearest hundred, I am 900. When rounded to the nearest ten, I am 900 too. What number am I?

2. When a number is rounded to the nearest thousand, it rounds to 4000. All its digits are the same. What number is it?

3. Rounding a number to the nearest ten, hundred, or thousand will give the same answer of 3000. And it is not 3000. What is the number?

4. When a number is rounded to the nearest hundred, the number is doubled. What is the number?

5. To the nearest hundred, a number rounds to 2800. Three digits of the number are the same. What is the number?

6. When a number is rounded to the nearest tens, hundreds, or thousands place, it gives the same answer of 1000. When you read it forward, it sounds the same as when you read it backwards. What is the number?

Name _____   Date _____

D. Number Patterns

Triangular numbers

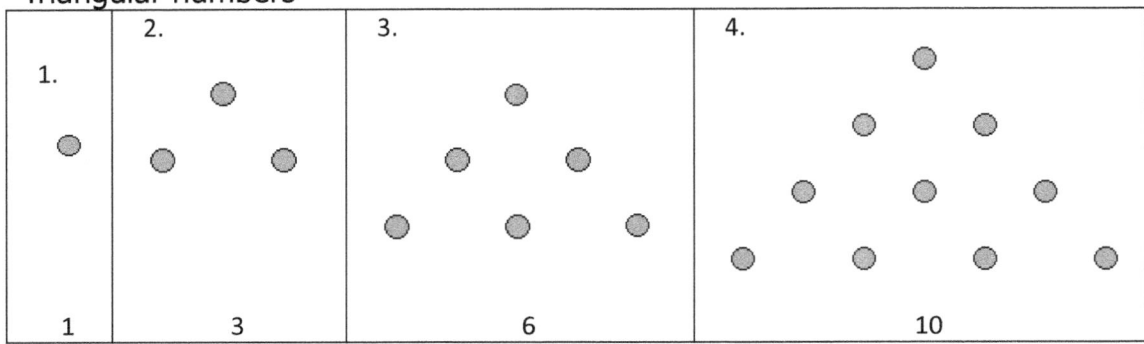

The next 4 triangular numbers are _____ , _____ , _____ and _____

Square numbers

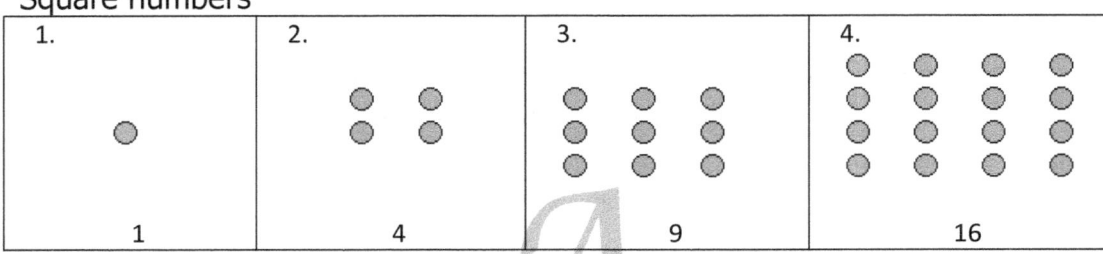

The next 4 square numbers are _____ , _____ , _____ and _____

Pentagonal numbers

1.	2.	3.	4.
1	5	12	22

The next 4 pentagonal numbers are _____ , _____ , _____ and _____

Name _____ Date _____

Triangular numbers and Square numbers
The following is a combination of 2 neighboring triangular numbers.

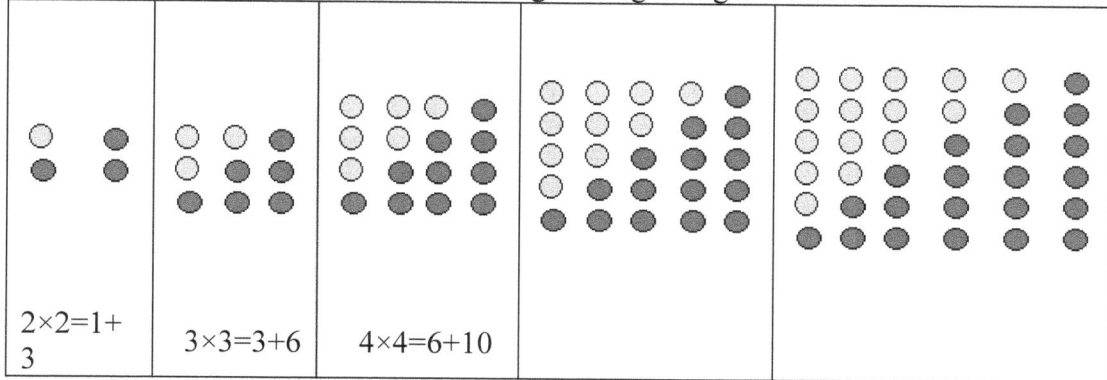

| 2×2=1+3 | 3×3=3+6 | 4×4=6+10 | | |

Fibonacci Numbers
Each number is the sum of the two previous numbers.

1 , 1 , 2 , 3 , 5 , 8 , 13 , 21 , ____ , ____ and ____

1 + 1 = 2
   1 + 2 = 3
      2 + 3 = 5
         3 + 5 = 8
           5 + 8 = 13
              8 + 13 = 21

Lucas Numbers
Each number is the sum of the two previous numbers.

1 , 3 , 4 , 7 , 11 , 18 , 29 , 47 , ____ , ____ and ____

1 + 3 = 4
   3 + 4 = 7
      4 + 7 = 11
         7 + 11 = 18
           11 + 18 = 29
              18 + 29 = 47

Palindromic Numbers
A natural number of two or more digits which are the same either read forwards or backwards.

55, 676, 7337, 45954, 987789

Give 3 examples of palindromic numbers. (Answer may vary)

_____, _____ and _____.

Pascal's Triangle

```
1=                              1
2=                          1       1
4=                      1       2       1
8=                  1       3       3       1
16=             1       4       6       4       1
32=         1       5      ___     ___     ___     ___
64=     1      ___     ___     ___     ___     ___     ___
128= 1    ___     ___     ___     ___     ___     ___     ___
```

Find the pattern and fill in blanks.

```
                        1
                    2       4
                3       6       9
            4       8      12      16
        5      10      ___     ___     ___
    6      ___     ___     ___     ___     ___
7     ___     ___     ___     ___     ___     ___
```

Follow the pattern and find the expansion of 7 × 7

    1 × 1   = 1

    2 × 2   = 1 + 3

    3 × 3   = 1 + 3 + 5

    4 × 4   = 1 + 3 + 5 + 7

    5 × 5   = 1 + 3 + 5 + 7 + 9

    6 × 6   = 1 + 3 + 5 + 7 + 9 + 11

7 × 7 = _____

Name _____ Date _____

D1. Patterns

1. 4   3   6   5   10 ___ ___ ___ ___
2. 2   6   7   21 22 ___ ___ ___ ___
3. 3   1   6   2   9   ___ ___ ___ ___
4. 7   15 6   13 5   ___ ___ ___ ___
5. 3   4   7   12 19 ___ ___ ___ ___
6. 2   4   8   14 22 ___ ___ ___ ___
7. 63 62 60 59 57 ___ ___ ___ ___
8. 35 36 38 39 41 ___ ___ ___ ___
9. 6   9   8   11 10 ___ ___ ___ ___
10. 50 45 46 41 42 ___ ___ ___ ___
11. 2   7   17 22 42 ___ ___ ___ ___
12. 4   9   19 34 54 ___ ___ ___ ___
13. 34 17 18 9   10 ___ ___ ___ ___
14. 2   5   11 23 47 ___ ___ ___ ___
15. 3   5   9   17 33 ___ ___ ___ ___

How are "A" and "B" related?

1.

A	B
2	8
3	7
4	6
5	
6	
7	

Rule: A + B = 10

2.

A	B
1	14
3	12
4	11
6	
8	
9	

Rule:

3.

A	B
4	9
5	11
6	13
7	
8	
9	

Rule:

4.

A	B
2	6
3	8
5	12
7	
9	
10	

Rule:

5.

A	B
3	15
4	20
6	30
7	
8	
9	

Rule:

6.

A	B
2	9
4	15
5	18
7	
8	
9	

Rule:

7.

A	B
1	3
2	6
4	18
6	
7	
8	

Rule:

8.

A	B
2	3
3	8
5	24
7	
8	
9	

Rule:

9.

A	B
1	6
2	11
3	16
6	
7	
9	

Rule:

10.

A	B
2	7
3	8
5	10
6	
7	
9	

Rule:

11.

A	B
1	11
3	9
4	8
5	
7	
8	

Rule:

12.

A	B
3	7
4	10
5	13
7	
8	
9	

Rule:

Name _____   Date _____

Find how A, B and C are related.

1.
A	B	C
2	3	5
3	7	10
5	8	13
7	4	11

A + B = C

2.
A	B	C
6	3	3
8	4	4
7	7	0
5	3	2

_____

3.
A	B	C
2	3	6
4	7	28
3	4	12
6	8	48

_____

4.
A	B	C
12	3	4
10	2	5
20	5	4
18	6	3

_____

5.
A	B	C
1	3	8
2	5	14
4	2	12
6	7	26

_____

6.
A	B	C
5	2	6
8	1	14
9	3	12
6	4	4

_____

7.
A	B	C
2	3	7
4	1	9
6	7	19
5	8	18

_____

8.
A	B	C
3	1	5
4	2	10
2	5	12
6	7	44

_____

9.
A	B	C
2	3	5
4	5	19
3	4	11
5	8	39

_____

10.
A	B	C
3	2	11
5	3	28
2	4	8
6	5	41

_____

11.
A	B	C
4	5	12
1	6	10
6	9	18
5	2	10

_____

12.
A	B	C
7	1	7
6	3	4
9	2	8
5	4	2

_____

D2. T-Tables

Observe the pattern below and answer questions.

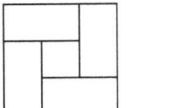 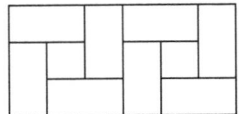 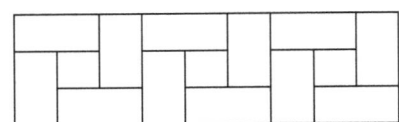

Pattern 1   Pattern 2   Pattern 3

Number of Pattern	Number of Tiles
1	4
2	
3	
4	
⋮	
10	

What pattern rule do you use to find the number of tiles?

How many tiles will you use in Pattern 20?

Observe the following pattern and answer question.

Pattern 1   Pattern 2   Pattern 3   Pattern 4

Pattern Number	Number of Stars
1	7
2	
3	
4	
⋮	
10	

What pattern rule do you use to find the number of Stars?

How many stars are there in Pattern 15?

Name _____   Date _____

Complete the table for this pattern.

Figure	Perimeter(units)	Area(square units)	Number of squares
1			
2			
3			
4			
5			

1. What pattern rule did you use to find the perimeter?

2. Which figure will have a perimeter of 40 units?

3. What pattern rule did you use to find the area?

4. Which figure will have an area of 81 square units?

5. What pattern rule did you use to find the number of squares?

6. How many squares are there in figure 8?

Name _____ Date _____

Solve the following question with the help of a T-table.

Emily works as a cashier in a coffee shop. Her hourly rate is $8.50. Complete the following table.

Hours worked	Salary
1	8.5
2	
3	
4	
5	
6	
7	
8	
⋮	
10	

1. If she works 8 hours a day, how much will she make in one day?

2. What pattern rule did you use?

If she works 40 hours a week, how much will she make in one week?

E. Time

E1. 12-hour clock and 24-hour clock

12-hour clock

24-hour clock

12-hour clock	1 a.m.	2 a.m.	...	11a.m.	12a.m.	1p.m.	...	11p.m.	12midnight
24-hour clock	01:00	02:00	...	11:00	12:00	13:00	...	23:00	24:00

Write the time using the 24-hour clock.

1. 2:00 a.m. _____
2. 2:15 a.m. _____
3. 5:35 a.m. _____
4. 8:00 p.m. _____
5. 7:20 p.m. _____
6. 3:10 p.m. _____
7. 1:00 a.m. _____
8. 4:40 p.m. _____
9. 11:35 p.m. _____
10. 5:25 a.m. _____
11. 0:10 p.m. _____
12. 9:25 p.m. _____

Write the time using 12-hour clock.

1. 04:00 _____
2. 14:10 _____
3. 05:00 _____
4. 13:00 _____
5. 03:15 _____
6. 13:30 _____
7. 9:20 _____
8. 23:05 _____
9. 23:10 _____
10. 20:40 _____
11. 17:00 _____
12. 12:50 _____

Find the duration.

1. from 05:00 to 11:00 _____
2. from 7:00a.m. to 11:00a.m. _____
3. from 06:15 to 13:30 _____
4. from 5:20a.m. to 3:30p.m. _____
5. from 09:45 to 20: 10 _____
6. from 9:20a.m. to 4:10p.m. _____
7. from 11:20 to 20:15 _____
8. from 10:30a.m. to 8:15p.m. _____

Elapsed Time

Example:

Departure time:	5: 10 a.m.	5 : 10
Elapsed time:	3 hrs. 30 min.	+ 3 : 30
Arrival time:	8: 40 a.m.	8 : 40

	Departure time	**+ Elapsed time**	**= Arrival time**
1.	5 : 10 a.m.	3 hrs. 30 min	8 : 40 a.m.
2.	8 : 40 a.m.	3 hrs. 05 min	
3.	5 : 10 a.m.	4 hrs. 25 min	
4.	4 : 25 a.m.	9 hrs. 15 min	
5.	7 : 35 a.m.	2 hrs. 10 min	
6.	6 : 25 p.m.	3 hrs. 35 min	
7.	9 : 24 p.m.	2 hrs. 16 min	

Example:

Departure time:	7: 25 p.m.	10 : 50
Arrival time:	10: 50 p.m.	− 7 : 25
Elapsed time:	3 hrs. 25 min.	3 : 25

	Departure time	**Elapsed time**	**Arrival time**
1.	7 : 25 a.m.		10 : 50 a.m.
2.	6 : 25 a.m.		11 : 40 a.m.
3.	10 : 30 p.m.		11 : 55 p.m.
4.	1 : 20 p.m.		6 : 30 p.m.
5.	5 : 15 p.m.		9 : 40 p.m.
6.	7 : 28 a.m.		9 : 50 a.m.

Name _____ Date _____

Elapsed Time

Example:

Departure time: 8 : 25 p.m.   8 : 25

Elapsed time: 2 hrs. 45 min.   +   2 : 45

Arrival time: 11 : 10 p.m.   10 : 70 = 11 : 10 (since 1 hr. = 60 min)

	Departure time	Elapsed time	Arrival time
1.	8 : 25 p.m.	2 hrs. 45 min	11 : 10 p.m.
2.	8 : 40 a.m.	1 hrs. 20 min	
3.	2 : 30 p.m.	8 hrs. 45 min	
4.	6 : 25 p.m.	4 hrs. 50 min	
5.	3 : 10 a.m.	6 hrs. 55 min	
6.	4 : 42 p.m.	3 hr. 27 min	
7.	9 : 26 a.m.	2 hrs. 58 min	

Example:

Departure time: 5: 45 p.m.   8 : 20 = 7 : 80

Arrival time: 8: 20 p.m.   −   5: 45   = 5 : 45

Elapsed time: 2 hrs. 35 min.   2 : 35

	Departure time	Elapsed time	Arrival time
1.	5: 45 a.m.		8 : 20 a.m.
2.	4: 20 a.m.		9 : 15 a. m.
3.	5 : 45 a.m.		11 : 20 a. m.
4.	2 : 35 p.m.		7 : 25 p.m.
5.	8 : 50 p.m.		10 : 30 p.m.
6.	1 : 30 p.m.		6 : 10 p.m.

Name _____ Date _____

The graph below shows the time of sunrise and sunset in a Canadian city on the 1st of each month.

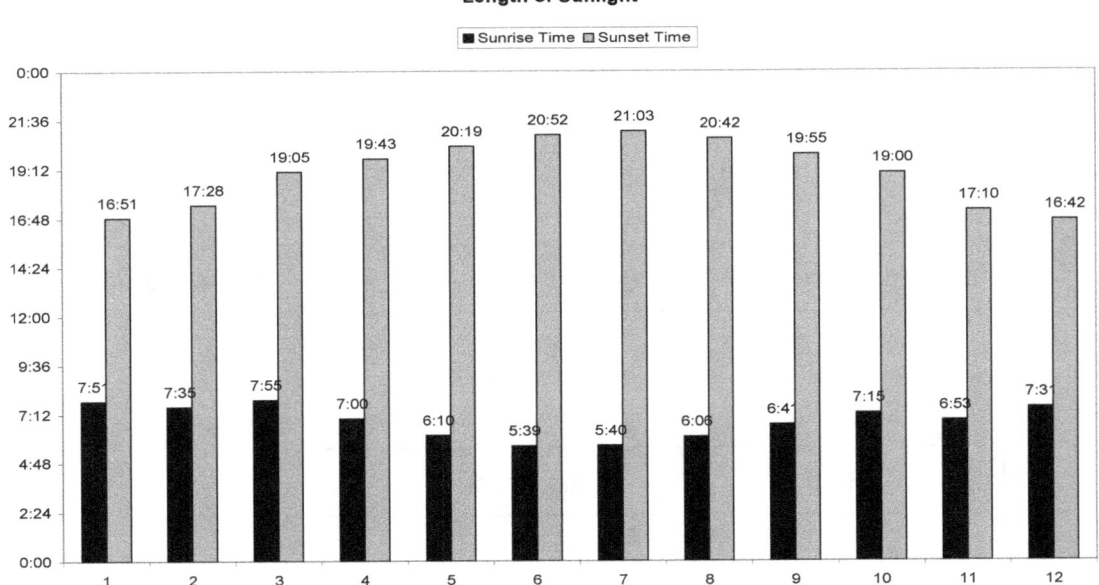

1. Find the length of daytime of the first day of each month.

Date	Sunrise	Sunset	Length
1-Jan	07:51	16:51	9 hrs.
1-Feb	07:35	17:28	
1-Mar	07:55	19:05	
1-Apr	07:00	19:43	
1-May	06:10	20:19	
1-Jun	05:39	20:52	
1-Jul	05:40	21:03	
1-Aug	06:06	20:42	
1-Sep	06:41	19:55	
1-Oct	07:15	19:00	
1-Nov	06:53	17:10	
1-Dec	07:31	16:42	

2. On which date in the table is the length of daytime:

a. the longest? _____   b. the shortest? _____

134

Name _____   Date _____

E2. Seconds, minutes, and hours

1 day = 24 hours   1 hour = 60 minutes   1 minute = 60 seconds

1. 2 hours = _____ minutes

2. 3 minutes = _____ seconds

3. 5 hours = _____ minutes

4. 10 minutes = _____ seconds

5. 2 hours 25 minutes = _____ minutes

6. 200 minutes = _____ hours _____ minutes

7. 6 hours 15 minutes = _____ minutes

8. 280 minutes = _____ hours _____ minutes

9. 7 minutes 25 seconds = _____ seconds

10. 345 seconds = _____ minutes _____ seconds

11. 10 hours = _____ minutes

12. 300 minutes = _____ hours _____ minutes

13. 190 seconds = _____ minutes and _____ seconds

14. 13 hours = _____ minutes

15. 520 minutes = _____ hours _____ minutes

16. 320 seconds = _____ minutes _____ seconds

17. 10 minutes 25 seconds = _____ seconds

18. 25 hours = _____ minutes

19. 630 minutes = _____ hours _____ minutes

20. 3 minutes and 5 seconds = _____ seconds

Name _____ Date _____

Addition and Multiplication

$$1 \text{ hour} = 60 \text{ minutes}, \quad 1 \text{ minute} = 60 \text{ seconds}$$

Example:

1. Susan took 3 hour 40 minutes to clean the house and 2 hour 45 minutes to cook dinner. How long did it take her to do household that day?

```
    h    min              h    min
    3     40              3     40
  + 2     45            + 2     45
  ─────────             ─────────
    5     85              5     85    (1 hr. = 60 min)
                       + 1    − 60
                       ─────────
                          6     25    6 hrs. 25 min
```

2. Sam does exercise for 1 hour 45 minutes every day. How long does he do exercise in 7 days?

```
    h    min              h    min
    1     45              1     45
  ×        7            ×        7
  ─────────             ─────────
    7    315              7    315    (5 hr. = 300 min)
                       + 5 ← − 300
                       ─────────
                         12     15    12 hrs. 15 min
```

Evaluate.

1.
```
    h    min
    4     45
  + 2     25
  ─────────
```

2.
```
  min    s
    4     20
  ×        7
  ─────────
```

3.
```
  min    s
    6     40
  + 4     30
  ─────────
```

4.
```
    h    min
    6     50
  ×        5
  ─────────
```

Name _____ Date _____

5.
```
      h    min
      5     28
   +  1     54
   ─────────────
```

6.
```
     min    s
      5    15
   ×         6
   ─────────────
```

7.
```
      h    min
      4     36
   +  2     47
   ─────────────
```

8.
```
      h    min
      3     32
   ×          5
   ─────────────
```

9.
```
     min    s
     20    37
   +  4    52
   ─────────────
```

10.
```
     min    s
     12    40
   ×         3
   ─────────────
```

11. Stanley traveled 2 hours 35 minutes from Vancouver to Hope and 2 hours 15 minutes back to Vancouver. How long did it take him to make the round trip?

12. It took Benjamin 25 minutes to go to school. He stayed at school for 5 hours and 30 minutes. And it took him another 25 minutes to go back home. How long did he stay away from home that day?

13. David planned to take a chess tournament of 8 games. It would take him an average of 55 minutes to finish a game. If he played with no stop, how long would it take him to finish the tournament?

14. It took Nick 3 minutes 12 seconds to swim one lap. If he kept the same speed, how long would it take him to swim 7 laps?

Name _____ Date _____

Subtraction and Division

Example:

1. In a marathon race, Steve finished in 3 hours 15 minutes. Michael won the first place in 2 hours 52 minutes. How much longer did Steve use to finish than Michael did?

```
   h    min              h      min
   3    15              3²      15⁷⁵
 - 2    52            - 2       52
                        0       23
```

Steve used 23 more minutes to finish.

2. In a chess tournament, Andrew finished 5 games in 3 hours 45 minutes. What was his average time to play one game?

```
    h  min         h        min          h         min
                                                    4 5
 5| 3  4 5     5| 3         4 5      5| 3          4 5
                 ×60  +   1 8 0         ×60   +  1 8 0
                 180      2 2 5         180      2 2 5
                                                 2 2 5
```

It took Andrew about 45 minutes to finish one game.

Evaluate.

1.
```
     h    min
     5    15
   - 1    40
```

2.
```
        h       min
   3 | 1        1 5
```

3.
```
    min    s
    10    30
  -  2    48
```

4.
```
        h     min
   6 | 4     4 8
```

138

5.
```
    min    s
    11    15
 -   9    25
```

6.
```
      h    min
  4 | 9    20
```

7.
```
    h    min
    5    05
 -  1    46
```

8.
```
      min    s
  5 | 3    05
```
(5 | 53 05)

9.
```
    min    s
    22    12
 -  15    36
```

10.
```
      min    s
  6 | 28    30
```

11. Linda finished a book in 3 hours 15 minutes. The same book took Ashley 2 hours 55 minutes. How much time shorter did Ashley use than Linda?

12. Fred finished a 5000 m race in 15 minutes 37 seconds. Sam did it in 17 minutes 45 seconds. How much faster is Fred than Sam?

13. Shirley painted 6 pictures in 3 hours 18 minutes. About how long did it take her to finish one painting?

14. Stanley is a math bizarre. He can finish 25 multiplication questions in 30 minutes 50 seconds. What is his average time to do one question?

E3. Hours, days, weeks, months, and years

1 year = 12 months = 52 weeks   1 month = 30 days

1 week = 7 days   1 day = 24 hours

1. 5 weeks = _____ days = _____ hours
2. 3 days = _____ hours
3. 7 months = _____ days
4. 3 years = _____ months = _____ days
5. 5 months = _____ days
6. 1 week = _____ days = _____ hours
7. 7 weeks = _____ days
8. 80 days = _____ weeks _____ days
9. 35 months = _____ years _____ months
10. 5 months 9 days = _____ days
11. 2 years 12 weeks = _____ weeks
12. 350 days = _____ months _____ days
13. 28 months = _____ years _____ months
14. 4 months = _____ days
15. 180 days = _____ weeks _____ days
16. 80 months = _____ years _____ months
17. 10 months 10 days = _____ days
18. 5 years 3 weeks = _____ weeks
19. 250 days = _____ months _____ days
20. 54 months = _____ years _____ months

Addition and Multiplication

Example:

	d		hr.		wk.	d			m	d			y	wk.
	2		8		6	5			2	12			3	14
+	4		21	+	8	3	×			7	×			8
	6		29		14	8			14	84			24	112
+	1	−	24	+	1	− 7	+		2	− 60	+		2	− 104
	7		5		15	1			16	24			26	8

Evaluate.

1.
  m   d
  4   23
+ 2   15

2.
  y   m
  4   6
×   7

3.
  m   wk
  5   3
+ 1   2

4.
  d   hr
  4   17
×   3

5.
  m   d
  6   28
+ 2   14

6.
  m   d
  3   23
×   4

7.
```
   d    hr
   4    16
+  3    11
─────────────
```

8.
```
   m    wk
   4    2
×        7
─────────────
```

9.
```
   y    wk
   5    37
+  1    21
─────────────
```

10.
```
   d    h
   7    14
×        4
─────────────
```

11.
```
   y    d
   3    126
+  1    258
─────────────
```

12.
```
   m    d
   7    11
×        4
─────────────
```

13.
```
   d    hr
   3    17
+  1    9
─────────────
```

14.
```
   y    m
   12   7
×        4
─────────────
```

15.
```
   m    d
   6    27
+  1    13
─────────────
```

16.
```
   d    hr
   8    17
×        3
─────────────
```

Subtraction and Division

Example:

```
  wk.   d        m    d           d        hr.        m          wk.
  5⁴   2⁹        4³   13⁴³        1         19        1           5
-  1    6      -  2    28      5)6          3 5    3)5            1
   3    3         1    15         5          6 0       3          1 4
                                  1  ×60     9 5       2   ×7     1 5
                                             9 5                  1 5
                                               0                    0
```

Evaluate.

1.   m   d
     4   6
   - 2   24

2.   m   wk.
   3)4   1 1

3.   y   d
     9   230
   - 6   325

4.   m   d
   7)10   4 3

5.   y   m
     9   5
   - 4   8

6.   y   m
   2)9   8

Name _____   Date _____

7.
```
     wk    d
      5    3
   -  2    5
   _____
```

8.
```
       m       d
      _____
   6 | 2 1    2 4
```

9.
```
     d    hr
     7    8
   - 5    21
   _____
```

10.
```
       y       m
      _____
   4 | 2 1     8
```

11.
```
      y    m
     31    4
   - 23    8
   _____
```

12.
```
       y       wk.
      _____
   3 | 1 3    3 5
```

13.
```
     wk    d
      8    9
   -  3    17
   _____
```

14.
```
       d       hr.
      _____
   5 | 1 8    1 3
```

Applications

1. There are 726 carrots. If a rabbit can eat 6 carrots a day, how many days will the rabbit finish all the carrots? How many months?

2. A little bear was 1.6 kg when it was born. If he gains 0.5 kg every week, how many months will it take him to grow to 7.6 kg?

3. Linda is 8 years 7 months years old. Her mom is 35 years 3 months years old. How many times older is her mom than her?

4. A mother is 4 times as old as her daughter. The daughter is 9 years 5 months old now. How old is the mom?

5. There is a snail at the bottom of a tree of 12m tall. If the snail climbs up 0.5m in one hour and rest for two hours, how many hours can the snail climb up to the top of the tree? How many days?

6. It takes 6 people 5 months 12 days to build a house. If there are 12 people to build the house, how long will it take them to finish?

7. It takes 8 people 4 months 18 days to build a house. If they plan to build 4 houses of the same kind, and there are 12 people, how long will it take them to finish??

8. Serena is training for a piano contest. She needs to finish 540 hours training in 30 weeks. If she practices 6 days a week, how many hours should she practice every day?

Name _____ Date _____

E4. Regular year and leap year

There are 365 days in a **regular year**.
There are 366 days in a **leap year**, with the extra day designated as February 29.
Leap Years are any year that can be evenly divided by 4, like 1948, 1988, 2016.

1. How many days are there in a leap year?

2. How many days are there in a regular year?

3. How many days are there in Febuary in a leap year?

4. How many days are there in Febuary in a regular year?

5. Is 2014 a leap year?

6. How many days are there in 2014?

7. Which year is the most recent leap year after 2017?

8. How many months in a year have 31 days? What are they?

9. How many months in a year have 30 days? What are they?

10. How many weeks are there in a regular year?

Name _____   Date _____

E5. Calendar

1. Today is Monday May 12; this coming Saturday will be   _____May 17._____

2. Today is Saturday, May 13; this coming Monday will be   _____

3. Today is Wednesday, Apr 8; last Thursday was   _____

4. Today is Monday, Dec 19; this coming Saturday will be   _____

5. Today is Saturday, June 28; this coming Monday will be   _____

6. Today is Wednesday, Jan 26; last Friday was   _____

7. Today is Tuesday 4, Aug 2; last Saturday was   _____

8. Today is Saturday, Mar 6; last Monday was   _____

9. Today is Wednesday, April 5; last Friday was   _____

10. Today is Monday, Nov 5; this coming Friday will be   _____

11. Today is Thursday, Jul 7; this coming Wednesday will be   _____

12. Today is Thursday, Aug 16; last Friday was   _____

13. Today is Tuesday, Sep 29; this coming Wednesday will be   _____

14. This month is April, 4 months later it will be   _____

15. This month is February, 5 months later will be   _____

16. This month is December, 3 months ago was   _____

17. This month is May, 6 months ago was   _____

18. This month is August, 5 months later will be   _____

19. This month is September, 21 months later will be   _____

20. This month is November, 24 months ago was   _____

Name _____ Date _____

F. Coins

       1 penny = 1 ¢   1 nickel = 5 ¢

       1 dime = 10 ¢   1 quarter = 25 ¢

Write each amount in decimal form.

1. 2 quarters, 3 dimes, 2 nickels, 5 pennies

    $0.95

2. 1 quarter, 2 dimes, 5 nickels, 6 pennies

3. 5 quarters, 4 nickels, 3 pennies

4. 3 quarters, 2 dimes, 6 nickels

5. 9 dimes, 3 nickels, 7 pennies

6. 8 quarters, 5 dimes, 2 pennies

7. 4 quarters, 2 dimes, 5 nickels

8. 7 dimes, 4 nickels, 8 pennies

Name _____ Date _____

F1. Coin problems

Use the fewest number of coins to make each amount.

1. 62 ¢

    _____ pennies _____ dimes

    _____ nickels _____ quarters

2. 36 ¢

    _____ pennies _____ dimes

    _____ nickels _____ quarters

3. 48 ¢

    _____ pennies _____ dimes

    _____ nickels _____ quarters

4. 74 ¢

    _____ pennies _____ dimes

    _____ nickels _____ quarters

5. 91 ¢

    _____ pennies _____ dimes

    _____ nickels _____ quarters

6. 56 ¢

    _____ pennies _____ dimes

    _____ nickels _____ quarters

7. 87 ¢

    _____ pennies _____ dimes

    _____ nickels _____ quarters

8. 19 ¢

    _____ pennies _____ dimes

    _____ nickels _____ quarters

9. $1.45

    _____ pennies _____ dimes

    _____ nickels _____ quarters

    _____ dollar

10. $5.39

    _____ pennies _____ dimes

    _____ nickels _____ quarters

    _____ dollar

11. $6.72

    _____ pennies _____ dimes

    _____ nickels _____ quarters

    _____ dollar

12. $3.56

    _____ pennies _____ dimes

    _____ nickels _____ quarters

    _____ dollar

Name _____ Date _____

Use exactly the number of coins to make each amount.

1. 47¢ with 5 coins

    _____ pennies _____ dimes

    _____ nickels _____ quarters

2. 53¢ with 5 coins

    _____ pennies _____ dimes

    _____ nickels _____ quarters

3. 36¢ with 4 coins

    _____ pennies _____ dimes

    _____ nickels _____ quarters

4. 73¢ with 8 coins

    _____ pennies _____ dimes

    _____ nickels _____ quarters

5. 87¢ with 8 coins

    _____ pennies _____ dimes

    _____ nickels _____ quarters

6. 81¢ with 5 coins

    _____ pennies _____ dimes

    _____ nickels _____ quarters

7. 69¢ with 10 coins

    _____ pennies _____ dimes

    _____ nickels _____ quarters

8. 56¢ with 9 coins

    _____ pennies _____ dimes

    _____ nickels _____ quarters

9. 42¢ with 11 coins

    _____ pennies _____ dimes

    _____ nickels _____ quarters

10. 99¢ with 9 coins

    _____ pennies _____ dimes

    _____ nickels _____ quarters

11. $1.12 with 9 coins

    _____ pennies _____ dimes

    _____ nickels _____ quarters

    _____ dollars

12. $2.08 with 6 coins

    _____ pennies _____ dimes

    _____ nickels _____ quarters

    _____ dollar

Name _____ Date _____

Represent each amount in two ways ('P' presents penny, 'N' presents nickel, 'D' presents dime, 'Q' presents quarter and 'T' presents total).

1. 30 ¢ with 6 coins	2. 40 ¢ with 4 coins
3. 45 ¢ with 9 coins	4. 54 ¢ with 11 coins
5. 51 ¢ with 7 coins	6. 58 ¢ with 9 coins

Represent each amount in three ways ('P' presents penny, 'N' presents nickel, 'D' presents dime, 'Q' presents quarter and 'T' presents total).

1. 57 ¢ with 9 coins

	P	N	D	Q	T
1.					
2.					
3.					

2. 85 ¢ with 12 coins

	P	N	D	Q	T
1.					
2.					
3.					

3. 73 ¢ with 15 coins

	P	N	D	Q	T
1.					
2.					
3.					

4. 55 ¢ with 7 coins

	P	N	D	Q	T
1.					
2.					
3.					

Name _____   Date _____

Represent each amount in as many ways as possible.

1. 80 ¢ with 8 coins

	P	N	D	Q	T
1.					
2.					
3.					
4.					

2. 85 ¢ with 13 coins

	P	N	D	Q	T
1.					
2.					
3.					
4.					

3. 96¢ with 11 coins

	P	N	D	Q	T
1.	1	1	9	0	
2.	6	1	1	3	
3.	1	4	5	1	
4.	1	7	1	2	

4. $1.00 with 18 coins

	P	N	D	Q	T
1.					
2.					
3.					
4.					
5.					

Name _____ Date _____

F2. Problem solving

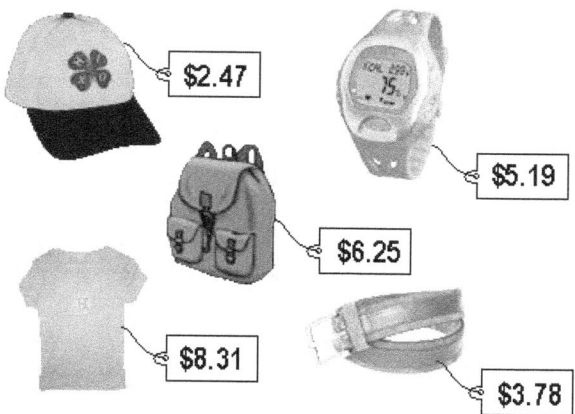

1. Linda bought a T-shirt and paid $10. How much change would she get?

2. Grace gave the clerk $6.25 for two items. Which two items did she buy?

3. Tom bought a bag and a watch. How much did the two items cost him?

   If he gave the clerk $15. How much change should he get back?

4. Steve bought 2 T-shirt and a bag. He had $20 with him. Does he have enough money? How much should he borrow to make the deal?

5. Isabel bought 3 items with $12. Which 3 items did she buy? How much change did she get back?

Name _____   Date _____

Problem solving

1. James bought a notebook for $1.75 and a pen for $2.46. How much did he spend?

2. Lollipop is $2.58 per pound. Chocolate bar is $7.84 per pound. Frank bought 5 pounds of lollipop and 2 pounds of chocolate bar. How much did he spend?

3. Kevin has some coins in his purse: 3 toonies, 4 loonies, 7 quarters, 3 dimes, 5s, and 15 pennies. How much does he have?

4. Three friends went for shopping for a picnic. They bought 3 loaves of bread for $1.27 each, 5 bottles of juice for $2.35 each, 2 pounds of sausage for $7.46 per pound. If they share the cost equally, how much should each person pay?

5. Aaron bought four goldfish for $0.28 each and a bag of fish food for $1.63. He gave the clerk $5. How much change did he get back?

Name _____ Date _____

F3. Rounding decimals

Example: Is $3.42 is closer to $3 or $4?

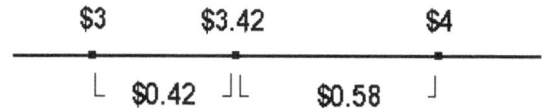

The difference between $3 and $3.42 is: $3.42 - $3 = $0.42
The difference between $4 and $3.42 is: $4 - $3.42 = $0.58
And we know that 0.58 > 0.42. So, when $3.42 is rounded to nearest dollar, the answer is $3.

Round each amount to the nearest dollar.

1. $ 4.78 _____   2. $ 0.63 _____

3. $ 23.52 _____   4. $ 8.41 _____

5. $ 7.89 _____   6. $ 5.09 _____

7. $ 27.91 _____   8. $ 81.32 _____

9. $ 48.19 _____   10. $ 31.87 _____

11. $ 157.37 _____   12. $ 642.61 _____

Round to the nearest ten dollars

1. $ 36.72 $40 _____   2. $ 81.32 _____

3. $ 68.07 _____   4. $ 55.67 _____

5. $ 43.98 _____   6. $ 37.21 _____

7. $ 582.71 _____   8. $ 695.86 _____

9. $ 472.96 _____   10. $ 892.65 _____

11. $ 531.53 _____   12. $ 637.09 _____

F4. Decimal estimations

Estimate the sums or differences

Example:

	$2.37 →	$2.00		$6.67 →		$7.00
+	$3.82 →	$4.00	−	$2.71 →	−	$3.00
	about	$6.00		about		$4.00

$ 2.74 + $ 5.08 + $ 12.57

= $ 3 + $ 5 + $ 13

= $ 21

$ 15.63 − $ 6.98

= $ 16 − $ 7

= $ 9

1.
$7.46 →
+ $4.73 → +
_____ _____

2.
$9.86 →
− $5.47 → −
_____ _____

3.
$32.65 →
+ $67.28 → +
_____ _____

4.
$72.58 →
− $18.36 → −
_____ _____

5. $ 4.75 + $ 3.17 + $ 8.69

=

=

6. $ 6.85 + $ 0.26 + $ 7.94

=

=

7. $ 17.95 − $ 3.62

=

=

8. $ 25.73 − $ 12.39

=

=

Name _____   Date _____

Estimate the products

Example:

$$\$2.83 \times 6 \qquad \$3.00 \times 6 = \text{about } \$18.00$$

$$\$18.93 \times 52$$
$$= \$20 \times 50$$
$$= \$1000$$

1. $\$5.08 \rightarrow$
   $\times \quad 9 \rightarrow \times$

2. $\$8.73 \rightarrow$
   $\times \quad 4 \rightarrow \times$

3. $\$12.66 \rightarrow$
   $\times \quad 7 \rightarrow \times$

4. $\$47.23 \rightarrow$
   $\times \quad 8 \rightarrow \times$

5. $\$5.14 \times 12$
   =
   =

6. $\$6.71 \times 8$
   =
   =

7. $\$15.31 \times 5$
   =
   =

8. $\$19.57 \times 13$
   =
   =

9. $\$21.47 \times 32$
   =
   =

10. $\$68.04 \times 79$
    =
    =

Name _____ Date _____

Estimate the quotients.

Example:

$6\overline{)\$23.27}$ *use compatible number* $6\overline{)\$24.00}$ $\begin{array}{r}\$4.00\\ \underline{24}\\ 0\end{array}$

$\$46.73 \div 7$
= $\$49.00 \div 7$ (round dividend with compatible number)
= $\$7$

1. $5\overline{)\$62.73}$ →

2. $4\overline{)\$33.59}$ →

3. $8\overline{)\$67.23}$ →

4. $7\overline{)\$81.36}$ →

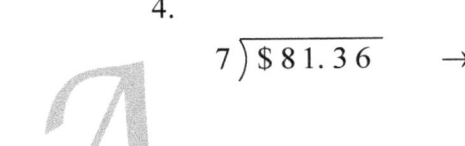

5. $\$53.87 \div 6$
    =
    =

6. $\$70.62 \div 9$
    =
    =

7. $\$43.09 \div 5$
    =
    =

8. $\$68.47 \div 6$
    =
    =

9. $\$39.72 \div 4$
    =
    =

10. $\$61.78 \div 7$
    =
    =

G. Decimals

G1. Units and tenths

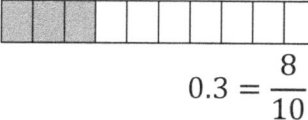
$0.3 = \dfrac{8}{10}$
It is read as three tenths.

  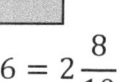
$2.6 = 2\dfrac{8}{10}$
It is read as two and eight tenths.

Express the shaded part in fractions and decimals.

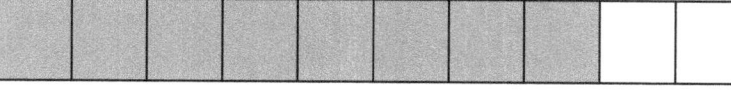 $\dfrac{8}{10}$ or 0.8

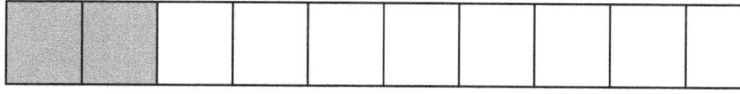 _____ or _____

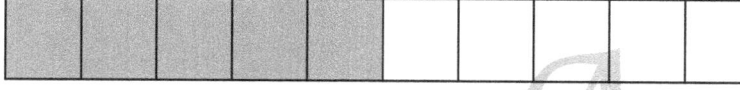 _____ or _____

 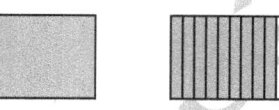 _____ or _____

  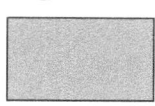 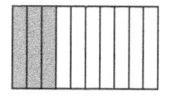 _____ or _____

  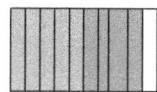 _____ or _____

Draw the length of AB

Example   3.8 cm
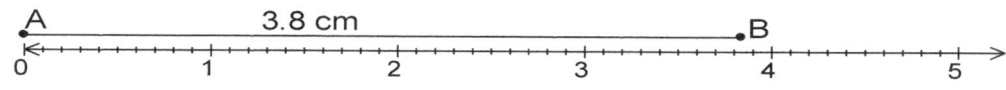

1)   3.6 cm
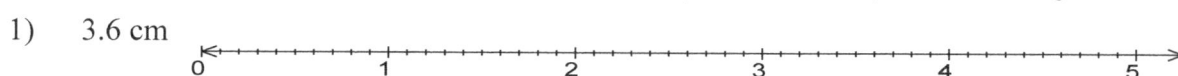

2)   1.3 cm

3)   0.9 cm
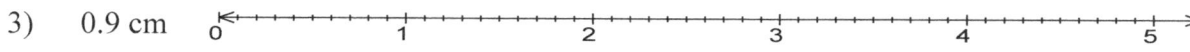

Name _____ Date _____

Write each fraction in decimal.

1) $\frac{2}{10}$ _____ 2) $2\frac{7}{10}$ _____

3) $8\frac{1}{10}$ _____ 4) $3\frac{4}{10}$ _____

Write each decimal in fraction or mixed number.

1) 0.5 _____ 2) 3.7 _____

3) 10.9 _____ 4) 7.1 _____

Write each numeral in decimal.

1) seven tenths _____ 2) two and six tenths _____

3) eight and three tenths _____ 4) three and one tenths _____

5) nine tenths _____ 6) ten and six tenths _____

7) forty and three tenths _____ 8) two hundred one and six tenths _____

9) fifteen and two tenth _____ 10) ninety and eight tenths _____

Write each decimal in word.

1) 0.7 _____ 2) 0.3 _____

3) 1.6 _____ 4) 5.9 _____

5) 4.7 _____ 6) 10.5 _____

7) 100.8 _____ 8) 38.2 _____

Count by tenths

1) from 0.2 to 0.9 _____

2) from 10.1 to 10.7 _____

Count by ones

1) from 1.4 to 8.4 _____

2) from 5.1 to 11.1 _____

G2. Equivalent decimals

Any number of zeros can be added onto the end of a decimal number without changing the value of the number. For example: 2=2.0

2

2.0

Give three decimal numbers which are equivalent to each of the following.

1) 2.1 _____ _____ _____

2) 10.2 _____ _____ _____

3) 100.01 _____ _____ _____

Compare by using < , > , or = in each ☐ to make each statement true.

1) 3.5 ____ 3.05   2) 10.5 ____ 15.00   3) 7.8 ____ 70.8

4) 5.6 ____ 5.60   5) 100.000 ____ 100.1   6) 6.000 ____ 6.0

7) 3.7 ____ 3.700   8) 6.300 ____ 6.30   9) 4.2 ____ 42.0

10) 5.3 ____ 5.1000   11) 1.20 ____ 1.3   12) 1.20 ____ 120

Circle the decimal that is equivalent to the number on the left.

1) 7.4   a. 7.04   b. 7.400   c. 0.74   d. 74.0

2) 11.0   a. 1.1   b. 110   c. 10.1   d. 11

3) 6.9   a. 9.6   b. 9.60   c. 6.90   d. 69

G3. Hundredths

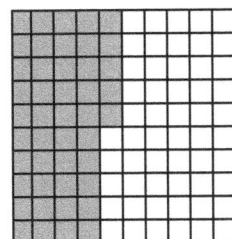

$0.45 = \dfrac{45}{100}$

It id read as forty-five hundredths

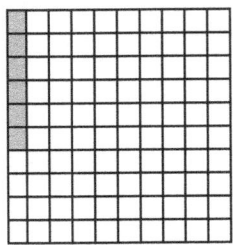

$0.06 = \dfrac{6}{100}$

It is read as six hundredths

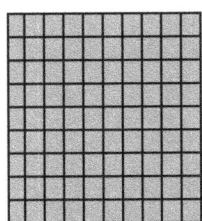 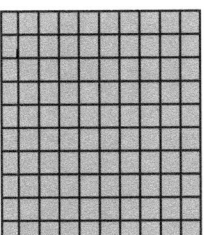 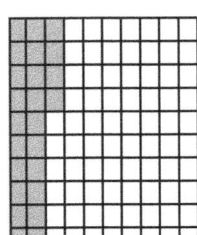

$2.24 = 2\dfrac{24}{100}$

It is read as two and Twenty-four hundredths

Express the following shaded parts in fraction and decimal

1.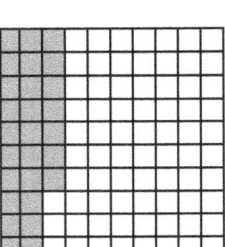

2.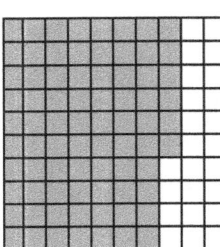

3.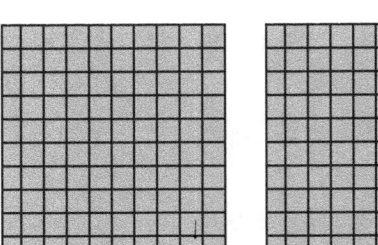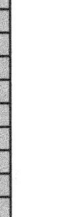

4.

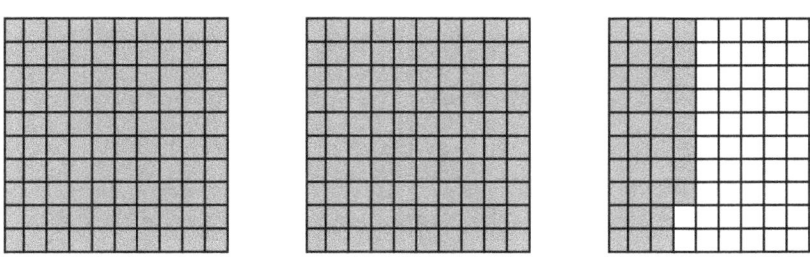

Graph each length on the number line.

1)   0.38 cm

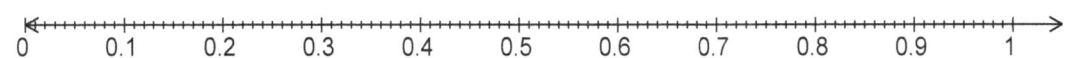

2)   1.85 cm

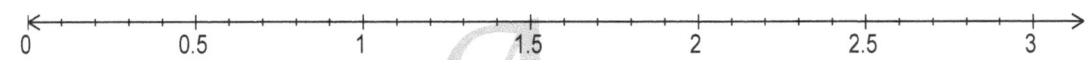

3)   2.35 cm

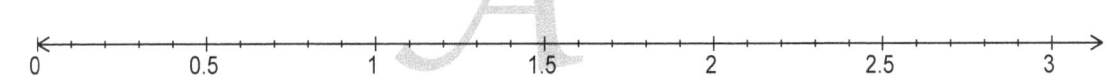

Circle the largest number.

1)   6.32   6.23   3.62   6.03

2)   8.52   7.82   8.25   8.72

Arrange these numbers in order from the smallest to the largest.

1)   3.04   5.03   3.05   3.45   3.54   3.40   3.50   5.34

_____

2)   1.05   5.01   10.5   1.51   1.15   5.11   6.17   7.61

_____

Name _____ Date _____

Write each decimal in standard form.

1) three and thirty-nine hundredths

2) five and two hundredths

3) fifteen and one hundredths

4) ten and three hundredths

5) one and one hundredth

6) forty-five and thirty hundredths

7) nine hundred and eighteen hundredths

8) one hundred and twenty-seven hundredths

Write each decimal in words.

1) 2.63

2) 10.50

3) 0.07

4) 43.21

5) 100.02

6) 12.15

7) 1.01

8) 20.50

Compare by using <, >, or = in each blank to make each statement true.

1) 0.25 _____ 0.21   2) 0.05 _____ 0.50   3) 3.21 _____ 3.12

4) 3.02 _____ 3.20   5) 10.00 _____ 1.000   6) 2.63 _____ 3.26

7) 9.60 _____ 9.6   8) 0.11 _____ 1.10   9) 00.02 _____ 100.20

10) 4.08 _____ 4.80   11) 3.30 _____ 33.0   12) 213.00 _____ 213

Name _____   Date _____

Write each fraction in decimal.

1) $\dfrac{21}{100} =$

2) $1\dfrac{43}{100} =$

3) $\dfrac{5}{10} =$

5) $2\dfrac{63}{100} =$

6) $10\dfrac{20}{100} =$

7) $8\dfrac{9}{100} =$

$\dfrac{6}{100} =$

$10\dfrac{30}{100} =$

$1\dfrac{1}{100} =$

9) $7\dfrac{16}{100} =$

10) $9\dfrac{4}{10} =$

11) $7\dfrac{2}{10} =$

Complete the following chart.

1.	Count in twos from 2	2	4	6	8	10
2.	Count in ones from 10					
3.	Count in tenths from 2.3					
4.	Count in tenths from 7					
5.	Count in tenths from 9.8					
6.	Count in hundredths from 10.05					
7.	Count in hundredths from 6					
8.	Count in hundredths from 0.5					
9.	Count in hundredths from 4.27					
10.	Count in hundredths from 9.98					

Name _____ Date _____

Write each number in expanded form in two ways.

Standard form   Expanded form

43.21 $= 4 \times 10 + 3 \times 1 + 2 \times 0.1 + 1 \times 0.01$

$= 40 + 3 + 0.2 + 0.01$

1) 0.45 = _____

= _____

2) 3.57 = _____

= _____

3) 8.62 = _____

= _____

4) 0.08 = _____

= _____

5) 7.05 = _____

= _____

6) 43.21 = _____

= _____

7) 53.09 = _____

= _____

G4. Thousandths

Write each decimal in standard form.

1) three hundred sixty-eight thousandths

   _____0.368_____

2) fifty-eight thousandths

   _____

3) ten and one thousandth

   _____

4) four and three thousandths

   _____

5) seven and eleven thousandths

   _____

6) eight thousandths

   _____

7) thirty and one hundred sixty thousandths

   _____

8) one and nine hundred sixteen thousandths

   _____

Write each decimal in words.

1) 4.321

2) 0.572

3) 1.056

4) 0.006

5) 2.780

6) 4.308

7) 0.072

8) 11.007

Compare by using <, >, or = in each blank to make each statement true.

1) 0.213 ____ 0.231   2) 0.963 ____ 1.043   3) 0.569 ____ 0.561

4) 0.32 ____ 3.210   5) 6.078 ____ 5.879   6) 0.473 ____ 0.453

7) 2.310 ____ 2.31   8) 5.286 ____ 52.86   9) 0.812 ____ 0.911

Name _____ Date _____

Write each fraction in decimal.

1. $\dfrac{729}{1000} =$ _____
2. $2\dfrac{849}{1000} =$ _____
3. $\dfrac{5}{1000} =$ _____

4. $4\dfrac{37}{1000} =$ _____
5. $\dfrac{50}{1000} =$ _____
6. $\dfrac{16}{1000} =$ _____

7. $3\dfrac{28}{1000} =$ _____
8. $10\dfrac{9}{1000} =$ _____
9. $1\dfrac{40}{1000} =$ _____

9. $6\dfrac{5}{1000} =$ _____
10. $\dfrac{7}{1000} =$ _____
11. $8\dfrac{16}{1000} =$ _____

Count in thousandths.

1) 0.004 _____ _____ _____ _____ _____

2) 1.247 _____ _____ _____ _____ _____

3) 2.995 _____ _____ _____ _____ _____

4) 5.6 _____ _____ _____ _____ _____

5) 8 _____ _____ _____ _____ _____

Write the value of digit '6' in each number.

1) 9.246   ___6 thousandths___
2) 7.06   _____

3) 6.725   _____
4) 3.176   _____

5) 0.967   _____
6) 36.532   _____

7) 5.916   _____
8) 6.009   _____

9) 7.628   _____
10) 4.746   _____

11) 61.75   _____
12) 0.673   _____

Write in expanded form in two ways.

Standard form | Expanded form
16.739 | $= 1 \times 10 + 6 \times 1 + 7 \times 0.1 + 3 \times 0.01 + 9 \times 0.001$
 | $= 10 + 6 + 0.7 + 0.03 + 0.009$

1) 7.846 = _____

    = _____

2) 10.673 = _____

    = _____

3) 0.078 = _____

    = _____

4) 8.904 = _____

    = _____

5) 6.235 = _____

    = _____

6) 0.952 = _____

    = _____

7) 67.009 = _____

    = _____

Review on Decimals

Thousands	Hundreds	Tens	Ones	.	tenths	hundredths	thousandths
5	2	7	3	decimal	4	6	9

Standard form   5273.469
Expanded form $5\,000 + 200 + 70 + 3 + 0.4 + 0.06 + 0.009$
    $5 \times 1000 + 2 \times 100 + 7 \times 10 + 3 \times 1 + 4 \times 0.1 + 6 \times 0.01 + 9 \times 0.001$
Words: five thousand two hundred seventy-three and four hundred sixty-nine thousandth

Write the following fractions in decimal form:

1) $5\dfrac{6}{10} =$

2) $\dfrac{82}{100} =$

3) $7\dfrac{57}{100} =$

4) $9\dfrac{475}{1000} =$

5) $3\dfrac{67}{1000} =$

6) $2\dfrac{9}{10} =$

7) $6\dfrac{8}{100} =$

8) $10\dfrac{7}{1000} =$

Express the following decimals in fraction form.

1) 1.6

2) 4.321

3) 3.12

4) 5.09

5) 0.74

6) 0.507

7) 0.005

8) 2.078

9) 0.01

10) 3.07

Name _____ Date _____

Write each number in decimal form.

1) one tenth _____

2) twenty-seven hundredths _____

3) sixty-four hundredths _____

4) eight thousandths _____

5) nineteen hundred and five hundred thirty-six thousandths _____

6) six hundred and one tenths _____

7) sixty-two hundred and five tenths _____

8) eight thousand five and thirty-six thousandths _____

9) nine thousand one hundred sixty and four tenths _____

10) seventy and four hundred fifty-four thousandths _____

11) three hundred fifteen and fourteen hundredths _____

12) sixty-eight and ninety-five thousandths _____

13) four hundred thirty-seven thousandths _____

14) seventy-two thousand and twenty-five hundredths _____

15) two hundred one thousandth _____

16) seven and twelve hundredths _____

17) three hundred seven and two hundredths _____

18) one and three hundredths _____

19) eighty-two and seven thousandths _____

20) fifty-three and seventeen thousandths _____

21) five tenths _____

22) fifteen thousandths _____

23) three hundred forty-five thousandths _____

24) ten hundred and two thousandths _____

25) four hundred and six tenths _____

Name _____ Date _____

Write each number in decimal form.

1) six and four tenths _____

2) nine and ninety-two hundredths _____

3) forty-eight and two thousandths _____

4) nine and three tenths _____

5) seven and three tenths _____

6) twenty-four hundred and nine thousandths _____

7) two and two hundredths _____

8) eight and five thousandths _____

9) six hundred and thirty-four thousandths _____

10) six and nine thousandths _____

11) five thousand nine hundred thirty-nine and seven hundredths _____

12) two and ninety-nine hundredths _____

13) one and eight hundred nine thousandths _____

14) nine thousand three hundred nine and six tenths _____

15) fifty-four hundred and thirty-seven thousandths _____

16) five thousand three and eight hundred one thousandths _____

17) forty thousand and nine hundredths _____

18) eight hundred and twenty-two hundredths _____

19) nine hundred forty-eight and nine thousandths _____

20) four thousand forty-nine and forty-seven hundredths _____

21) three hundred nine and four tenths _____

22) fifteen hundred and seven thousandths _____

23) four and nine hundred six thousandths _____

24) nine hundred and twenty-five hundredths _____

25) eight thousand five and seven tenths _____

Name _____ Date _____

Write each number in decimal form.

1) $5000 + 300 + 1 + \dfrac{1}{10} + \dfrac{4}{100} + \dfrac{6}{1000} =$

2) $300 + 80 + 5 + \dfrac{1}{10} + \dfrac{7}{100} + \dfrac{5}{1000} =$

3) $100 + 3 + \dfrac{5}{10} + \dfrac{8}{1000} =$

4) $700 + 1 + \dfrac{9}{1000} =$

5) $70000 + 3000 + 60 + \dfrac{4}{10} + \dfrac{9}{100} + \dfrac{2}{1000} =$

6) $5000 + 90 + \dfrac{3}{10} + \dfrac{4}{1000} =$

7) $50000 + 900 + 4 + \dfrac{3}{10} + \dfrac{2}{1000} =$

8) $1000 + 1 + \dfrac{1}{10} + \dfrac{1}{100} + \dfrac{1}{1000} =$

9) $70000 + 3000 + 20 + 5 + \dfrac{1}{10} + \dfrac{8}{100} + \dfrac{6}{1000} =$

10) $6000 + 200 + 4 + \dfrac{3}{10} + \dfrac{8}{1000} =$

11) $50 + 4 + \dfrac{3}{10} + \dfrac{2}{100} + \dfrac{1}{1000} =$

12) $7000 + 1 + \dfrac{8}{10} + \dfrac{2}{100} + \dfrac{5}{1000} =$

13) $70 + 6 + \dfrac{4}{100} + \dfrac{9}{1000} =$

14) $5000 + 700 + 3 + \dfrac{3}{10} + \dfrac{5}{1000} =$

15) $9000 + 600 + \dfrac{5}{100} + \dfrac{2}{1000} =$

Name _____   Date _____

Order the following numbers from smallest to largest.

1)   8.1   6.3   5.7   6.9   2.0

_____

2)   1.03   10.30   6.52   5.29   5.52

_____

3)   3.56   35.6   3.06   5.26   0.56

_____

4)   1.438   1.408   1.038   1.409   0.438

_____

5)   0.056   0.506   0.605   0.256   0.206

_____

Find the digit that is in specified place value.

1) 37.24   tenths place   2   2) 105.74   One's place   _____

3) 29.51   tens place   _____   4) 6.915   Thousandths place _____

5) 1.078   hundredths place _____   6) 9.423   tenths place   _____

7) 300.68   hundreds place   _____   8) 57.149   tens place   _____

9) 107.916 thousandths place _____ 10) 38.051   hundredths place   _____

In number 68.391, what number is in the:

1) tens place   6   2) tenths place   _____

3) hundredths place   _____   4) thousandths place _____

Name _____ Date _____

In 693.157, what is the value of the

1) 6   _6 hundreds_   2) 7 _____

3) 1 _____   4) 5 _____

5) 9 _____   6) 3 _____

Write four decimals that are equivalent to 45.70. (answer may vary)

1)   2)

3)   4)

Write a decimal number that is between each pair of numbers. (answer may vary)

1) 4 and 5 _____   2) 9.9 and 10.0 _____

3) 6.3 and 6.4 _____   4) 5.32 and 6 _____

5) 2.4 and 3.0 _____   6) 1.03 and 1.3 _____

Write the decimal for each dot shown on the number line.

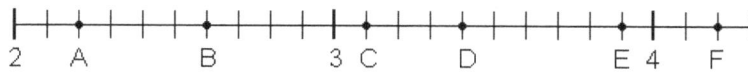

1) A   2) B   3) C

4) D   5) E   6) F

1) A   2) B   3) C

4) D   5) E   6) F

Name _____   Date _____

Choose the correct answer.

1. 6 tenths
   a. 0.06   b. 0.6   c. 6.0   d. 0.006

2. 7 hundredths
   a. 700   b. 0.70   c. 7.0   d. 0.07

3. 16 hundredths
   a. 0.16   b. 0.016   c. 1.6   d. 16

4. 10 thousandths
   a. 10000   b. 10   c. 0.01   d. 1000

5. 1 ten 4 hundredths
   a. 10.04   b. 1.04   c. 1.004   d. 1.400

6. 3 ones 23 hundredths
   a. 323   b. 3.23   c. 0.323   d. 3.023

7. 2 tens 4 ones three hundredth
   a. 20.03   b. 24.30   c. 23.04   d. 24.03

8. 5 ones two hundred thirty-six thousandths
   a. 5.236   b. 52.36   c. 6.235   d. 5236

9. 7 tens 2 ones four hundredths
   a. 72.4   b. 72.40   c. 72.04   d. 7.240

10. 2 hundred 5 tenths
    a. 205.0   b. 200.5   c. 0.205   d. 250

G5. Adding decimals

2 + 0.6 = 2.6

1) 1 + 0.1 =
2) 5 + 0.7 =
3) 7 + 0.9 =
4) 1 + 0.01 =
5) 6 + 0.05 =
6) 9 + 0.09 =
7) 4 + 0.12 =
8) 3 + 0.59 =
9) 5 + 0.75 =
10) 8 + 0.002 =
11) 2 + 0.001 =
12) 6 + 0.008 =
13) 8 + 0.106 =
14) 9 + 0.528 =
15) 5 + 0.837 =
16) 10 + 1.3 =
17) 2 + 8.4 =
18) 3 + 4.2 =
19) 7 + 3.06 =
20) 4 + 3.815 =
21) 8 + 0.74 =
22) 2 + 1.065 =
23) 1 + 7.208 =
24) 7 + 15.9 =
25) 6 + 100.6 =
26) 3 + 10.75 =
27) 20 + 11.072 =
28) 30 + 2.31 =
29) 100 + 10.54 =
30) 200 + 25.64 =

Column Addition

When do decimal addition, we should line the decimal points up.

```
    2 7 . 6 4
  +   5 . 9
  ─────────────
    3 3 . 5 4
```

1.
```
    5 . 2 6
  + 6 . 6 2
  ─────────
```

2.
```
    2 . 3 5
  + 8 . 5 3
  ─────────
```

3.
```
    9 .
  + 0 . 0 8
  ─────────
```

4.
```
    4 . 4 6
  + 9 . 8 7
  ─────────
```

5.
```
    6 . 7 5
  + 8 . 5 7
  ─────────
```

6.
```
    0 . 4 6
  + 0 . 7
  ─────────
```

7.
```
    6 . 7
  + 0 . 8 3
  ─────────
```

8.
```
    4 . 8 4
  + 6 . 5 2
  ─────────
```

9.
```
    7 . 4 1
  + 3 . 7
  ─────────
```

10.
```
    6 . 5 7
  + 0 . 9 1
  ─────────
```

11.
```
    5 . 7 4
  + 8 .
  ─────────
```

12.
```
    8 . 4 6
  + 6 . 0 7
  ─────────
```

13.
```
    5 . 6 9
  +     9
  ─────────
```

14.
```
    7
  + 8 . 6 4
  ─────────
```

15.
```
    2 . 5 8
  + 5 . 9 3
  ─────────
```

16.
```
    0 . 8
  + 0 . 3 6
  ─────────
```

17.
```
    0 . 5 5
  + 5 . 7
  ─────────
```

18.
```
    8 . 3 3
  + 6 . 1 5
  ─────────
```

Name _____   Date _____

Across Addition

1)   2.36 + 6.84 = _____

2)   9.04 + 8.47 = _____

3)   5.005 + 3.7 = _____

4)   0.734 + 6.85 = _____

5)   10.09 + 0.25 = _____

6)   7.6 + 0.08 = _____

7)   8.38 + 7.39 = _____

8)   25.7 + 6.009 = _____

9)   3.96 + 0.5 = _____

10)   4.7 + 0.53 = _____

11) 8.63 + 4.09 = _____

12)   0.06 + 12.5 = _____

13) 9.63 + 7.05 = _____

14) 0.12 + 4.85 = _____

15) 10 + 6.95 = _____

Name _____ Date _____

16) 5.68 + 0.09 = ___

17) 8.004 + 12.5 = ___

18) 53.7 + 6.58 = ___

19) 24.08 + 7.65 = ___

20) 86 + 13.75 = ___

21) 89.07 + 0.05 = ___

22) 15.9 + 0.26 = ___

23) 7.85 + 5.9 = ___

24) 9.65 + 6.08 = ___

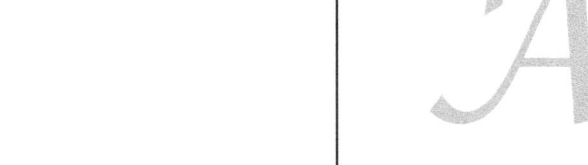

25) 8.93 + 10.53 = ___

26) 8.95 + 0.361 = ___

27) 7.856 + 0.15 = ___

28) 8.5 + 25.73 = ___

29) 8.95 + 0.842 = ___

30) 1.85 + 37.661 = ___

Name _____   Date _____

31) 8.43 + 7.12 + 5.76 = _____

32) 5.8 + 7.35 + 4.23 = _____

33) 0.97 + 3.35 + 12.51 = _____

34) 9.67 + 0.04 + 2.73 = _____

35) 23 + 6.88 + 5.93 = _____

36) 68.45 + 8.7 + 11.63 = _____

37) 9.75 + 15.08 + 0.47 = _____

38) 10.64 + 6.3 + 0.095 = _____

Name _____ Date _____

Calculate the total payment of each receipt, and then find the change.

1.	2.	3.	4.
$ 2.51	$ 3.31	$ 4.21	$ 14.22
$ 3.53	$ 7.79	$ 2.65	$ 2.50
$ 0.37	$ 1.43	$ 0.48	$ 0.36
$ 4.22	$ 0.86	$ 2.82	$ 3.79
$ 3.79	$ 5.60	$ 7.20	$ 2.34
$ 2.84	$ 3.33	$ 4.06	$ 20.98
$ 10.72	$ 7.86	$ 11.93	$ 4.54
$ 0.35	$ 10.21	$ 1.24	$ 5.73

Change from $30   Change from $50   Change from $40   Change from $60

5.	6.	7.	8.
$ 20.16	$ 2.01	$ 2.30	$ 12.30
$ 3.48	$ 38.79	$ 6.53	$ 5.65
$ 7.33	$ 4.34	$ 23.25	$ 3.28
$ 31.49	$ 70.27	$ 5.58	$ 20.83
$ 0.84	$ 5.93	$ 43.72	$ 5.64
$ 6.60	$ 34.55	$ 0.90	$ 0.81
$ 12.06	$ 29.02	$ 6.21	$ 13.40
$ 8.31	$ 1.55	$ 10.84	$ 2.73

Change from $100   Change from $200   Change from $100   Change from $75

G6. Subtracting decimals

The same as addition, always line the decimal points up.

```
   6 1 . 7 3
 − 2 7 . 3 5
 ─────────
   3 4 . 3 8
```

1. 5.73 − 2.56

2. 5.7 − 2.32

3. 8 − 3.39

4. 7.09 − 2.31

5. 4.61 − 0.08

6. 7.03 − 0.05

7. 4.07 − 1.82

8. 7.94 − 2.6

9. 4 − 2.25

10. 9.07 − 1.58

11. 6.43 − 5.34

12. 5 − 0.99

13. 8.62 − 0.35

14. 1.53 − 0.08

15. 7 − 0.54

16. 7 − 4.59

17. 4.53 − 3.54

18. 4.36 − 2.37

Name _____ Date _____

Across Subtraction

1) 6.72 − 5.46 = ____

2) 6.08 − 1.27 = ____

3) 1.45 − 0.08 = ____

4) 8 − 4.25 = _____

5) 5 − 2.06 = _____

6) 13.64 − 0.68 = ___

7) 7.3 − 2.61 = _____

8) 5.84 − 3 = _____

9) 10.23 − 4.78 = ___

10) 7.23 − 3.27 = ____

11) 10 − 9.99 = _____

12) 5.16 − 3.61 = ____

13) 8.38 − 3.44 = ____

14) 1 − 0.05 = _____

15) 10 − 0.05 = _____

Name _____   Date _____

16) 7.18 − 2.05 = ____

17) 8.27 − 1.62 = _____

18) 4.71 − 0.06 = ____

19) 9.6 − 9.06 = _____

20) 4.3 − 0.68 = _____

21) 8 − 0.01 = _____

22) 7 − 3.16 = _____

23) 8.92 − 6 = _____

24) 5.13 − 0.05 = ____

25) 6.3 − 0.35 = _____

26) 6 − 0.005 = _____

27) 8.1 − 0.26 = _____

28) 8.41 − 2.63 = ____

29) 9.48 − 8.49 = ____

30) 3.62 − 2.65 = ____

Name _____   Date _____

Addition and Subtraction

31) $8.78 - 5.21 - 1.37 =$ _____

32) $14.71 - 1.5 - 2.16 =$ _____

33) $3.62 + 3.07 - 0.39 =$ _____

34) $6.35 + 5.14 - 7.92 =$ _____

35) $2.38 - 1.07 + 0.08 =$ _____

36) $6.74 - 2.15 + 4.2 =$ _____

37) $7.2 - 1.68 - 3 =$ _____

38) $8 + 4.7 - 5.62 =$ _____

G7. Multiplying decimals

Different from decimal addition and subtraction, we should line the digits up instead of decimal points up. Then count the total digits after decimal point and place the decimal point the same number of places from the right.

```
        3.  2  6
    ×           2
    ─────────────
        6.  5  2
```

1. 2.53 × 4

2. 1.52 × 7

3. 0.32 × 6

4. 0.07 × 8

5. 3.07 × 7

6. 5.23 × 5

7. 4.28 × 6

8. 4.05 × 3 = 12.15

9. 3.35 × 4 = 13.40

10. 0.25 × 4

11. 24.7 × 8

12. 27.6 × 5

13. 6.17 × 9

14. 3.5 × 7

15. 61.8 × 8

16. 0.39 × 2

17. 1.72 × 6

18. 0.58 × 5

Name _____ Date _____

Column Multiplication

```
            2. 4 3
        ×      0. 7
        ─────────────
         1. 7 0 1
```

1.   1. 6 5
  ×   0. 6

2.   0. 6 1 7
  ×   0. 2

3.   4. 7 3 6
  ×   0. 5

4.   2 1. 5 3
  ×   0. 6

5.   0. 0 0 7
  ×   0. 4

6.   4 9 2. 6
  ×   0. 4

7.   9. 4 3
  ×   0. 7

8.   1. 7 4 2
  ×   0. 1

9.   7. 3 3 1
  ×   0. 9

10.   0. 0 2 7
  ×   0. 8

11.   0. 0 0 6
  ×   0. 8

12.   2 3. 5 6
  ×   0. 5

13.   4 1. 8
  ×   0. 3

14.   0. 0 4 9
  ×   0. 3

15.   2 1. 4 3
  ×   0. 6

16.   0. 0 9 3
  ×   0. 5

17.   0. 0 0 9
  ×   0. 2

18.   3 1 0. 5
  ×   0. 6

Name _____ Date _____

1. 46.28 × 0.04

2. 637.1 × 0.03

3. 0.06 × 0.08

4. 45.25 × 0.08

5. 0.035 × 7

6. 8.367 × 0.005

7. 0.583 × 0.5

8. 45.15 × 0.06

9. 0.537 × 0.02

10. 780.3 × 0.03

11. 0.507 × 0.8

12. 47.08 × 0.04

13. 2095 × 0.08

14. 24.68 × 0.5

15. 386.5 × 0.04

16. 2.074 × 0.5

17. 1.009 × 0.5

18. 58.05 × 0.06

1. 2.6
  × 5.9

2. 0.73
  × 0.16

3. 5.3
  × 0.14

4. 0.47
  × 12

5. 2.37
  × 1.5

6. 6.1
  × 1.9

7. 0.32
  × 0.47

8. 0.17
  × 5.8

9. 0.52
  × 2.3

10. 52.8
  × 3.1

11. 8.4
  × 2.1

12. 0.66
  × 0.15

13. 0.27
  × 8.1

14. 6.2
  × 0.31

15. 5.07
  × 0.48

1. 5.17 × 0.32

2. 0.521 × 0.35

3. 8.09 × 5.3

4. 0.613 × 4.1

5. 1.82 × 0.17

6. 4.09 × 0.78

7. 0.003 × 0.08

8. 47.1 × 0.24

9. 0.428 × 3.5

10. 43.8 × 3.6

11. 2.53 × 0.15

12. 0.052 × 0.25

13. 73.4 × 0.35

14. 70.6 × 0.45

15. 0.519 × 0.62

Name _____ Date _____

Across Multiplication

1) 42.6 × 0.9 = ___

2) 8.34 × 0.5 = ___

3) 0.67 × 0.6 = ___

4) 5.18 × 0.3 = ___

5) 0.426 × 0.7 = ___

6) 5.27 × 0.03 = ___

7) 6.24 × 0.05 = ___

8) 0.057 × 0.4 = ___

9) 8.06 × 0.2 = ___

10) 0.846 × 1 = ___

11) 42.5 × 0.08 = ___

12) 72.6 × 0.09 = ___

Name _____   Date _____

13) 2.7 × 6.5 = ___

14) 8.6 × 2.3 = ___

15) 8.3 × 2.6 = ___

16) 0.63 × 0.45 = ___

17) 0.67 × 0.41 = ___

18) 0.39 × 0.52 = ___

19) 9.2 × 0.35 = ___

20) 0.59 × 1.4 = ___

21) 8.9 × 31 = ___

22) 73 × 0.24 = ___

23) 0.054 × 2.7 = ___

24) 9.6 × 0.028 = ___

Name _____   Date _____

25) 56.1 × 1.2 = ___

26) 7.49 × 5.1 = ___

27) 7.36 × 3.2 = ___

28) 0.609 × 0.37 = ___

29) 8.17 × 25 = ___

30) 5.27 × 0.16 = ___

31) 9.52 × 0.73 = ___

32) 0.724 × 0.15 = ___

33) 0.435 × 72 = ___

34) 9.67 × 1.7 = ___

35) 8.35 × 6.2 = ___

36) 523 × 0.024 = ___

G8. Multiplying decimals by 10s

```
      2. 3 5         2.35 × 10 = 23.5     The decimal point moved to
   ×     1 0                              the right the same number of
   ─────────                               places as the number of zeros
       0 0 0                               in the other multiplier.
     2 3 5
   ─────────
     2 3. 5 0
   Or 23.5
```

```
1.      0. 6 8 3    2.      2. 5 7 2    3.       3. 1 4 2
     ×      1 0          ×    1 0 0          ×  1 0 0 0
     ──────────          ──────────          ───────────
        6. 8 3
```

4. 6.327 × 10 =   5. 2.35 × 100 = **235**

6. 12.8 × 10 =   7. 2.89 × 10 =

8. 45.67 × 100 =   9. 1.50 × 100 =

10. 1.2 × 10 =   11. 3.007 × 1000 =

12. 3.61 × 10 =   13. 0.034 × 10 =

14. 0.24 × 10 =   15. 2.024 × 1000 =

16. 2.07 × 100 =   17. 0.05 × 10 =

Name _____ Date _____

Multiplying decimals by tenth, hundredth, and thousandth.

1.   2.7 4 3
    ×   0.1

2.   6 3.4 7
    ×   0.0 1

3.   2.1 6
    ×   0.0 1

4. 3.57 × 0.1 =

5. 6.38 × 0.1 =

6. 2.09 × 0.01 =

7. 0.36 × 0.01 =

8. 0.36 × 0.1 =

9. 30.7 × 0.1 =

10. 20.4 × 0.001 =

11. 100 × 0.01 =

12. 219 × 0.01 =

13. 0.57 × 0.1 =

14. 0.25 × 0.1 =

15. 2.24 × 0.001 =

16. 4.68 × 0.001 =

17. 60 × 0.001 =

Name _____ Date _____

G9. Dividing decimals

$5.6 \div 4 = 1.4$

$$\begin{array}{r} 1.4 \\ 4{\overline{\smash{\big)}\,5.6}} \\ \underline{4} \\ 16 \\ \underline{16} \\ 0 \end{array}$$

1. $3{\overline{\smash{\big)}\,5.1}}$

2. $2{\overline{\smash{\big)}\,9.8}}$

3. $3{\overline{\smash{\big)}\,15.3}}$

4. $3{\overline{\smash{\big)}\,0.69}}$

5. $6{\overline{\smash{\big)}\,24.72}}$

6. $5{\overline{\smash{\big)}\,60.5}}$

7. $4{\overline{\smash{\big)}\,7.52}}$

8. $3{\overline{\smash{\big)}\,7.08}}$

9. $7{\overline{\smash{\big)}\,9.24}}$

10. $8{\overline{\smash{\big)}\,95.9}}$

11. $6{\overline{\smash{\big)}\,7.08}}$

12. $4{\overline{\smash{\big)}\,9.72}}$

Name _____ Date _____

13. $7 \overline{) 9.45}$

14. $5 \overline{) 62.5}$

15. $6 \overline{) 0.714}$

16. $9 \overline{) 7.47}$

17. $8 \overline{) 4.64}$

18. $6 \overline{) 4.56}$

19. $4 \overline{) 32.8}$

20. $6 \overline{) 82.8}$

21. $4 \overline{) 4.28}$

22. $8 \overline{) 8.56}$

23. $7 \overline{) 7.63}$

24. $5 \overline{) 5.35}$

25. $9 \overline{) 6.21}$

26. $6 \overline{) 2.58}$

27. $4 \overline{) 1.36}$

Name _____ Date _____

28.

$6 \overline{)0.816}$

29.

$5 \overline{)0.725}$

30.

$4 \overline{)0.952}$

31.

$5 \overline{)0.635}$

32.

$7 \overline{)0.728}$

33.

$8 \overline{)0.936}$

34.

$4 \overline{)0.348}$

35.

$9 \overline{)0.648}$

36.

$7 \overline{)0.259}$

37.

$6 \overline{)0.276}$

38.

$8 \overline{)0.256}$

39.

$7 \overline{)0.364}$

40. $2\overline{)31.24}$

41. $5\overline{)72.65}$

42. $7\overline{)65.45}$

43. $7\overline{)0.056}$

44. $4\overline{)0.032}$

45. $5\overline{)0.035}$

46. $3\overline{)251.4}$

47. $8\overline{)6.256}$

48. $4\overline{)0.528}$

50. $6\overline{)562.2}$

51. $9\overline{)0.5724}$

52. $8\overline{)0.056}$

Name _____ Date _____

1. $23 \overline{)25.3}$

2. $23 \overline{)78.2}$

3. $35 \overline{)59.5}$

4. $52 \overline{)9.36}$

5. $27 \overline{)9.18}$

6. $19 \overline{)7.98}$

7. $30 \overline{)84.0}$

8. $50 \overline{)60.0}$

9. $40 \overline{)92.0}$

10. $14 \overline{)0.196}$

11. $16 \overline{)0.496}$

12. $23 \overline{)0.621}$

Name _____   Date _____

22. $43 \overline{) 26.66}$

23. $53 \overline{) 24.91}$

24. $27 \overline{) 15.12}$

25. $61 \overline{) 2.135}$

26. $26 \overline{) 1.898}$

27. $48 \overline{) 1.728}$

28. $43 \overline{) 0.2881}$

29. $31 \overline{) 0.2852}$

30. $65 \overline{) 0.3185}$

31. $29 \overline{) 15.66}$

32. $19 \overline{) 0.1482}$

33. $29 \overline{) 162.4}$

Name _____ Date _____

Add Zeros: Divide a decimal by a whole number with no reminder.

$$6 \div 5 = 1.2 \qquad 5 \overline{) \begin{array}{r} 1.2 \\ 6.0 \\ \underline{5} \\ 1.0 \\ \underline{1.0} \\ 0 \end{array}}$$

1. $2\overline{)1}$

2. $4\overline{)2}$

3. $5\overline{)4}$

4. $2\overline{)0.21}$

5. $6\overline{)45}$

6. $4\overline{)0.62}$

7. $4\overline{)0.51}$

8. $4\overline{)3}$

9. $5\overline{)2.6}$

10. $8\overline{)4.2}$

11. $8\overline{)2.5}$

12. $6\overline{)2.7}$

Name _____ Date _____

Divide a whole number by a decimal: Add Zeros.

$$5 \div 0.2 = 50 \div 2 = 25 \qquad 2\overline{)50} \begin{array}{r} 25 \\ \underline{4} \\ 10 \\ \underline{10} \\ 0 \end{array}$$

1. $0.5\overline{)12}$

2. $0.9\overline{)27}$

3. $0.6\overline{)9}$

4. $0.8\overline{)4}$

5. $0.3\overline{)12}$

6. $0.6\overline{)54}$

7. $0.7\overline{)42}$

8. $0.4\overline{)3}$

9. $0.4\overline{)17}$

10. $0.3\overline{)36}$

11. $0.4\overline{)62}$

12. $0.5\overline{)50}$

Name _____ Date _____

Divide a decimal by a decimal.

```
         4.3                          25
    ┌────────                    ┌────────
0.6 )  2.58                 0.15 )  3.75
       24                           30
       ──                           ──
       18                           75
       18                           75
       ──                           ──
        0                            0
```

1.
$$1.2 \overline{) 8.04}$$

2.
$$1.5 \overline{) 9.45}$$

3.
$$2.4 \overline{) 1.272}$$

4.
$$3.2 \overline{) 3.008}$$

5.
$$0.16 \overline{) 0.368}$$

6.
$$0.45 \overline{) 1.125}$$

Name _____   Date _____

7.

$$0.12 \overline{\smash{)}0.0552}$$

8.

$$0.042 \overline{\smash{)}0.0756}$$

9.

$$0.36 \overline{\smash{)}0.504}$$

10.

$$0.028 \overline{\smash{)}10.64}$$

11.

$$0.35 \overline{\smash{)}59.5}$$

12.

$$0.63 \overline{\smash{)}3.024}$$

13.

$$5.2 \overline{\smash{)}2.496}$$

14.

$$0.28 \overline{\smash{)}0.0952}$$

Name _____   Date _____

Across Division

1. $0.36 \div 0.2 =$

2. $0.63 \div 0.09 =$

3. $1.35 \div 0.3 =$

4. $2.64 \div 0.6 =$

5. $0.345 \div 0.05 =$

6. $47.6 \div 0.07 =$

7. $62.1 \div 0.9 =$

8. $6.08 \div 0.008 =$

9. $7.85 \div 0.005 =$

10. $0.512 \div 0.04 =$

11. $0.672 \div 0.3 =$

12. $3.92 \div 0.08 =$

Name _____ Date _____

13. 4.8 ÷ 2 =	14. 9.6 ÷ 4 =	15. 3.5 ÷ 5 =
16. 0.64 ÷ 8 =	17. 0.21 ÷ 3 =	18. 0.39 ÷ 6 =
19. 8 ÷ 0.2 =	20. 12 ÷ 0.4 =	21. 28 ÷ 0.07 =
22. 54 ÷ 0.05 =	23. 39 ÷ 0.03 =	24. 27 ÷ 0.06 =

Name _____ Date _____

25. 3.18 ÷ 0.02 =

26. 0.234 ÷ 0.6 =

27. 0.612 ÷ 0.09 =

28. 8.19 ÷ 0.7 =

29. 0.805 ÷ 0.5 =

30. 56.4 ÷ 0.06 =

31. 58.2 ÷ 0.3 =

32. 20.5 ÷ 0.05 =

33. 0.912 ÷ 0.08 =

34. 0.683 ÷ 0.1 =

35. 4.77 ÷ 0.9 =

36. 45.5 ÷ 0.07 =

Name _____ Date _____

37. 24 ÷ 0.3 =	38. 4.6 ÷ 0.02 =	39. 7.5 ÷ 0.05 =
40. 7.3 ÷ 0.08 =	41. 4.5 ÷ 0.04 =	42. 5.4 ÷ 0.06 =
43. 7.07 ÷ 0.07 =	44. 9.4 ÷ 0.8 =	45. 72 ÷ 0.09 =
46. 61 ÷ 0.4 =	47. 0.27 ÷ 0.6 =	48. 6.2 ÷ 0.08 =

Name _____   Date _____

49. 9.45 ÷ 3.5 =

50. 10.81 ÷ 2.3 =

51. 7.82 ÷ 4.6 =

52. 1.736 ÷ 5.6 =

53. 1.326 ÷ 3.9 =

54. 0.624 ÷ 1.6 =

55. 0.425 ÷ 0.25 =

56. 0.512 ÷ 0.32 =

57. 2.624 ÷ 0.41 =

58. 0.1272 ÷ 0.53 =

59. 0.2684 ÷ 0.44 =

60. 0.0476 ÷ 0.28 =

61. 0.81 ÷ 0.45 =	62. 8.64 ÷ 3.6 =	63. 1.922 ÷ 6.2 =
64. 1.044 ÷ 7.2 =	65. 1.272 ÷ 0.53 =	66. 3.57 ÷ 21 =
67. 0.875 ÷ 0.25 =	68. 0.253 ÷ 11 =	69. 0.8 ÷ 3.2 =
70. 0.56 ÷ 0.35 =	71. 4 ÷ 0.16 =	72. 0.6 ÷ 15 =

G10. Rounding when divide decimals

Divide. Round your answer to the nearest tenth.

$5.2 \div 3 = ?$

Round off your answer to the nearest tenth.

$5.2 \div 3 = 1.7$

```
       1.73
    ┌──────
  3 ) 5.2
      3
      ──
      2 2
      2 1
      ───
        10
         9
        ──
         1
```

1. $0.3 \overline{) 2.5}$

2. $0.6 \overline{) 2.8}$

3. $0.7 \overline{) 5.2}$

4. $0.4 \overline{) 2.51}$

5. $7 \overline{) 9}$

6. $9 \overline{) 12.5}$

7. $5 \overline{) 0.82}$

8. $0.7 \overline{) 15.02}$

9. $9 \overline{) 14.63}$

Name _____ Date _____

Divide. Round your answer to the nearest hundredth.

$$0.412 \div 0.6 = ?$$

Round off your answer to the nearest tenth.

$$0.412 \div 0.6 = 0.69$$

$$\begin{array}{r} 0.686 \\ 0.6\overline{)0.412} \\ \underline{36} \\ 52 \\ \underline{48} \\ 40 \\ \underline{36} \\ 4 \end{array}$$

1. $0.9\overline{)0.262}$

2. $0.7\overline{)1.352}$

3. $0.9\overline{)3.251}$

4. $6\overline{)4}$

5. $7\overline{)5}$

6. $3\overline{)5}$

7. $4\overline{)0.71}$

8. $0.7\overline{)0.085}$

9. $6\overline{)0.74}$

Name _____   Date _____

Divide. Round your answer to the nearest tenth.

1. 6 ÷ 0.9 =	2. 4 ÷ 0.7 =	3. 0.52 ÷ 0.3 =
4. 0.26 ÷ 0.7 =	5. 3.2 ÷ 0.12 =	6. 4.2 ÷ 1.8 =
7. 3.3 ÷ 0.18 =	8. 25 ÷ 11 =	9. 0.27 ÷ 0.13 =

Name _____ Date _____

Divide. Round your answer to the nearest hundredth.

1. 1 ÷ 8 =

2. 2 ÷ 9 =

3. 4 ÷ 7 =

4. 0.241 ÷ 0.3 =

5. 0.362 ÷ 0.9 =

6. 4.21 ÷ 1.2 =

7. 3.05 ÷ 0.15 =

8. 0.527 ÷ 1.1 =

9. 0.538 ÷ 0.13 =

Name _____ Date _____

Divided by Tens

$2.51 \div 10 = ?$

$$\begin{array}{r} 0.251 \\ 10\overline{)2.51} \\ \underline{20} \\ 51 \\ \underline{51} \\ 10 \\ \underline{10} \\ 0 \end{array}$$

$2.51 \div 10 = 0.251$

1. $10\overline{)3.3}$

2. $100\overline{)3.72}$

3. $10\overline{)70.3}$

What did you find from the above? Follow the same pattern and evaluate.

1. $1 \div 10 =$ _____
2. $0.1 \div 10 =$ _____
3. $1 \div 100 =$ _____
4. $0.1 \div 100 =$ _____
5. $2.3 \div 10 =$ _____
6. $51.3 \div 10 =$ _____
7. $2.5 \div 100 =$ _____
8. $3.6 \div 1000 =$ _____
9. $0.28 \div 10 =$ _____
10. $321 \div 10 =$ _____
11. $4.08 \div 100 =$ _____
12. $23.5 \div 1000 =$ _____
13. $63.2 \div 1000 =$ _____
14. $0.45 \div 10 =$ _____
15. $0.03 \div 10 =$ _____
16. $52 \div 100 =$ _____
17. $1 \div 1000 =$ _____
18. $0.2 \div 100 =$ _____
19. $3 \div 1000 =$ _____
20. $8.05 \div 10 =$ _____

Name _____ Date _____

Divided by tenths, hundredths, and thousandths

$3.62 \div 0.1 = ?$

$3.62 \div 0.1 = 36.2$

$$0.1 \overline{)3.62} = 36.2$$

$$\begin{array}{r} 3 \\ \hline 6 \\ 6 \\ \hline 2 \\ 2 \\ \hline 0 \end{array}$$

1. $0.1 \overline{)2.63}$

2. $0.01 \overline{)4.93}$

3. $0.1 \overline{)0.26}$

What did you find from the above? Follow the same pattern and evaluate.

1. $1 \div 0.1 =$ _____
2. $0.1 \div 0.1 =$ _____
3. $1 \div 0.01 =$ _____
4. $0.1 \div 0.01 =$ _____
5. $3.5 \div 0.1 =$ _____
6. $42.5 \div 0.1 =$ _____
7. $4.8 \div 0.01 =$ _____
8. $4.7 \div 0.001 =$ _____
9. $0.37 \div 0.1 =$ _____
10. $51 \div 0.1 =$ _____
11. $2.06 \div 0.01 =$ _____
12. $31.46 \div 0.001 =$ _____
13. $18.4 \div 0.001 =$ _____
14. $0.29 \div 0.1 =$ _____
15. $0.052 \div 0.1 =$ _____
16. $32 \div 0.01 =$ _____
17. $1 \div 0.001 =$ _____
18. $0.5 \div 0.01 =$ _____
19. $5 \div 0.001 =$ _____
20. $2.31 \div 0.1 =$ _____

Name _____   Date _____

Compare by fill in each blank with <, =, or > to make each statement true.

4. 2.47 × 10 _____ 2.47 × 0.1   13. 1.73 × 10 _____ 1.73 × 0.1

5. 3.58 × 10 _____ 3.58 ÷ 0.1   14. 0.45 × 10 _____ 0.45 ÷ 0.1

6. 3.6 × 100 _____ 3.6 ÷ 0.1   15. 4.8 × 10 _____ 4.8 ÷ 0.01

7. 1.8 ÷ 10 _____ 1.8 ÷ 0.1   16. 7.2 ÷ 10 _____ 7.2 ÷ 0.1

8. 3.5 × 10 _____ 0.35 ÷ 0.1   17. 1.2 × 10 _____ 0.12 ÷ 0.1

9. 27 ÷ 10 _____ 2.7 ÷ 0.1   18. 6.4 × 10 _____ 0.64 × 0.1

10. 0.93 × 10 _____ 9.3 ÷ 0.1   19. 9.08 ÷ 100 _____ 9.08 ÷ 0.01

11. 4.16 ÷ 100 _____ 0.416 ÷ 0.1   20. 0.624 × 10 _____ 6.24 ÷ 0.01

12. 0.527 × 0.1 _____ 5.27 × 0.01   21. 0.835 × 0.1 _____ 8.35 ÷ 0.01

13. 30.8 ÷ 0.01 _____ 0.308 ÷ 0.1   22. 45.7 ÷ 10 _____ 0.457 ÷ 0.1

14. 61.4 ÷ 100 _____ 0.614 ÷ 0.1   23. 279 × 0.01 _____ 27.9 × 0.1

15. 47.3 × 0.1 _____ 4.73 ÷ 0.1   24. 5.37 × 10 _____ 53.7 ÷ 0.01

Name _____ Date _____

Fill in each blank.

1. 3.65 × _____ = 365
2. 4.07 × _____ = 40.7
3. 2.6 × _____ = 0.26
4. 0.462 ÷ _____ = 46.2
5. 7.25 ÷ _____ = 0.725
6. 97.4 × _____ = 0.974
7. 206 × _____ = 2.06
8. 4.72 ÷ _____ = 47.2
9. 0.728 × _____ = 728
10. 28.4 ÷ _____ = 2.84
11. 0.916 ÷ _____ = 91.6
12. 8.36 ÷ _____ = 83.6
13. 0.604 × _____ = 60.4
14. 9.13 × _____ = 0.913
15. 582 × _____ = 5820
16. 5.37 ÷ _____ = 537
17. 4.69 ÷ _____ = 46.9
18. 0.825 × _____ = 82.5
19. 90.7 × _____ = 0.907
20. 0.982 × _____ = 9.82
21. 0.824 ÷ _____ = 82.4
22. 0.584 × _____ = 584
23. 54.7 × _____ = 0.547
24. 9.36 ÷ _____ = 0.936
25. 0.736 ÷ _____ = 73.6
26. 6.36 ÷ _____ = 6360
27. 49.2 × _____ = 0.492
28. 9.46 ÷ _____ = 94.36
29. 0.53 × _____ = 530
30. 3 × _____ = 0.03
31. 0.05 × _____ = 50
32. 200 ÷ _____ = 0.2
33. 9.36 ÷ _____ = 936
34. 0.574 ÷ _____ = 5.74
35. 59 × _____ = 0.59
36. 0.534 × _____ = 4.62
37. 673 × _____ = 0.673
38. 462 ÷ _____ = 4.62
39. 0.5 × _____ = 50
40. 0.1 ÷ _____ = 0.01

G11. Decimal operations

Evaluate.

1. $3.6 + 0.38$

2. 4.2×0.7

3. $5.2 - 1.7$

4. $5.4 \div 0.09$

5. $10 - 5.3 + 7.2$

6. $10 + (5.3 + 7.2)$

7. $10 + 5.3 - 7.2$

8. $7.4 + 0.37 + 0.08$

9. $6.7 - 0.92 - 3.1$

10. $7.8 - (2.5 - 0.8)$

11. $3.5 \div 0.5 + 0.08$

12. $0.36 \times 0.7 + 10$

13. $6.4 + 7.1 \times 3$

14. $7.5 + 2.8 \times 0.6$

15. $(2.5 + 4.6) \div 0.5$

16. $(7.2 - 1.9) \times 0.4$

Name _____   Date _____

17. 2.4 × 0.2 × 0.7

18. 4.8 × 0.5 × 5.1

19. 4.5 × 0.8 ÷ 0.3

20. 5.6 ÷ 0.08 × 6.2

21. 2.31 × (0.09 ÷ 0.3)

22. 2.6 × (7.2 ÷ 1.2)

23. 16.5 − 7.11 ÷ 0.9

24. 5.01 + 3.1 ÷ 0.8

25. 2.6 ÷ 0.4 − 1.8 ÷ 0.9

26. 7.8 ÷ 1.2 + 2.1 × 0.6

27. 5.2 ÷ 0.4 × 0.2 + 0.54

28. 4.25 + 2.1 × 0.6 × 0.5

29. 2 × 0.1 ÷ 0.01 − 5

30. 5.4 × 0.2 ÷ 0.6 + 0.06

31. (3.4 + 1.7) ÷ 0.17 ÷ 0.1

32. (6.3 − 0.09) × 0.4 ÷ 0.5

Name _____ Date _____

G12. Problem solving

The price of:

Name	Gross Price	Unit Price
2 lb of cherries	$11	
3 lb of apples	$6	
4 lb of pears	$10	
5 lb of oranges	$8	
5 lb of bananas	$4	

1. What is the total cost of 4 lb of cherries?

2. If I buy 2 lb of pears and 2 lb of cherry, how much do I have to pay?
Hint: The cost of 2 lb of pears _____

    The cost of 2 lb of cherries _____

    The amount I have to pay _____

3. If I buy 6 lb of apples and 2 lb of oranges, how much do I have to pay?
Hint: The cost of 6 lb of apples _____

    The cost of 2 lb of oranges _____

    The amount I must pay _____

4. What is the change for $30 if I buy 4 lb of bananas and 3 lb of cherries?
Hint: The cost of 4 lb of bananas _____

    The cost of 3 lb of cherries _____

    The change for $30 is _____

5. If I buy 2 lb of apples and 4 lb of pears with a $1 discount, how much do I have to pay?
Hint: The cost of 2 lb of apples _____

    The cost of 4 lb of pears _____

    The amount I must pay _____

6. What is the change for $20 if I buy 3 lb of pears and 3 lb of bananas?
Hint: The cost of 3 lb of pears _____

    The cost of 3 lb of bananas _____

    The change for $20 is _____

7. What is the change for $40 if I buy 1 lb of each item in the list?
Hint: The total cost of 1 lb. of each item is _____

    The change is _____

Name _____ Date _____

The price of:	Name	Gross Price	Unit Price
	2 lb of lettuce	$1.50	
	3 lb of celery	$2.40	
	4 lb of potatoes	$3	
	5 lb of onion	$2	
	2 lb of mushroom	$5	

1. What is the total cost of 6 lb of celery?

2. If I buy 2 lb of potatoes and 2 lb of onion, how much do I have to pay?

Hint: The cost of 2 lb of potatoes _____

The cost of 2 lb of onion _____

The amount I must pay _____

3. If I buy 4 lb of lettuce and 3 lb of mushroom, how much do I have to pay?

Hint: The cost of 4 lb of lettuce _____

The cost of 3 lb of mushroom _____

The amount I must pay _____

4. What is the change for $10 if I buy 2 lb of celery and 3 lb of potatoes?

Hint: The cost of 2 lb of celery _____

The cost of 3 lb of potatoes

The change for $10 is _____

5. If I buy 5 lb of potatoes and 5 lb of mushroom with a $2 discount, how much do I have to pay?

Hint: The cost of 5 lb of potatoes _____

The cost of 5 lb of mushroom _____

The amount I must pay _____

6. What is the change for $10 if I buy 3 lb of lettuces and 3 lb of onion?

Hint: The cost of 3 lb of lettuce _____

The cost of 3 lb of onion _____

The change for $10 is _____

7. What is the change for $40 if I buy 1 lb of each item in the list?

Hint: The total cost of 1 lb of each item is _____

The change is _____

H. Number Sense

H1. Factors

Example: $12 = 1 \times 12 = 2 \times 6 = 3 \times 4$, so factors of 12 are: 1, 2, 3, 4, 6, and 12.

Find all the factors of each given number.

1. 15 _____
2. 18 _____
3. 22 _____
4. 47 _____
5. 36 _____
6. 45 _____
7. 51 _____
8. 56 _____
9. 72 _____
10. 48 _____
11. 91 _____
12. 66 _____
13. 18 _____
14. 75 _____
15. 87 _____

Name _____ Date _____

H2. Multiples

Example: Find the first five multiples of 6:
$$1 \times 6 = 6, 2 \times 6 = 12, 3 \times 6 = 18, 4 \times 6 = 24, 5 \times 6 = 30$$
So, the first five multiples of 6 are: 6, 12, 18, 24, and 30.

1. The first five multiples of 4 are _____

2. The first five multiples of 8 are _____

3. The first five multiples of 10 are _____

4. The first five multiples of 12 are _____

5. The first five multiples of 19 are _____

6. The first five multiples of 21 are _____

7. The first five multiples of 15 are _____

8. The first five multiples of 51 are _____

9. The first five multiples of 9 are _____

10. The first five multiples of 25 are _____

11. The fifth multiple of 14 is _____

12. The ninth multiple of 8 is _____

13. The twentieth multiple of 5 is _____

14. The fifteenth multiple of 8 is _____

15. The sixth multiple of 45 is _____

Multiple and Factor Problems (I)

1. How many numbers are multiples of 6 from 1 to 100 inclusive?

2. How many numbers are not multiples of 8 from 1 to 100 inclusive?

3. How many numbers are multiples of 4 but not multiples of 6 from 1 to 100 inclusive?

4. How many numbers are multiples of 8 or multiples of 12 from 1 to 1000 inclusive?

5. 500 people go to cinema. Every 12 people receive a free chocolate and every 18 people receive a free drink. How many people receive at least one item?

Multiple and Factor Problems (II)

1. Cathy has 80 chocolate bars and 96 lollipops. She plans to invite friends to her party in a way that each person will share her goodies of every kind equally with her. How many friends should she invite? List all the possible answers.

2. I'm a number. I'm a multiple of 8. I'm between 50 and 60. What number am I?

3. Susan has a square piece of cloth of 5 feet long. She wants to cut it into rectangular pieces with width of 5 inches and length of 6 inches. How many pieces can she get?

4. Julia has a book with 500 pages. She draws a star on every 12 pages and a cat on every 16 pages. How many pages in her book have at least one mark?

5. There is a number. When it is divided by 4, leaves a reminder of 3. When it is divided by 6, leaves a reminder of 1. What is the smallest possible value of this number?

Name _____   Date _____

Multiple and Factor Problems (III)

1. Katherine is between 20 and 30 years old. Last year her age was a multiple of 4. This year her age is a multiple of 5. How old is Katherine?

2. Adam is between 30 and 40 years old. Last year his age was a multiple of 4. This year his age is a multiple of 3. How old is Adam?

3. I'm a number. I'm a multiple of 8. I'm also a multiple of 12. I'm between 40 and 50. What number am I?

4. I'm a number. I'm a multiple of 16. I'm also a multiple of 24. I'm not 48. I'm less than 100. What number am I?

Name _____ Date _____

H3. Even and odd numbers

> even + even = even
> odd + odd = even
> odd + even = odd
> even × even = even
> odd × odd = odd
> odd × even = even

Circle the correct answer without calculating the result.

1. $19575 + 205947$ a. even   b. odd
2. 59999×628127 a. even   b. odd
3. $53748 - 18765$ a. even   b. odd
4. $158 \times 256 - 158 \times 109$ a. even   b. odd
5. $327 \times 457 - 327 \times 219$ a. even   b. odd
6. $629 \times 315 - 384 \times 315$ a. even   b. odd
7. $247 \times 109 + 125 \times 109$ a. even   b. odd
8. $65 \times 18 + 65 \times 47 + 65 \times 36$ a. even   b. odd
9. $72 \times 35 + 72 \times 17 - 72 \times 41$ a. even   b. odd
10. $243 \div 3 + 276 \div 3$ a. even   b. odd
11. $2871 \div 9 - 1503 \div 9$ a. even   b. odd
12. $1347 \times 175 + 7519 \times 308$ a. even   b. odd
13. $3147 \times 134 - 1684 \times 419$ a. even   b. odd
14. $418 \times 519 - 234 \times 137 + 249 \times 354$ a. even   b. odd
15. $307 \times 165 + 129 \times 217 - 497 \times 321$ a. even   b. odd
16. $412 \times 649 - 167 \times 198 + 149 \times 425$ a. even   b. odd

H4. Divisibility rules

A number is divisible by 2 if and only if the last digit is divisible by 2.

A number is divisible by 3 if and only if the sum of all the digits is divisible by 3.

A number is divisible by 4 if and only if the last 2 digit of the number is divisible by 4.

A number is divisible by 5 if and only if the last digit is 0 or 5.

A number is divisible by 6 if and only if the number is divisible by 2 and 3.

A number is divisible by 7 when we take the last digit, double it, and then subtract it from the rest of the number, if the answer is divisible by 7.

A number is divisible by 8 if and only if the last 3 digits of the number is divisible by 8.

A number is divisible by 9 if and only if the sum of all the digits is divisible by 9 (same rule as 3).

A number is divisible by 10 if and only if the last digit is 0.

A number is divisible by 11 if and only if the difference between the sum of the odd numbered digits and the sum of the even numbered digits is 0 or divisible by 11.

A number is divisible by 12 if and only if the number is divisible by 3 and 4.

A number is divisible by 14 if and only if the number is divisible by 2 and 7.

A number is divisible by 15 if and only if the number is divisible by 3 and 5.

A number is divisible by 25 if and only if the number ends with 00, 25, 50, or 75.

Put a "√" if the number is divisible by the following.

	144	792	312	135	204	715	336	480	750
By 2									
By 3									
By 4									
By 5									
By 6									
By 7									
By 8									
By 9									
By 10									
By 11									
By 12									
By 15									
By 18									
By 20									
By 25									

H5. Prime and composite numbers

Prime number is a number that has no divisor other than 1 and itself.
Composite number is exactly divisible by at least one number other than 1 or itself.
1 is neither a prime number nor a composite number.

Use the Sieve of Eratosthenes to find prime numbers.

1. Cross out 1 because 1 is not a prime number.
2. Cross out all multiples of 2, except 2 itself.
3. Cross out all multiples of 3, except 3 itself.
4. Cross out all multiples of 5, except 5 itself.
5. Cross out all multiples of 7, except 7 itself.
6. Put a circle around each of the remaining numbers. They are all prime numbers.
7. Write the prime numbers within 100. There should be 25 prime numbers within 100.

1	2	3	4	5	6
7	8	9	10	11	12
13	14	15	16	17	18
19	20	21	22	23	24
25	26	27	28	29	30
31	32	33	34	35	36
37	38	39	40	41	42
43	44	45	46	47	48
49	50	51	52	53	54
55	56	57	58	59	60
61	62	63	64	65	66
67	68	69	70	71	72
73	74	75	76	77	78
79	80	81	82	83	84
85	86	87	88	89	90
91	92	93	94	95	96
97	98	99	100	101	102

Name _____ Date _____

Use divisibility rules to decide whether the following number is a prime or composite number. Put a "√" on the right answers.

Divisible by	2	3	5	7	11	13	Prime	Composite
28								
33								
47								
59								
101								
121								
187								
211								
169								
91								
495								
151								
143								
97								
133								

Name _____ Date _____

What digit could each blank be?

1. The number 3109☐ is divisible by 4. What digit could ☐ be? _____

2. The number 17☐56 is divisible by 6. What digit could ☐ be? _____

3. The number 2☐472 is divisible by 9. What digit could ☐ be? _____

4. The number 7103☐ is divisible by 6. What digit could ☐ be? _____

5. The number 4791☐ is divisible by 15. What digit could ☐ be? _____

6. The number 511☐6 is divisible by 8. What digit could ☐ be? _____

7. The number 7089☐ is divisible by 8. What digit could ☐ be? _____

8. The number 4276☐ is divisible by 12. What digit could ☐ be? _____

9. The number 45☐18 is divisible by 11. What digit could ☐ be? _____

True or false

1. If a number is divisible by 3, then it is also divisible by 9. _____

2. If a number is divisible by 2 and 4, then it is also divisible by 8. _____

3. If a number is divisible by 2 and 3, then it is also divisible by 6. _____

4. If a number is divisible by 6, then it is also divisible by 3. _____

5. If a number is even and divisible by 5, then it ends with a zero. _____

6. If a number is divisible by 15, then it is also divisible by 10. _____

7. If a number is divisible by 6, then it must be even. _____

8. If the last digit of a number is 3, then it must be divisible by 3. _____

9. If the last digit of a number is 0, then it must be divisible by 5. _____

10. If you write down three consecutive numbers, one of them must be divisible by 3. _____

Name _____ Date _____

Decide whether the following statements are always true, sometimes true, or never true.

1. The sum of two prime numbers is a prime. _____

2. The product of two prime numbers is a prime. _____

3. The sum of two composite numbers is a composite. _____

4. The product of two composite numbers is a composite. _____

5. The sum of a prime and a composite number is a composite. _____

6. The product of a prime and a composite number is a composite. _____

7. "1" is a prime number. _____

8. The sum of 1 and a prime number is a composite number. _____

9. The product of 1 and a prime number is a composite number. _____

10. The sum of three consecutive numbers is a composite number. _____

11. The product of two consecutive numbers is a composite number. _____

12. The sum of two odd numbers is a prime number. _____

13. If the last digit of a two-digit number is 2, then it is a composite. _____

14. If the last digit of a two-digit number is 3, then it is a composite. _____

15. Prime numbers are odd numbers. _____

Decide whether the answer to the following is even or odd.

1. Odd + Odd = _____ 2. Even + Even = _____

3. Odd + Even = _____ 4. Even + Odd = _____

5. Odd × Odd = _____ 6. Odd × Even = _____

7. Even × Even = _____ 8. Even × Odd = _____

I. Integers

I1. Representing integers

Graph each number on the number line.

```
<---|---|---|---|---|---|---|---|---|---|---|---|---|---|---|---|--->
   -7  -6  -5  -4  -3  -2  -1   0   1   2   3   4   5   6   7   8
```

I = −4   H = +3   G = −2   R = −6   T = +7

What do you notice?

The further the number to the right, the _____ the number.

The further the number to the left, the _____ the number.

Compare each pair of numbers using < or >.

1. +7 ____ +24
2. 0 ____ +15
3. −5 ____ +7
4. −13 ____ −28
5. −4 ____ −9
6. +52 ____ −87
7. +20 ____ +8
8. −37 ____ +21
9. −18 ____ 0
10. −29 ____ −63

Order the following number from least to largest.

1. +7, −3, +20, −16, 0 _____
2. −4, +8, −21, −62, +15 _____
3. +5, +23, −10, −17, −42 _____
4. +39, −16, −25, +2, +17 _____
5. −9, −26, +3, +37, +14 _____
6. −17, −29, −6, +9, −45 _____
7. −32, −18, −4, −15, −1 _____
8. +6, −2, −16, −29, −25 _____

Name _____ Date _____

Graph each number on the number line.

1.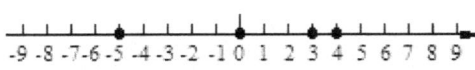

    Integers -5, 0, 3, 4

2. ⊢⊢⊢⊢⊢⊢⊢⊢⊢⊢⊢⊢⊢⊢⊢→

    Integers -3, 2, 5, 6

3. ⊢⊢⊢⊢⊢⊢⊢⊢⊢⊢⊢⊢⊢⊢⊢→

    Integers -4, -2, -1, 3

4. ⊢⊢⊢⊢⊢⊢⊢⊢⊢⊢⊢⊢⊢⊢⊢→

    Integers -6, -4, -3, 2

5. ⊢⊢⊢⊢⊢⊢⊢⊢⊢⊢⊢⊢⊢⊢⊢→

    Integers -8, -5, -1, 4

6. ⊢⊢⊢⊢⊢⊢⊢⊢⊢⊢⊢⊢⊢⊢⊢→

    Integers -4, -1, 0, 3

7. ⊢⊢⊢⊢⊢⊢⊢⊢⊢⊢⊢⊢⊢⊢⊢→

    Integers -4, -2, 0, 1

8. ⊢⊢⊢⊢⊢⊢⊢⊢⊢⊢⊢⊢⊢⊢⊢→

    Integers -4, -3, -2, -1

Find the opposite of each number.

1. +8
2. +(-3)
3. -(+6)
4. -5
5. +(+10)
6. -(+15)
7. -(-2)
8. -(-7)
9. +(-23)

Name _____   Date _____

Multiple choices

1. Which of the following has the greatest value?
   a. −1.5   b. −10.5   c. −15   d. −50   e. −150

2. Which of the following has the least value?
   a. −21   b. −201   c. −0.21   d. −20.1   e. −2.1

3. Which of the following is the greatest even integer less than 49?
   a. −28   b. 20.2   c. −9   d. −12   e. 52

4. Which of the following is the least odd integer greater than 36?
   a. −5   b. 40   c. 41   d. 11   e. 38

5. How many numbers are there from 100 to 200 inclusive?
   a. 99   b. 100   c. 101   d. 199   e. 200

6. How many odd numbers are there from 100 to 200 inclusive?
   a. 49   b. 50   c. 51   d. 52   e. 100

7. How many even numbers are there from 1000 to 2000 inclusive?
   a. 999   b. 1000   c. 1001   d. 1002   e. 101

8. How many multiples of 4 are there from 1000 to 2000 inclusive?
   a. 250   b. 251   c. 252   d. 100   e. 400

9. How many factors does 56 have?
   a. 2   b. 4   c. 6   d. 8   e. 10

10. How many factors does 36 have?
    a. 5   b. 6   c. 7   d. 8   e. 9

11. Which of the following is divisible by 6?
    a. 222   b. 316   c. 611   d. 614   e. 333

12. Which of the following is divisible by 8?
    a. 246   b. 426   c. 462   d. 642   e. 624

13. Which of the following is divisible by 9?
    a. 113   b. 114   c. 115   d. 116   e. 117

14. Which of the following is a multiple of 12?
    a. 1   b. 2   c. 3   d. 6   e. 12

15. Which of the following is a factor of 6?
    a. 6   b. 12   c. 15   d. 24   e. 60

Name _____   Date _____

Multiple choices

1. Which of the following is a prime?
   a. 31   b. 57   c. 51   d. 77   e. 63

2. Which of the following is not a prime?
   a. 91   b. 11   c. 37   d. 53   e. 97

3. Which of the following is a composite?
   a. 1   b. 5   c. 7   d. 11   e. 15

4. Which of the following is not a composite?
   a. 1   b. 40   c. 49   d. 91   e. 87

5. Which of the following is a multiple of 11?
   a. 101   b. 408   c. 506   d. 606   e. 708

6. Which of the following has a factor of 27?
   a. 72   b. 162   c. 99   d. 96   e. 160

7. Which of the following has 5 factors?
   a. 12   b. 16   c. 25   d. 27   e. 32

8. Which of the following has 6 as its factor?
   a. 53   b. 54   c. 55   d. 56   e. 57

9. Which of the following is a perfect square?
   a. 21   b. 22   c. 23   d. 24   e. 25

10. Which of the following is not a perfect square?
    a. 0   b. 1   c. 2   d. 4   e. 9

11. Which of the following has only one factor?
    a. 1   b. 2   c. 4   d. 5   e. 8

12. Which of the following has the most number of factors?
    a. 32   b. 40   c. 48   d. 50   e. 60

13. Which of the following has the least number of factors?
    a. 20   b. 25   c. 32   d. 35   e. 36

14. Which of the following has the most number of prime factors?
    a. 12   b. 28   c. 30   d. 32   e. 35

15. Which of the following has the least number of prime factors?
    a. 50   b. 51   c. 52   d. 53   e. 54

12. Word problems

1. Arrange the numbers from 1 to 9 in such a way that the number in the middle row is twice that in the top row and the number in the bottom row is triple of that in the top row. For example,

   Find 3 more ways of arranging the numbers.

2. There are 3 boys who share 3 apples in a basket. Each boy got one whole apple but there was still one whole apple in the basket, explain how?

   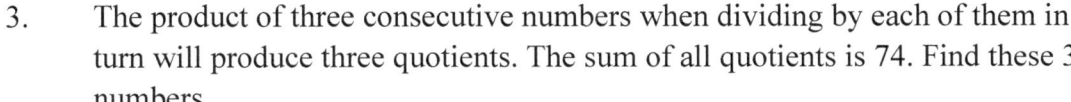

3. The product of three consecutive numbers when dividing by each of them in turn will produce three quotients. The sum of all quotients is 74. Find these 3 numbers.

4. What is the median of seven consecutive whole numbers whose sum is 42?

241

5. What number between 120 and 149 is exactly divisible by both 3 and 5?

6. Students in Gina's class gave each other 55 high fives in total, how many students are there in Gina's class (including Gina)?

7. With 4 weeks remaining, Adrian has collected 27 more cans than Jasmine. If Jasmine is to collect more cans than Adrian, at least how many more cans she must collect in average per week than Adrian?

8. Austin vacuumed his room from 10:00 am to 10:30 am and finished one third of his room. He wants to finish vacuuming his entire room by 5:30 pm at the same rate, what is the latest time that he must start vacuuming the room again?

9. If a taxi can take at least 2 passengers but no more than 7 passengers and no taxis have the same number of passengers, what is the smallest number of taxis required to take all 27 passengers?

Name _____   Date _____

J. Fractions

J1. Representing fractions

1. A fraction is a number written in the form: $\frac{N}{D}$ where **N** is called the **numerator** and **D** is called the **denominator**.
In the typical case, the numerator and denominator are whole numbers. However, the denominator **cannot** be zero. Here are some typical fractions: $\frac{1}{2}, \frac{7}{3}, 2\frac{3}{7}$

1. Divide the figure and shade the portion the fraction represented.

1.

$\frac{1}{2}$

2.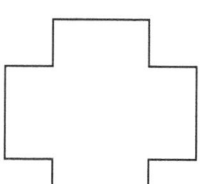

$\frac{1}{4}$

3.

$\frac{1}{5}$

4.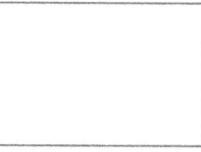

$\frac{1}{5}$

5.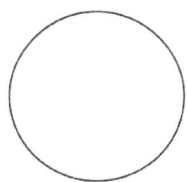

$\frac{2}{4}$

6.

$\frac{3}{8}$

7.

$\frac{5}{8}$

8.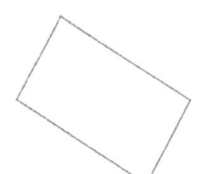

$\frac{2}{6}$

9.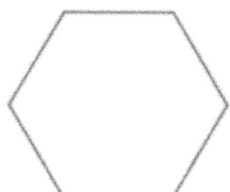

$\frac{5}{12}$

10.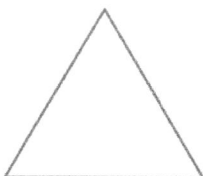

$\frac{3}{4}$

11.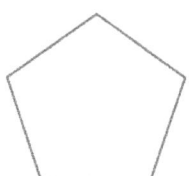

$\frac{7}{10}$

12.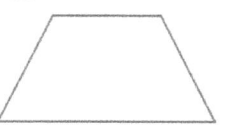

$\frac{2}{3}$

Name _____ Date _____

J2. Fractions to decimals

If the denominator can be changed to multiples of 10s

$$\frac{7}{10} = 0.7 \qquad 6\frac{8}{10} = 6.8$$

$$\frac{9}{100} = 0.09 \qquad 10\frac{1}{100} = 10.01$$

$$\frac{5}{1000} = 0.005 \qquad 3\frac{6}{1000} = 3.006$$

1. Convert the following fractions to decimals.

1. $\dfrac{3}{10} =$

2. $5\dfrac{6}{10} =$

3. $\dfrac{8}{100} =$

4. $9\dfrac{75}{100} =$

5. $6\dfrac{17}{100} =$

6. $\dfrac{4}{10} =$

7. $7\dfrac{9}{100} =$

8. $3\dfrac{23}{100} =$

9. $\dfrac{5}{10} =$

10. $23\dfrac{19}{100} =$

11. $24\dfrac{8}{10} =$

12. $6\dfrac{89}{100} =$

13. $3\dfrac{8}{10} =$

14. $\dfrac{1}{10} =$

15. $\dfrac{39}{1000} =$

16. $\dfrac{7}{10} =$

17. $72\dfrac{8}{100} =$

18. $25\dfrac{15}{100} =$

19. $\dfrac{2}{10} =$

20. $30\dfrac{33}{100} =$

21. $\dfrac{321}{1000} =$

22. $51\dfrac{72}{1000} =$

23. $15\dfrac{42}{100} =$

24. $30\dfrac{8}{100} =$

Name _____   Date _____

2. Convert the following fractions to decimals.

1. $\dfrac{2}{5} = \dfrac{2\times 2}{5\times 2} = \dfrac{4}{10} = 0.4$

2. $\dfrac{6}{25} = \dfrac{6\times 4}{25\times 4} = \dfrac{24}{100} = 0.24$

3. $\dfrac{7}{50} = \dfrac{}{100} =$

4. $\dfrac{1}{2} = \dfrac{}{10} =$

5. $\dfrac{3}{25} = \dfrac{}{100} =$

6. $\dfrac{9}{20} = \dfrac{}{100} =$

7. $\dfrac{1}{2} = \dfrac{}{10} =$

8. $\dfrac{12}{25} = \dfrac{}{100} =$

9. $\dfrac{3}{4} = \dfrac{}{100} =$

10. $\dfrac{1}{4} = \dfrac{}{100} =$

11. $\dfrac{17}{25} = \dfrac{}{100} =$

12. $\dfrac{13}{20} = \dfrac{}{100} =$

13. $\dfrac{6}{25} = \dfrac{}{100} =$

14. $\dfrac{7}{25} = \dfrac{}{100} =$

15. $\dfrac{11}{25} = \dfrac{}{100} =$

16. $\dfrac{19}{20} = \dfrac{}{100} =$

17. $\dfrac{5}{8} = \dfrac{}{1000} =$

18. $\dfrac{33}{125} = \dfrac{}{1000} =$

19. $\dfrac{13}{500} = \dfrac{}{1000} =$

20. $\dfrac{42}{125} = \dfrac{}{1000} =$

21. $\dfrac{32}{500} = \dfrac{}{1000} =$

22. $\dfrac{7}{20} = \dfrac{}{100} =$

23. $\dfrac{3}{20} = \dfrac{}{100} =$

24. $\dfrac{23}{50} = \dfrac{}{100} =$

Name _____   Date _____

3. Convert the following fractions to decimals.

1. $\dfrac{4}{20} = \dfrac{4 \div 2}{20 \div 2} = \dfrac{2}{10} = 0.2$

2. $\dfrac{36}{40} = \dfrac{36 \div 4}{40 \div 4} = \dfrac{9}{10} = 0.9$

3. $\dfrac{8}{20} = \dfrac{}{10} =$

4. $\dfrac{12}{60} = \dfrac{}{10} =$

5. $\dfrac{69}{300} = \dfrac{}{100} =$

6. $\dfrac{24}{800} = \dfrac{}{100} =$

7. $\dfrac{56}{700} = \dfrac{}{100} =$

8. $\dfrac{2}{200} = \dfrac{}{100} =$

9. $\dfrac{35}{500} = \dfrac{}{100} =$

10. $\dfrac{54}{600} = \dfrac{}{100} =$

11. $5\dfrac{25}{500} = 5\dfrac{}{100} =$

12. $9\dfrac{16}{400} = 9\dfrac{}{100} =$

13. $10\dfrac{25}{500} = 10\dfrac{}{100} =$

14. $12\dfrac{45}{50} = 12\dfrac{}{10} =$

15. $7\dfrac{20}{500} = 7\dfrac{}{100} =$

16. $9\dfrac{12}{400} = 9\dfrac{}{100} =$

17. $2\dfrac{63}{700} = 2\dfrac{}{100} =$

18. $\dfrac{120}{500} = \dfrac{}{100} =$

19. $21\dfrac{75}{250} = 21\dfrac{}{10} =$

20. $19\dfrac{64}{800} = 19\dfrac{}{100} =$

21. $32\dfrac{24}{80} = 32\dfrac{}{10} =$

22. $55\dfrac{32}{40} = 55\dfrac{}{10} =$

23. $9\dfrac{72}{400} = 9\dfrac{}{100} =$

24. $7\dfrac{324}{3000} = 7\dfrac{}{1000} =$

Name _____ Date _____

4. Convert the following fractions to decimals.

1. $\dfrac{7}{20} =$

2. $\dfrac{13}{25} =$

3. $\dfrac{9}{20} =$

4. $\dfrac{6}{8} =$

5. $\dfrac{3}{6} =$

6. $\dfrac{2}{20} =$

7. $1\dfrac{12}{24} =$

8. $6\dfrac{4}{16} =$

9. $\dfrac{60}{125} =$

10. $2\dfrac{3}{20} =$

11. $3\dfrac{8}{40} =$

12. $2\dfrac{3}{12} =$

13. $5\dfrac{5}{20} =$

14. $7\dfrac{28}{100} =$

15. $7\dfrac{12}{48} =$

16. $3\dfrac{17}{50} =$

17. $6\dfrac{80}{500} =$

18. $3\dfrac{45}{200} =$

19. $11\dfrac{24}{60} =$

20. $6\dfrac{6}{24} =$

21. $9\dfrac{20}{25} =$

22. $5\dfrac{6}{20} =$

23. $24\dfrac{15}{50} =$

24. $16\dfrac{35}{50} =$

5. Decimal fractions and decimal numbers.

Decimal fractions or decimals are fractions with denominators of 10, 100, 1000, and so on.
$\frac{1}{10} = 0.1 \qquad \frac{1}{100} = 0.01 \qquad \frac{1}{1000} = 0.001$

1. $\frac{1}{10} =$

2. $\frac{1}{100} =$

3. $\frac{1}{1000} =$

4. $\frac{1}{10} =$

5. $\frac{1}{10000} =$

6. $\frac{1}{1000} =$

7. $\frac{1}{100} =$

8. $\frac{1}{100000} =$

9. $\frac{1}{10000} =$

10. $\frac{1}{100000} =$

11. $\frac{1}{100000000} =$

12. $\frac{1}{10000000000} =$

13. $\frac{1}{100000} =$

14. $\frac{1}{1000000} =$

15. $\frac{1}{10000000} =$

16. $\frac{1}{10000} =$

17. $\frac{1}{1000000} =$

18. $\frac{1}{100000000} =$

Name _____   Date _____

6. Convert the following fractions to decimals.

You can also use division method to convert fraction to decimal.

Convert $\dfrac{5}{8}$ into decimal

$so, \dfrac{5}{8} = 0.625$

```
      0.625
   8)5.000
     48
     ---
      20
      16
      ---
       40
       40
       ---
        0
```

1. $\dfrac{1}{2} =$

2. $\dfrac{1}{4} =$

3. $\dfrac{3}{8} =$

4. $\dfrac{3}{6} =$

5. $3\dfrac{6}{8} =$

6. $1\dfrac{3}{4} =$

7. $2\dfrac{4}{25} =$

8. $8\dfrac{7}{8} =$

9. $\dfrac{16}{50} =$

10. $7\dfrac{19}{20} =$

11. $4\dfrac{32}{80} =$

12. $5\dfrac{30}{48} =$

13. $4\dfrac{7}{20} =$

14. $6\dfrac{25}{80} =$

15. $6\dfrac{17}{80} =$

16. $5\dfrac{42}{60} =$

Name _____ Date _____

7. Convert the following fractions to decimals by division, and round your answer to the nearest tenths.

Convert $\frac{1}{3}$ to decimal. Round off to the nearest tenth.

$\frac{1}{3}$ = 0.33... = 0.3

```
   0.33
3)1.00
   9
   ‾
   10
    9
    ‾
    1
```

1. $\frac{3}{25} =$ 　　　　2. $\frac{5}{13} =$

3. $\frac{3}{7} =$ 　　　　4. $\frac{9}{16} =$

5. $\frac{4}{13} =$ 　　　　6. $\frac{1}{7} =$

7. $\frac{2}{9} =$ 　　　　8. $\frac{12}{17} =$

9. $\frac{11}{23} =$ 　　　　10. $\frac{2}{11} =$

11. $\frac{4}{11} =$ 　　　　12. $\frac{5}{9} =$

13. $\frac{12}{13} =$ 　　　　14. $\frac{11}{17} =$

15. $\frac{12}{16} =$ 　　　　16. $\frac{11}{20} =$

Name _____ Date _____

8. Convert the following fractions to decimals by division, and round your answer to the nearest hundredths.

$2\dfrac{2}{7} = 2 + \dfrac{2}{7}$

$2\dfrac{2}{7} = 2 + \dfrac{2}{7} = 2 + 0.285\ldots$
$= 2.285\ldots$
$= 2.29$

```
    0.285
7)2.000
    14
    ――
     60
     56
     ――
      40
      35
      ――
       5
```

1. $3\dfrac{2}{3} =$

2. $1\dfrac{1}{7} =$

3. $2\dfrac{5}{6} =$

4. $4\dfrac{2}{9} =$

5. $5\dfrac{3}{14} =$

6. $3\dfrac{4}{11} =$

7. $8\dfrac{5}{12} =$

8. $3\dfrac{7}{13} =$

9. $3\dfrac{8}{15} =$

10. $2\dfrac{9}{14} =$

11. $10\dfrac{7}{18} =$

12. $43\dfrac{5}{12} =$

13. $7\dfrac{8}{21} =$

14. $5\dfrac{7}{19} =$

Name _____   Date _____

Convert the following decimals to fractions in their simplest form

1. $0.3 =$

2. $1.35 = 1\dfrac{35}{100} = 1\dfrac{\cancel{35}^{7}}{\cancel{100}_{20}} = 1\dfrac{7}{20}$

3. $0.7 =$

4. $1.3 =$

5. $3.25 =$

6. $8.75 =$

7. $9.56 =$

8. $4.321 =$

9. $0.506 =$

10. $3.008 =$

11. $2.045 =$

12. $10.24 =$

13. $0.0012 =$

14. $1.0001 =$

15. $5.021 =$

16. $7.705 =$

17. $10.005 =$

18. $6.325 =$

19. $9.010 =$

20. $32.41 =$

21. $100.4 =$

22. $26.73 =$

23. $12.16 =$

24. $0.0091 =$

25. $20.76 =$

26. $6.007 =$

27. $50.532 =$

28. $10.56 =$

J3. Equivalent fractions

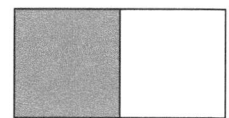 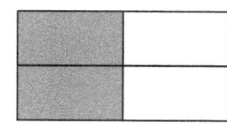 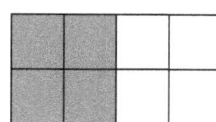

We can see from above, $\frac{2}{4}$ and $\frac{4}{8}$ are different ways of writing $\frac{1}{2}$. So $\frac{1}{2}$, $\frac{2}{4}$ and $\frac{4}{8}$ are **equivalent fractions**.

Fill in the missing numbers.

1. $\frac{1}{4}$ 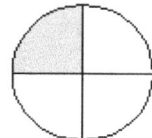 is equivalent to (the same as) 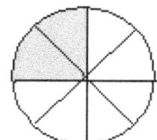 $\frac{2}{8}$ ∴ $\frac{1}{4} = \frac{2}{8}$

2. $\frac{3}{4}$ 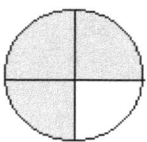 is equivalent to (the same as) 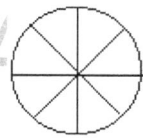 $\frac{6}{8}$ ∴ $\frac{3}{4} = \frac{6}{8}$

3. $\frac{1}{2}$ is equivalent to (the same as) 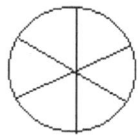 $\frac{3}{6}$ ∴ $\frac{1}{2} = \frac{3}{6}$

4. $\frac{2}{6}$ is equivalent to (the same as) 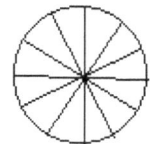 $\frac{4}{12}$ ∴ $\frac{2}{6} = \frac{4}{12}$

5. $\frac{1}{3}$ 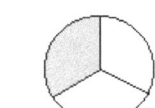 is equivalent to (the same as) 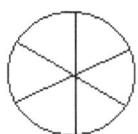 $\frac{2}{6}$ ∴ $\frac{1}{3} = \frac{2}{6}$

Name _____ Date _____

Fill in the missing numbers.

When the numerator and denominator of a fraction are multiplied or divided by the same number, the value of the fraction remains the same.

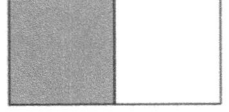 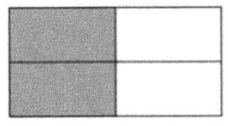 $\dfrac{1}{2} = \dfrac{1 \times 2}{2 \times 2} = \dfrac{2}{4}$

1. $\dfrac{1}{2} = \dfrac{1 \times \square}{2 \times \square} = \dfrac{}{10}$

2. $\dfrac{1}{3} = \dfrac{1 \times \square}{3 \times \square} = \dfrac{}{18}$

3. $\dfrac{3}{5} = \dfrac{3 \times \square}{5 \times \square} = \dfrac{}{40}$

4. $\dfrac{3}{7} = \dfrac{3 \times \square}{7 \times \square} = \dfrac{}{41}$

5. $\dfrac{5}{7} = \dfrac{5 \times \square}{7 \times \square} = \dfrac{}{35}$

6. $\dfrac{3}{8} = \dfrac{3 \times \square}{8 \times \square} = \dfrac{}{48}$

7. $\dfrac{5}{9} = \dfrac{5 \times \square}{9 \times \square} = \dfrac{}{54}$

8. $\dfrac{2}{3} = \dfrac{2 \times \square}{3 \times \square} = \dfrac{}{33}$

9. $\dfrac{6}{11} = \dfrac{6 \times \square}{ \times \square} = \dfrac{}{55}$

10. $\dfrac{3}{13} = \dfrac{3 \times \square}{13 \times \square} = \dfrac{}{52}$

11. $\dfrac{4}{9} = \dfrac{4 \times \square}{9 \times \square} = \dfrac{20}{}$

12. $\dfrac{7}{12} = \dfrac{7 \times \square}{12 \times \square} = \dfrac{42}{}$

13. $\dfrac{8}{13} = \dfrac{8 \times \square}{13 \times \square} = \dfrac{56}{}$

14. $\dfrac{11}{13} = \dfrac{11 \times \square}{13 \times \square} = \dfrac{66}{}$

15. $\dfrac{7}{15} = \dfrac{7 \times \square}{15 \times \square} = \dfrac{63}{}$

16. $\dfrac{8}{17} = \dfrac{8 \times \square}{17 \times \square} = \dfrac{88}{}$

17. $\dfrac{9}{11} = \dfrac{9 \times \square}{11 \times \square} = \dfrac{99}{}$

18. $\dfrac{8}{21} = \dfrac{8 \times \square}{21 \times \square} = \dfrac{88}{}$

19. $\dfrac{7}{34} = \dfrac{7 \times \square}{34 \times \square} = \dfrac{77}{}$

20. $\dfrac{6}{23} = \dfrac{6 \times \square}{23 \times \square} = \dfrac{66}{}$

Name _____ Date _____

Fill in the missing numbers.

1. $\dfrac{5}{8} = \dfrac{}{40}$
2. $\dfrac{3}{7} = \dfrac{}{49}$
3. $\dfrac{5}{9} = \dfrac{}{45}$

4. $\dfrac{3}{8} = \dfrac{}{32}$
5. $\dfrac{5}{6} = \dfrac{}{24}$
6. $\dfrac{3}{5} = \dfrac{}{50}$

7. $\dfrac{2}{5} = \dfrac{}{35}$
8. $\dfrac{2}{9} = \dfrac{16}{}$
9. $\dfrac{6}{11} = \dfrac{24}{}$

10. $\dfrac{5}{12} = \dfrac{}{60}$
11. $\dfrac{7}{10} = \dfrac{}{100}$
12. $\dfrac{9}{11} = \dfrac{}{33}$

13. $\dfrac{4}{7} = \dfrac{40}{}$
14. $\dfrac{3}{10} = \dfrac{}{100}$
15. $\dfrac{4}{9} = \dfrac{}{81}$

16. $\dfrac{4}{9} = \dfrac{}{108}$
17. $\dfrac{4}{7} = \dfrac{}{105}$
18. $\dfrac{8}{15} = \dfrac{96}{}$

19. $\dfrac{6}{13} = \dfrac{}{52}$
20. $\dfrac{7}{12} = \dfrac{}{84}$
21. $\dfrac{8}{17} = \dfrac{104}{}$

22. $\dfrac{5}{19} = \dfrac{}{95}$
23. $\dfrac{1}{15} = \dfrac{}{225}$
24. $\dfrac{6}{17} = \dfrac{84}{}$

25. $\dfrac{7}{12} = \dfrac{}{144}$
26. $\dfrac{6}{17} = \dfrac{66}{}$
27. $\dfrac{6}{25} = \dfrac{150}{}$

28. $\dfrac{11}{12} = \dfrac{}{156}$
29. $\dfrac{13}{17} = \dfrac{169}{}$
30. $\dfrac{16}{19} = \dfrac{320}{}$

31. $\dfrac{10}{16} = \dfrac{}{176}$
32. $\dfrac{7}{17} = \dfrac{77}{}$
33. $\dfrac{7}{25} = \dfrac{}{150}$

34. $\dfrac{12}{37} = \dfrac{}{111}$
35. $\dfrac{15}{22} = \dfrac{}{66}$
36. $\dfrac{12}{13} = \dfrac{156}{}$

37. $\dfrac{9}{16} = \dfrac{}{176}$
38. $\dfrac{31}{37} = \dfrac{}{111}$
39. $\dfrac{12}{25} = \dfrac{}{625}$

Name _____   Date _____

Fill in the missing numbers.

1. $\dfrac{4}{8} = \dfrac{4 \div \square}{8 \div \square} = \dfrac{}{2}$

2. $\dfrac{3}{9} = \dfrac{3 \div \square}{9 \div \square} = \dfrac{}{3}$

3. $\dfrac{15}{18} = \dfrac{15 \div \square}{18 \div \square} = \dfrac{5}{}$

4. $\dfrac{21}{49} = \dfrac{21 \div \square}{49 \div \square} = \dfrac{3}{}$

5. $\dfrac{40}{75} = \dfrac{40 \div \square}{75 \div \square} = \dfrac{}{15}$

6. $\dfrac{16}{36} = \dfrac{16 \div \square}{36 \div \square} = \dfrac{4}{}$

7. $\dfrac{10}{100} = \dfrac{10 \div \square}{100 \div \square} = \dfrac{}{10}$

8. $\dfrac{16}{40} = \dfrac{16 \div \square}{40 \div \square} = \dfrac{2}{}$

9. $\dfrac{27}{117} = \dfrac{27 \div \square}{117 \div \square} = \dfrac{3}{}$

10. $\dfrac{55}{132} = \dfrac{55 \div \square}{132 \div \square} = \dfrac{5}{}$

Reduce the following fractions by 2.

1. $\dfrac{\cancel{2}^{\,1}}{\cancel{4}_{\,2}} = \dfrac{1}{2}$

2. $\dfrac{8}{10} =$

3. $\dfrac{2}{6} =$

4. $\dfrac{4}{14} =$

5. $\dfrac{6}{16} =$

6. $\dfrac{8}{18} =$

7. $\dfrac{12}{14} =$

8. $\dfrac{14}{16} =$

9. $\dfrac{16}{18} =$

10. $\dfrac{22}{24} =$

11. $\dfrac{18}{20} =$

12. $\dfrac{8}{22} =$

13. $\dfrac{24}{34} =$

14. $\dfrac{26}{36} =$

15. $\dfrac{28}{38} =$

16. $\dfrac{16}{46} =$

17. $\dfrac{14}{44} =$

18. $\dfrac{24}{46} =$

19. $\dfrac{10}{52} =$

20. $\dfrac{16}{82} =$

21. $\dfrac{18}{76} =$

Name _____   Date _____

Reduce the following fractions by 3.

1. $\dfrac{3}{9} =$ 2. $\dfrac{12}{15} =$ 3. $\dfrac{9}{12} =$

4. $\dfrac{6}{15} =$ 5. $\dfrac{12}{21} =$ 6. $\dfrac{15}{24} =$

7. $\dfrac{18}{33} =$ 8. $\dfrac{15}{36} =$ 9. $\dfrac{15}{42} =$

10. $\dfrac{27}{30} =$ 11. $\dfrac{18}{57} =$ 12. $\dfrac{21}{63} =$

13. $\dfrac{33}{63} =$ 14. $\dfrac{24}{51} =$ 15. $\dfrac{24}{45} =$

16. $\dfrac{27}{57} =$ 17. $\dfrac{39}{81} =$ 18. $\dfrac{63}{78} =$

Reduce the following fractions by 5.

1. $\dfrac{5}{25} =$ 2. $\dfrac{10}{35}$ 3. $\dfrac{15}{25} =$

4. $\dfrac{15}{40} =$ 5. $\dfrac{25}{55} =$ 6. $\dfrac{10}{25} =$

7. $\dfrac{25}{60} =$ 8. $\dfrac{30}{65} =$ 9. $\dfrac{30}{35} =$

10. $\dfrac{15}{50} =$ 11. $\dfrac{20}{45} =$ 12. $\dfrac{35}{100} =$

13. $\dfrac{30}{85} =$ 14. $\dfrac{35}{75} =$ 15. $\dfrac{50}{95} =$

16. $\dfrac{40}{85} =$ 17. $\dfrac{55}{75} =$ 18. $\dfrac{60}{85} =$

Name _____ Date _____

Reduce the following fractions by 7.

1. $\dfrac{7}{77} =$ 2. $\dfrac{21}{35} =$ 3. $\dfrac{21}{49} =$

4. $\dfrac{14}{63} =$ 5. $\dfrac{14}{77} =$ 6. $\dfrac{28}{49} =$

7. $\dfrac{56}{77} =$ 8. $\dfrac{35}{63} =$ 9. $\dfrac{28}{77} =$

10. $\dfrac{42}{91} =$ 11. $\dfrac{49}{84} =$ 12. $\dfrac{77}{84} =$

13. $\dfrac{35}{98} =$ 14. $\dfrac{42}{91} =$ 15. $\dfrac{35}{84} =$

16. $\dfrac{63}{77} =$ 17. $\dfrac{63}{98} =$ 18. $\dfrac{49}{84} =$

Reduce the following fractions by 10.

1. $\dfrac{10}{100} =$ 2. $\dfrac{20}{50} =$ 3. $\dfrac{30}{40} =$

4. $\dfrac{70}{200} =$ 5. $\dfrac{40}{150} =$ 6. $\dfrac{50}{160} =$

7. $\dfrac{20}{230} =$ 8. $\dfrac{120}{350} =$ 9. $\dfrac{100}{1000} =$

10. $\dfrac{80}{130} =$ 11. $\dfrac{60}{700} =$ 12. $\dfrac{160}{900} =$

13. $\dfrac{200}{900} =$ 14. $\dfrac{300}{800} =$ 15. $\dfrac{400}{700} =$

16. 600/1100 =   17. $\dfrac{700}{1000} =$ 18. $\dfrac{400}{9000} =$

Name _____ Date _____

Fill in the missing numbers.

1. $\dfrac{2}{7} = \dfrac{(2 \times 3)}{7 \times 3} = \dfrac{(6)}{21}$ 2. $\dfrac{8}{12} = \dfrac{(8 \div 4)}{12 \div 4} = \dfrac{2}{3}$ 3. $\dfrac{3}{8} = \dfrac{9}{}$

4. $\dfrac{6}{15} = \dfrac{}{30}$ 5. $\dfrac{7}{16} = \dfrac{21}{}$ 6. $\dfrac{6}{14} = \dfrac{}{42}$

7. $\dfrac{5}{9} = \dfrac{}{63}$ 8. $\dfrac{28}{49} = \dfrac{}{7}$ 9. $\dfrac{12}{21} = \dfrac{}{7}$

10. $\dfrac{24}{42} = \dfrac{}{7}$ 11. $\dfrac{12}{32} = \dfrac{}{64}$ 12. $\dfrac{21}{30} = \dfrac{}{10}$

13. $\dfrac{28}{52} = \dfrac{7}{}$ 14. $\dfrac{16}{84} = \dfrac{}{21}$ 15. $\dfrac{6}{15} = \dfrac{24}{}$

16. $\dfrac{35}{77} = \dfrac{5}{}$ 17. $\dfrac{55}{66} = \dfrac{}{6}$ 18. $\dfrac{22}{33} = \dfrac{2}{}$

19. $\dfrac{40}{70} = \dfrac{}{7}$ 20. $\dfrac{5}{8} = \dfrac{50}{}$ 21. $\dfrac{11}{13} = \dfrac{}{52}$

22. $\dfrac{24}{40} = \dfrac{}{5}$ 23. $\dfrac{13}{15} = \dfrac{52}{}$ 24. $\dfrac{9}{11} = \dfrac{99}{}$

25. $\dfrac{11}{17} = \dfrac{}{187}$ 26. $\dfrac{45}{72} = \dfrac{5}{}$ 27. $\dfrac{12}{13} = \dfrac{}{156}$

28. $\dfrac{18}{21} = \dfrac{378}{}$ 29. $\dfrac{2}{70} = \dfrac{20}{}$ 30. $\dfrac{5}{90} = \dfrac{}{900}$

Name _____ Date _____

J4. Lowest term fractions

A fraction in which the numerator and denominator have no factors in common (other than 1) is said to be **irreducible** or **in lowest terms (or simplest form).** For instance, ³⁄₉ is not in lowest terms because both 3 and 9 can be evenly divided by 3. In contrast, ³⁄₈ *is* in lowest terms — the only number that's a factor of both 3 and 8 is 1.

Express each fraction in its lowest term.

1. $\dfrac{4}{16} =$
2. $\dfrac{5}{25} =$
3. $\dfrac{6}{36} =$

4. $\dfrac{15}{45} =$
5. $\dfrac{21}{42} =$
6. $\dfrac{12}{36} =$

7. $\dfrac{6}{24} =$
8. $\dfrac{8}{12} =$
9. $\dfrac{12}{18} =$

10. $\dfrac{12}{42} =$
11. $\dfrac{13}{26} =$
12. $\dfrac{11}{22} =$

13. $\dfrac{12}{24} =$
14. $\dfrac{22}{44} =$
15. $\dfrac{33}{66} =$

16. $\dfrac{22}{55} =$
17. $\dfrac{35}{63} =$
18. $\dfrac{30}{42} =$

19. $\dfrac{18}{45} =$
20. $\dfrac{21}{56} =$
21. $\dfrac{14}{49} =$

22. $\dfrac{16}{56} =$
23. $\dfrac{15}{45} =$
24. $\dfrac{25}{30} =$

25. $\dfrac{30}{50} =$
26. $\dfrac{30}{60} =$
27. $\dfrac{40}{60} =$

28. $\dfrac{121}{132} =$
29. $\dfrac{77}{121} =$
30. $\dfrac{55}{154} =$

Name _____ Date _____

Express each fraction in its lowest term.

1. $\dfrac{6}{144} =$
2. $\dfrac{30}{80} =$
3. $\dfrac{49}{98} =$

4. $\dfrac{27}{36} =$
5. $\dfrac{24}{34} =$
6. $\dfrac{28}{84} =$

7. $\dfrac{20}{80} =$
8. $\dfrac{33}{66} =$
9. $\dfrac{84}{91} =$

10. $\dfrac{15}{35} =$
11. $\dfrac{16}{42} =$
12. $\dfrac{32}{56} =$

13. $\dfrac{8}{18} =$
14. $\dfrac{25}{45} =$
15. $\dfrac{21}{30} =$

16. $\dfrac{18}{30} =$
17. $\dfrac{36}{63} =$
18. $\dfrac{15}{45} =$

19. $\dfrac{45}{63} =$
20. $\dfrac{32}{72} =$
21. $\dfrac{42}{63} =$

22. $\dfrac{35}{65} =$
23. $\dfrac{50}{70} =$
24. $\dfrac{24}{42} =$

25. $\dfrac{15}{51} =$
26. $\dfrac{11}{66} =$
27. $\dfrac{46}{92} =$

28. $\dfrac{70}{80} =$
29. $\dfrac{30}{75} =$
30. $\dfrac{26}{52} =$

31. $\dfrac{36}{48} =$
32. $\dfrac{16}{64} =$
33. $\dfrac{14}{56} =$

34. $\dfrac{33}{99} =$
35. $\dfrac{24}{72} =$
36. $\dfrac{33}{121} =$

37. $\dfrac{19}{38} =$
38. $\dfrac{17}{51} =$
39. $\dfrac{13}{39} =$

40. $\dfrac{56}{88}=\dfrac{7}{11}$	41. $\dfrac{28}{84}=\dfrac{1}{3}$	42. $\dfrac{15}{60}=\dfrac{1}{4}$
43. $\dfrac{22}{44}=\dfrac{1}{2}$	44. $\dfrac{35}{70}=\dfrac{1}{2}$	45. $\dfrac{60}{90}=\dfrac{2}{3}$
46. $\dfrac{14}{52}=\dfrac{7}{26}$	47. $\dfrac{17}{51}=\dfrac{1}{3}$	48. $\dfrac{22}{88}=\dfrac{1}{4}$
49. $\dfrac{62}{93}=\dfrac{2}{3}$	50. $\dfrac{28}{63}=\dfrac{4}{9}$	51. $\dfrac{16}{48}=\dfrac{1}{3}$
52. $\dfrac{45}{60}=\dfrac{3}{4}$	53. $\dfrac{12}{60}=\dfrac{1}{5}$	54. $\dfrac{41}{82}=\dfrac{1}{2}$
55. $\dfrac{23}{92}=\dfrac{1}{4}$	56. $\dfrac{33}{60}=\dfrac{11}{20}$	57. $\dfrac{66}{90}=\dfrac{11}{15}$
58. $\dfrac{16}{64}=\dfrac{1}{4}$	59. $\dfrac{27}{72}=\dfrac{3}{8}$	60. $\dfrac{14}{56}=\dfrac{1}{4}$
61. $\dfrac{45}{54}=\dfrac{5}{6}$	62. $\dfrac{44}{66}=\dfrac{2}{3}$	63. $\dfrac{24}{60}=\dfrac{2}{5}$
64. $\dfrac{28}{82}=\dfrac{14}{41}$	65. $\dfrac{20}{200}=\dfrac{1}{10}$	66. $\dfrac{30}{300}=\dfrac{1}{10}$
67. $\dfrac{15}{51}=\dfrac{5}{17}$	68. $\dfrac{33}{121}=\dfrac{3}{11}$	69. $\dfrac{45}{400}=\dfrac{9}{80}$
70. $\dfrac{200}{400}=\dfrac{1}{2}$	71. $\dfrac{56}{84}=\dfrac{2}{3}$	72. $\dfrac{78}{87}=\dfrac{26}{29}$
73. $\dfrac{300}{900}=\dfrac{1}{3}$	74. $\dfrac{57}{75}=\dfrac{19}{25}$	75. $\dfrac{55}{75}=\dfrac{11}{15}$
76. $\dfrac{12}{144}=\dfrac{1}{12}$	77. $\dfrac{23}{92}=\dfrac{1}{4}$	78. $\dfrac{25}{75}=\dfrac{1}{3}$

J5. Equivalent fractions

Find the pattern rule, then fill in each blank.

1. $\dfrac{1}{2}$, $\dfrac{2}{4}$, $\dfrac{3}{6}$, _____, _____, _____, _____, _____

2. $\dfrac{1}{3}$, $\dfrac{2}{6}$, $\dfrac{3}{9}$, _____, _____, _____, _____, _____

3. $\dfrac{1}{4}$, $\dfrac{2}{8}$, $\dfrac{3}{12}$, _____, _____, _____, _____, _____

4. $\dfrac{2}{3}$, $\dfrac{4}{6}$, $\dfrac{6}{9}$, _____, _____, _____, _____, _____

5. $\dfrac{2}{5}$, $\dfrac{4}{10}$, $\dfrac{6}{15}$, _____, _____, _____, _____, _____

6. $\dfrac{3}{7}$, $\dfrac{6}{14}$, $\dfrac{9}{21}$, _____, _____, _____, _____, _____

7. $\dfrac{3}{4}$, $\dfrac{6}{8}$, $\dfrac{9}{12}$, _____, _____, _____, _____, _____

8. $\dfrac{5}{6}$, $\dfrac{10}{12}$, $\dfrac{15}{18}$, _____, _____, _____, _____, _____

J6. Proper fraction, improper fractions, and mixed numbers

Proper fraction is a fraction in which the numerator is less than the denominator, such as $\frac{1}{4}$.

2.   **Improper fraction** is a fraction in which the numerator is larger than or equal to the denominator, such as $\frac{29}{4}$

3.   **Mixed number** is a number consisting of an integer and a fraction, such as $7\frac{1}{4}$

What fraction of the following shape is shaded? Give your answer as improper fraction, then as a mixed number.

1.
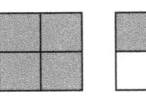
$\frac{5}{4}$ $1\frac{1}{4}$

2.

$\frac{10}{4}$ $2\frac{2}{4}$

3.
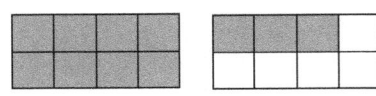
$\frac{11}{8}$ $1\frac{3}{8}$

4.
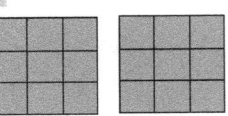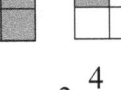
$\frac{31}{9}$ $3\frac{4}{9}$

5.
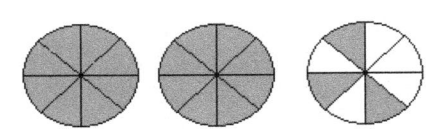
$\frac{19}{8}$ $\mathbf{2\frac{3}{8}}$

6.
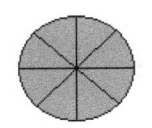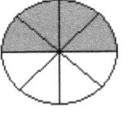
$\frac{12}{8}$ $1\frac{4}{8}$

7.
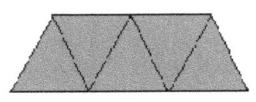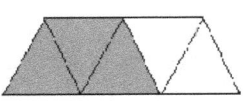
$\frac{8}{5}$ $1\frac{3}{5}$

8.

$\frac{11}{8}$ $1\frac{3}{8}$

264

Cross out the misplaced numbers.

Proper Fractions	a. $\dfrac{3}{5}$	b. $2\dfrac{3}{7}$	c. $\dfrac{5}{9}$	d. $\dfrac{6}{5}$	e. $\dfrac{9}{10}$
Improper Fractions	a. $\dfrac{7}{3}$	b. $\dfrac{13}{6}$	c. $\dfrac{7}{12}$	d. $\dfrac{4}{3}$	e. $3\dfrac{4}{5}$
Mixed Numbers	a. $6\dfrac{3}{4}$	b. $\dfrac{7}{4}$	c. $6\dfrac{3}{14}$	d. $\dfrac{2}{3}$	e. $3\dfrac{5}{9}$

J7. Improper fraction to mixed number

$$\frac{7}{4} = 7 \div 4 = 1\frac{3}{4} \qquad 4\overline{)7}$$

Convert the following numbers to mixed numbers or whole numbers.

1. $\frac{6}{5} =$ 2. $\frac{3}{2} =$ 3. $\frac{5}{3} =$

4. $\frac{8}{5} =$ 5. $\frac{13}{3} =$ 6. $\frac{20}{7} =$

7. $\frac{14}{5} =$ 8. $\frac{36}{5} =$ 9. $\frac{28}{9} =$

10. $\frac{51}{7} =$ 11. $\frac{64}{8} =$ 12. $\frac{77}{9} =$

13. $\frac{25}{12} =$ 14. $\frac{36}{25} =$ 15. $\frac{24}{11} =$

16. $\frac{46}{15} =$ 17. $\frac{75}{16} =$ 18. $\frac{47}{13} =$

19. $\frac{98}{15} =$ 20. $\frac{76}{19} =$ 21. $\frac{68}{15} =$

22. $\frac{51}{25} =$ 23. $\frac{67}{16} =$ 24. $\frac{85}{17} =$

25. $\frac{81}{25} =$ 26. $\frac{57}{20} =$ 27. $\frac{71}{30} =$

28. $\frac{48}{21} =$ 29. $\frac{73}{12} =$ 30. $\frac{83}{21} =$

Name _____   Date _____

Convert each improper fraction to a mixed number or whole number.

1. $\dfrac{45}{7} =$ 2. $\dfrac{34}{7} =$ 3. $\dfrac{28}{3} =$

4. $\dfrac{55}{4} =$ 5. $\dfrac{56}{7} =$ 6. $\dfrac{27}{8} =$

7. $\dfrac{36}{5} =$ 8. $\dfrac{66}{13} =$ 9. $\dfrac{31}{6} =$

10. $\dfrac{37}{7} =$ 11. $\dfrac{53}{9} =$ 12. $\dfrac{48}{7} =$

13. $\dfrac{47}{10} =$ 14. $\dfrac{39}{10} =$ 15. $\dfrac{71}{10} =$

16. $\dfrac{43}{6} =$ 17. $\dfrac{79}{9} =$ 18. $\dfrac{64}{13} =$

19. $\dfrac{84}{3} =$ 20. $\dfrac{65}{7} =$ 21. $\dfrac{53}{10} =$

22. $\dfrac{37}{12} =$ 23. $\dfrac{53}{11} =$ 24. $\dfrac{64}{16} =$

25. $\dfrac{37}{11} =$ 26. $\dfrac{73}{6} =$ 27. $\dfrac{63}{10} =$

28. $\dfrac{48}{11} =$ 29. $\dfrac{68}{13} =$ 30. $\dfrac{49}{12} =$

31. $\dfrac{39}{7} =$ 32. $\dfrac{47}{10} =$ 33. $\dfrac{60}{12} =$

34. $\dfrac{34}{15} =$ 34. $\dfrac{31}{14} =$ 36. $\dfrac{100}{10} =$

37. $\dfrac{85}{21} =$ 36. $\dfrac{29}{14} =$ 39. $\dfrac{43}{11} =$

J8. Mixed number to improper fraction

Example: $2\dfrac{5}{6} = \dfrac{2\times 6+5}{6} = \dfrac{17}{6}$

1. $1\dfrac{2}{5} = \dfrac{}{5}$ 2. $2\dfrac{1}{3} = \dfrac{}{3}$ 3. $3\dfrac{2}{5} = \dfrac{}{5}$

4. $3\dfrac{1}{4} = \dfrac{}{4}$ 5. $2\dfrac{3}{5} = \dfrac{}{5}$ 6. $1\dfrac{5}{6} = \dfrac{}{6}$

7. $4\dfrac{2}{7} = \dfrac{}{7}$ 8. $2\dfrac{3}{8} = \dfrac{}{8}$ 9. $4\dfrac{1}{6} = \dfrac{}{6}$

10. $3\dfrac{4}{9} = \dfrac{}{9}$ 11. $5\dfrac{3}{10} = \dfrac{}{10}$ 12. $4\dfrac{5}{8} = \dfrac{}{8}$

13. $2\dfrac{7}{10} = \dfrac{}{10}$ 14. $6\dfrac{4}{7} = \dfrac{}{7}$ 15. $6\dfrac{7}{8} = \dfrac{}{12}$

16. $10\dfrac{5}{7} = \dfrac{}{7}$ 17. $10\dfrac{4}{9} = \dfrac{}{9}$ 18. $10\dfrac{2}{5} = \dfrac{}{5}$

19. $4\dfrac{7}{10} = \dfrac{}{10}$ 20. $5\dfrac{1}{5} = \dfrac{}{5}$ 21. $3\dfrac{3}{11} = \dfrac{}{11}$

22. $11\dfrac{7}{12} = \dfrac{}{12}$ 23. $9\dfrac{5}{13} = \dfrac{}{13}$ 24. $7\dfrac{7}{11} = \dfrac{}{11}$

25. $10\dfrac{2}{9} = \dfrac{}{9}$ 26. $6\dfrac{3}{11} = \dfrac{}{11}$ 27. $6\dfrac{7}{9} = \dfrac{}{9}$

28. $3\dfrac{11}{37} = \dfrac{}{37}$ 29. $2\dfrac{7}{20} = \dfrac{}{20}$ 30. $3\dfrac{6}{17} = \dfrac{}{17}$

31. $4\dfrac{7}{15} = \dfrac{}{15}$ 32. $2\dfrac{8}{25} = \dfrac{}{25}$ 33. $2\dfrac{11}{30} = \dfrac{}{30}$

Name _____   Date _____

Convert the following mixed numbers into improper fractions.

1. $1\dfrac{4}{5}$
2. $2\dfrac{1}{3}$
3. $4\dfrac{5}{6}$
4. $3\dfrac{2}{7}$
5. $6\dfrac{3}{8}$
6. $7\dfrac{2}{9}$
7. $6\dfrac{5}{7}$
8. $3\dfrac{7}{8}$
9. $4\dfrac{8}{9}$
10. $2\dfrac{3}{7}$
11. $8\dfrac{5}{8}$
12. $8\dfrac{4}{5}$
13. $3\dfrac{5}{6}$
14. $10\dfrac{5}{7}$
15. $3\dfrac{7}{10}$
16. $2\dfrac{6}{11}$
17. $4\dfrac{5}{12}$
18. $5\dfrac{7}{12}$
19. $8\dfrac{2}{11}$
20. $11\dfrac{6}{11}$
21. $5\dfrac{7}{11}$
22. $3\dfrac{12}{37}$
23. $9\dfrac{9}{10}$
24. $2\dfrac{3}{5}$
25. $3\dfrac{10}{13}$
26. $12\dfrac{2}{3}$
27. $25\dfrac{3}{4}$
28. $2\dfrac{7}{15}$
29. $3\dfrac{9}{17}$
30. $6\dfrac{4}{15}$
31. $5\dfrac{4}{9}$
32. $3\dfrac{3}{13}$
33. $4\dfrac{7}{12}$
34. $5\dfrac{4}{15}$
35. $6\dfrac{9}{14}$
36. $12\dfrac{5}{12}$

J9. Comparing fractions

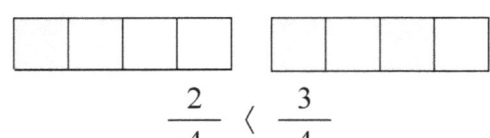

Order from least to greatest:
$$\frac{3}{8}, \frac{5}{8}, \frac{1}{8}$$

Least to greatest: $\frac{1}{8}, \frac{3}{8}, \frac{5}{8}$

Compare by using > , < or = to make each statement true.

1. $\frac{3}{7} \square \frac{5}{7}$
2. $\frac{4}{9} \square \frac{5}{9}$
3. $\frac{5}{8} \square \frac{3}{8}$

4. $\frac{5}{12} \square \frac{5}{12}$
5. $\frac{6}{16} \square \frac{9}{16}$
6. $\frac{4}{15} \square \frac{7}{15}$

7. $\frac{1}{3} \square \frac{1}{5}$
8. $\frac{4}{7} \square \frac{4}{9}$
9. $\frac{3}{10} \square \frac{3}{4}$

10. $\frac{5}{13} \square \frac{5}{6}$
11. $\frac{5}{7} \square \frac{5}{12}$
12. $\frac{4}{11} \square \frac{4}{7}$

13. $\frac{2}{8} \square \frac{7}{8}$
14. $\frac{3}{8} \square \frac{3}{9}$
15. $\frac{7}{24} \square \frac{7}{15}$

16. $\frac{8}{13} \square \frac{5}{13}$
17. $\frac{7}{18} \square \frac{13}{18}$
18. $\frac{7}{13} \square \frac{7}{25}$

19. $\frac{6}{7} \square \frac{6}{13}$
20. $\frac{2}{7} \square \frac{4}{14}$
21. $\frac{5}{9} \square \frac{5}{12}$

22. $\frac{6}{13} \square \frac{6}{13}$
23. $\frac{9}{10} \square \frac{9}{17}$
24. $\frac{8}{17} \square \frac{7}{17}$

25. $\frac{10}{13} \square \frac{10}{25}$
26. $\frac{7}{16} \square \frac{7}{13}$
27. $\frac{2}{4} \square \frac{1}{2}$

28. $\frac{8}{21} \square \frac{15}{21}$
29. $\frac{9}{11} \square \frac{9}{16}$
30. $\frac{12}{15} \square \frac{12}{25}$

Name _____ Date _____

Order the following numbers from least to largest.

1. $\dfrac{7}{9}, \dfrac{5}{9}, \dfrac{2}{9}$

2. $\dfrac{3}{7}, \dfrac{6}{7}, \dfrac{4}{7}$

3. $\dfrac{5}{13}, \dfrac{9}{13}, \dfrac{12}{13}$

4. $\dfrac{4}{15}, \dfrac{2}{15}, \dfrac{7}{15}$

5. $\dfrac{7}{10}, \dfrac{3}{10}, \dfrac{4}{10}$

6. $\dfrac{3}{8}, \dfrac{7}{8}, \dfrac{4}{8}$

7. $\dfrac{4}{11}, \dfrac{4}{31}, \dfrac{4}{21}$

8. $\dfrac{7}{24}, \dfrac{7}{15}, \dfrac{7}{30}$

Order the following numbers from least to largest.

1. $\dfrac{6}{7}, \dfrac{2}{7}, \dfrac{4}{7}$

2. $\dfrac{5}{10}, \dfrac{7}{10}, \dfrac{3}{10}$

3. $\dfrac{3}{11}, \dfrac{6}{11}, \dfrac{5}{11}$

4. $\dfrac{5}{12}, \dfrac{11}{12}, \dfrac{7}{12}$

5. $\dfrac{5}{13}, \dfrac{5}{6}, \dfrac{5}{9}$

6. $\dfrac{3}{20}, \dfrac{3}{7}, \dfrac{3}{13}$

Name _____ Date _____

Fill in each blank with appropriate fraction.

1					
$\frac{1}{2}$			$\frac{1}{2}$		
$\frac{1}{4}$					
$\frac{1}{5}$					

Compare by using >, < or = to make each statement true. Use the diagram above to help thinking.

1. $\dfrac{1}{3}$ ☐ $\dfrac{2}{3}$ 2. $\dfrac{1}{4}$ ☐ $\dfrac{1}{5}$ 3. $\dfrac{1}{6}$ ☐ $\dfrac{1}{8}$

4. $\dfrac{2}{3}$ ☐ $\dfrac{3}{4}$ 5. $\dfrac{4}{5}$ ☐ $\dfrac{3}{4}$ 6. $\dfrac{6}{7}$ ☐ $\dfrac{7}{8}$

7. $\dfrac{2}{4}$ ☐ $\dfrac{4}{8}$ 8. $\dfrac{2}{3}$ ☐ $\dfrac{2}{6}$ 9. $\dfrac{4}{5}$ ☐ $\dfrac{2}{3}$

10. $\dfrac{3}{5}$ ☐ $\dfrac{2}{4}$ 11. $\dfrac{4}{8}$ ☐ $\dfrac{1}{2}$ 12. $\dfrac{3}{6}$ ☐ $\dfrac{2}{5}$

13. $\dfrac{3}{5}$ ☐ $\dfrac{2}{7}$ 14. $\dfrac{2}{3}$ ☐ $\dfrac{4}{6}$ 15. $\dfrac{3}{7}$ ☐ $\dfrac{4}{5}$

16. $\dfrac{6}{8}$ ☐ $\dfrac{3}{4}$ 17. $\dfrac{2}{6}$ ☐ $\dfrac{3}{8}$ 18. $\dfrac{3}{5}$ ☐ $\dfrac{6}{7}$

Name _____ Date _____

Compare fractions by finding LCD (lowest common denominator).

Example:

Compare: $\dfrac{3}{5}\ \square\ \dfrac{4}{7}$

$\dfrac{3}{5} = \dfrac{21}{35}$, $\dfrac{4}{7} = \dfrac{20}{35}$, so $\dfrac{3}{5}\ \boxed{>}\ \dfrac{4}{7}$

1. $\dfrac{2}{5}\ \square\ \dfrac{1}{3}$

    $\dfrac{2}{5} = \dfrac{}{15}$, $\dfrac{1}{3} = \dfrac{}{15}$

2. $\dfrac{2}{7}\ \square\ \dfrac{1}{5}$

    $\dfrac{2}{7} = \dfrac{}{35}$, $\dfrac{1}{5} = \dfrac{}{35}$

3. $\dfrac{3}{8}\ \square\ \dfrac{1}{3}$

    $\dfrac{3}{8} = \dfrac{}{24}$, $\dfrac{1}{3} = \dfrac{}{24}$

4. $\dfrac{5}{9}\ \square\ \dfrac{3}{4}$

    $\dfrac{5}{9} = \dfrac{}{36}$, $\dfrac{3}{4} = \dfrac{}{36}$

5. $\dfrac{2}{7}\ \square\ \dfrac{3}{10}$

    $\dfrac{2}{7} = \dfrac{}{70}$, $\dfrac{3}{10} = \dfrac{}{70}$

6. $\dfrac{3}{7}\ \square\ \dfrac{5}{9}$

    $\dfrac{3}{7} = \dfrac{}{63}$, $\dfrac{5}{9} = \dfrac{}{63}$

7. $\dfrac{5}{11}\ \square\ \dfrac{4}{9}$

    $\dfrac{5}{11} = \dfrac{}{}$, $\dfrac{4}{9} = \dfrac{}{}$

8. $\dfrac{4}{5}\ \square\ \dfrac{7}{8}$

    $\dfrac{4}{5} = \dfrac{}{}$, $\dfrac{7}{8} = \dfrac{}{}$

9. $\dfrac{2}{7}\ \square\ \dfrac{4}{9}$

    $\dfrac{2}{7} = \dfrac{}{}$, $\dfrac{4}{9} = \dfrac{}{}$

10. $\dfrac{5}{9}\ \square\ \dfrac{7}{11}$

    $\dfrac{5}{9} = \dfrac{}{}$, $\dfrac{7}{11} = \dfrac{}{}$

11. $\dfrac{5}{6}\ \square\ \dfrac{7}{9}$

    $\dfrac{5}{6} = \dfrac{}{}$, $\dfrac{7}{9} = \dfrac{}{}$

12. $\dfrac{6}{11}\ \square\ \dfrac{5}{9}$

    $\dfrac{6}{11} = \dfrac{}{}$, $\dfrac{5}{9} = \dfrac{}{}$

Name _____   Date _____

Rewrite the following fractions from least to greatest.

1. $\frac{2}{5}, \frac{2}{3}, \frac{1}{2}$ 	$\frac{2}{5}, \frac{1}{2}, \frac{2}{3}$ 	2. $\frac{6}{7}, \frac{3}{4}, \frac{1}{2}$

_____	_____

$\frac{2}{5} = \frac{12}{30}, \quad \frac{2}{3} = \frac{20}{30}, \quad \frac{1}{2} = \frac{15}{30}$ 	$\frac{6}{7} = \frac{}{28}, \quad \frac{3}{4} = \frac{}{28}, \quad \frac{1}{2} = \frac{}{28}$

3. $\frac{5}{6}, \frac{7}{18}, \frac{2}{9}$ 	4. $\frac{5}{7}, \frac{9}{14}, \frac{23}{28}$

_____	_____

$\frac{5}{6} = \frac{}{18}, \quad \frac{7}{18} = \frac{}{18}, \quad \frac{2}{9} = \frac{}{18}$ 	$\frac{5}{7} = \frac{}{28}, \frac{9}{14} = \frac{}{28}, \frac{23}{28} = \frac{}{28}$

5. $\frac{2}{9}, \frac{1}{3}, \frac{1}{5}$ 	6. $\frac{5}{6}, \frac{1}{2}, \frac{2}{3}$

_____	_____

$\frac{2}{9} = \frac{}{}, \quad \frac{1}{3} = \frac{}{}, \quad \frac{1}{5} = \frac{}{}$ 	$\frac{5}{6} = \frac{}{}, \quad \frac{1}{2} = \frac{}{}, \quad \frac{2}{3} = \frac{}{}$

7. $1\frac{3}{5}, 1\frac{1}{4}, 1\frac{1}{3}$ 	8. $\frac{2}{5}, \frac{3}{10}, \frac{1}{4}$

_____	_____

$1\frac{3}{5} = \frac{}{}, 1\frac{1}{4} = \frac{}{}, 1\frac{1}{3} = \frac{}{}$ 	$\frac{2}{5} = \frac{}{}, \quad \frac{3}{10} = \frac{}{}, \quad \frac{1}{4} = \frac{}{}$

9. $\frac{4}{9}, \frac{3}{7}, \frac{2}{3}$ 	10. $\frac{3}{4}, \frac{7}{12}, \frac{2}{3}$

_____	_____

$\frac{4}{9} = \frac{}{}, \quad \frac{3}{7} = \frac{}{}, \quad \frac{2}{3} = \frac{}{}$ 	$\frac{3}{4} = \frac{}{}, \quad \frac{7}{12} = \frac{}{}, \quad \frac{2}{3} = \frac{}{}$

11. $\frac{3}{5}, \frac{1}{6}, \frac{1}{2}$ 	12. $\frac{2}{9}, \frac{1}{3}, \frac{3}{4}$

_____	_____

$\frac{3}{5} = \frac{}{}, \quad \frac{1}{6} = \frac{}{}, \quad \frac{1}{2} = \frac{}{}$ 	$\frac{2}{9} = \frac{}{}, \quad \frac{1}{3} = \frac{}{}, \quad \frac{3}{4} = \frac{}{}$

Name _____ Date _____

Rewrite the following fractions from greatest to least.

1. $\dfrac{2}{5}, \dfrac{7}{10}, \dfrac{1}{2}$

   _____

   $\dfrac{2}{5} = \dfrac{4}{10}$, $\dfrac{7}{10} = \dfrac{7}{10}$, $\dfrac{1}{2} = \dfrac{5}{10}$

2. $\dfrac{1}{3}, \dfrac{2}{3}, \dfrac{5}{9}$

   _____

   $\dfrac{1}{3} = —$, $\dfrac{2}{3} = —$, $\dfrac{5}{9} = —$

3. $\dfrac{1}{2}, \dfrac{2}{3}, \dfrac{1}{6}$

   _____

   $\dfrac{1}{2} = —$, $\dfrac{2}{3} = —$, $\dfrac{1}{6} = —$

4. $\dfrac{1}{3}, \dfrac{7}{15}, \dfrac{3}{5}$

   _____

   $\dfrac{1}{3} = —$, $\dfrac{7}{15} = —$, $\dfrac{3}{5} = —$

5. $\dfrac{3}{2}, \dfrac{11}{10}, \dfrac{6}{5}$

   _____

   $\dfrac{3}{2} = —$, $\dfrac{11}{10} = —$, $\dfrac{6}{5} = —$

6. $\dfrac{3}{4}, \dfrac{7}{20}, \dfrac{1}{5}$

   _____

   $\dfrac{3}{4} = —$, $\dfrac{7}{20} = —$, $\dfrac{1}{5} = —$

7. $\dfrac{11}{24}, \dfrac{3}{4}, \dfrac{7}{12}$

   _____

   $\dfrac{11}{24} = —$, $\dfrac{3}{4} = —$, $\dfrac{7}{12} = —$

8. $\dfrac{4}{9}, \dfrac{7}{18}, \dfrac{5}{6}$

   _____

   $\dfrac{4}{9} = —$, $\dfrac{7}{18} = —$, $\dfrac{5}{6} = —$

9. $\dfrac{7}{9}, \dfrac{2}{9}, \dfrac{13}{27}$

   _____

   $\dfrac{7}{9} = —$, $\dfrac{2}{9} = —$, $\dfrac{13}{27} = —$

10. $\dfrac{4}{7}, \dfrac{2}{3}, \dfrac{3}{5}$

    _____

    $\dfrac{4}{7} = —$, $\dfrac{2}{3} = —$, $\dfrac{3}{5} = —$

11. $\dfrac{2}{3}, \dfrac{5}{6}, \dfrac{7}{12}$

    _____

    $\dfrac{2}{3} = —$, $\dfrac{5}{6} = —$, $\dfrac{7}{12} = —$

12. $\dfrac{1}{5}, \dfrac{3}{10}, \dfrac{2}{7}$

    _____

    $\dfrac{1}{5} = —$, $\dfrac{3}{10} = —$, $\dfrac{2}{7} = —$

J10. Addition with like denominators

Rewrite each of the following fractions as a mixed number in simplest form.

Example: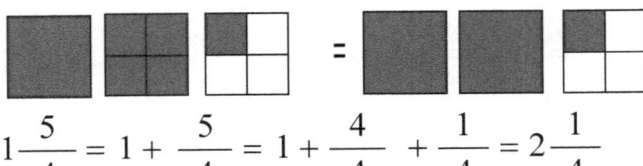

$$1\frac{5}{4} = 1 + \frac{5}{4} = 1 + \frac{4}{4} + \frac{1}{4} = 2\frac{1}{4}$$

1. $1\dfrac{3}{2} = 2\dfrac{1}{2}$
2. $3\dfrac{6}{4} = \quad 4\dfrac{1}{2}$

3. $6\dfrac{4}{4} =$
4. $5\dfrac{18}{12} =$

5. $2\dfrac{14}{7} =$
6. $8\dfrac{20}{15} =$

7. $2\dfrac{8}{5} =$
8. $9\dfrac{24}{16} =$

9. $3\dfrac{10}{8} =$
10. $5\dfrac{9}{9} =$

11. $7\dfrac{9}{6} =$
12. $5\dfrac{21}{12} =$

13. $7\dfrac{19}{13} =$
14. $15\dfrac{24}{14} =$

15. $13\dfrac{8}{4} =$
16. $10\dfrac{20}{16} =$

17. $6\dfrac{6}{4} =$
18. $7\dfrac{16}{12} =$

19. $8\dfrac{36}{20} =$
20. $5\dfrac{14}{8} =$

Name _____   Date _____

Add. Write each sum in its simplest form.

Example: 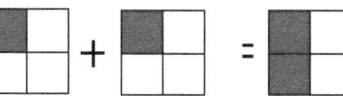 $\dfrac{1}{4} + \dfrac{1}{4} = \dfrac{1+1}{4} = \dfrac{2}{4} = \dfrac{1}{2}$

1. $\dfrac{1}{3} + \dfrac{1}{3} =$
2. $\dfrac{2}{5} + \dfrac{1}{5} =$

3. $\dfrac{1}{6} + \dfrac{5}{6} =$
4. $\dfrac{2}{7} + \dfrac{3}{7} =$

5. $\dfrac{2}{5} + \dfrac{2}{5} =$
6. $\dfrac{1}{8} + \dfrac{3}{8} =$

7. $\dfrac{3}{10} + \dfrac{1}{10} =$
8. $\dfrac{2}{11} + \dfrac{5}{11} =$

9. $\dfrac{5}{12} + \dfrac{1}{12} =$
10. $\dfrac{7}{12} + \dfrac{5}{12} =$

11. $\dfrac{4}{15} + \dfrac{7}{15} =$
12. $\dfrac{2}{15} + \dfrac{8}{15} =$

13. $\dfrac{3}{10} + \dfrac{7}{10} =$
14. $\dfrac{3}{12} + \dfrac{7}{12} =$

15. $\dfrac{4}{17} + \dfrac{6}{17} =$
16. $\dfrac{5}{18} + \dfrac{7}{18} =$

17. $\dfrac{1}{7} + \dfrac{2}{7} + \dfrac{3}{7} =$
18. $\dfrac{1}{9} + \dfrac{4}{9} + \dfrac{2}{9} =$

19. $\dfrac{4}{11} + \dfrac{2}{11} + \dfrac{3}{11} =$
20. $\dfrac{3}{16} + \dfrac{5}{16} + \dfrac{7}{16} =$

21. $\dfrac{2}{15} + \dfrac{7}{15} + \dfrac{4}{15} =$
22. $\dfrac{5}{13} + \dfrac{2}{13} + \dfrac{6}{13} =$

Add. Write each sum in simplest form.

Example:

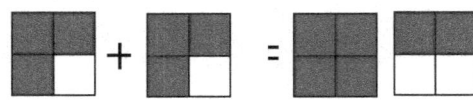

$$\frac{3}{4}+\frac{3}{4}=\frac{3+3}{4}=\frac{6}{4}=\frac{3}{2}=1\frac{1}{2}$$

1. $\dfrac{2}{3}+\dfrac{2}{3}=$ 2. $\dfrac{2}{5}+\dfrac{4}{5}=$

3. $\dfrac{4}{7}+\dfrac{5}{7}=$ 4. $\dfrac{4}{9}+\dfrac{8}{9}=$

5. $\dfrac{3}{5}+\dfrac{4}{5}=$ 6. $\dfrac{5}{8}+\dfrac{7}{8}=$

7. $\dfrac{3}{10}+\dfrac{9}{10}=$ 8. $\dfrac{5}{9}+\dfrac{6}{9}=$

9. $\dfrac{5}{8}+\dfrac{5}{8}=$ 10. $\dfrac{7}{15}+\dfrac{11}{15}=$

11. $\dfrac{13}{24}+\dfrac{17}{24}=$ 12. $\dfrac{16}{21}+\dfrac{8}{21}=$

13. $\dfrac{7}{18}+\dfrac{13}{18}=$ 14. $\dfrac{21}{25}+\dfrac{14}{25}=$

15. $\dfrac{15}{26}+\dfrac{17}{26}=$ 16. $\dfrac{4}{15}+\dfrac{14}{15}=$

17. $\dfrac{1}{8}+\dfrac{7}{8}+\dfrac{5}{8}=$ 18. $\dfrac{5}{7}+\dfrac{4}{7}+\dfrac{5}{7}=$

19. $\dfrac{5}{12}+\dfrac{7}{12}+\dfrac{11}{12}=$ 20. $\dfrac{11}{15}+\dfrac{7}{15}+\dfrac{2}{15}=$

21. $\dfrac{9}{20}+\dfrac{7}{20}+\dfrac{17}{20}=$ 22. $\dfrac{6}{13}+\dfrac{9}{13}+\dfrac{11}{13}=$

Name _____ Date _____

Add. Write each sum in simplest form.

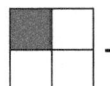 +  =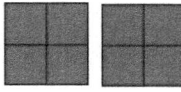

$1\frac{1}{4} + 2\frac{1}{4} = (1+2) + (\frac{1}{4} + \frac{1}{4}) = 3 + \frac{2}{4} = 3 + \frac{1}{2} = 3\frac{1}{2}$

1. $1\frac{1}{3} + 2\frac{1}{3} =$
2. $2\frac{1}{5} + 3\frac{2}{5} =$
3. $2\frac{1}{7} + \frac{4}{7} =$
4. $3\frac{1}{8} + 2\frac{3}{8} =$
5. $\frac{2}{9} + 6\frac{4}{9} =$
6. $2\frac{3}{10} + 7\frac{1}{10} =$
7. $5\frac{4}{11} + \frac{6}{11} =$
8. $3\frac{5}{12} + 5\frac{1}{12} =$
9. $3\frac{3}{8} + 6\frac{1}{8} =$
10. $2\frac{4}{15} + 5\frac{7}{15} =$
11. $5\frac{7}{20} + 4\frac{9}{20} =$
12. $5\frac{7}{24} + 10\frac{11}{24} =$
13. $5\frac{5}{16} + 7\frac{7}{16} =$
14. $4\frac{9}{25} + 9\frac{11}{25} =$
15. $6\frac{5}{18} + 7\frac{7}{18} =$
16. $8\frac{5}{16} + 9\frac{9}{16} =$
17. $10\frac{5}{21} + 5\frac{4}{21} =$
18. $4\frac{7}{18} + \frac{5}{18} =$
19. $8\frac{7}{27} + 5\frac{17}{27} =$
20. $9\frac{17}{24} + 5\frac{1}{24} =$

Name _____ Date _____

Add. Write each answer in simplest form.

  +  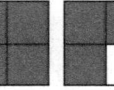 =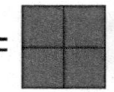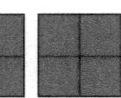

$1\dfrac{3}{4} + 2\dfrac{3}{4} = (1+2)+(\dfrac{3}{4}+\dfrac{3}{4})=3+\dfrac{6}{4}=3+\dfrac{3}{2}=3+1\dfrac{1}{2}=4\dfrac{1}{2}$

1. $1\dfrac{3}{4} + 3\dfrac{3}{4} =$

2. $2\dfrac{5}{9} + 1\dfrac{7}{9} =$

3. $6\dfrac{5}{8} + \dfrac{7}{8} =$

4. $\dfrac{7}{9} + 2\dfrac{8}{9} =$

5. $4\dfrac{7}{12} + 2\dfrac{11}{12} =$

6. $10\dfrac{7}{12} + 2\dfrac{11}{12} =$

7. $3\dfrac{5}{14} + 6\dfrac{11}{14} =$

8. $2\dfrac{7}{10} + 4\dfrac{9}{10} =$

9. $5\dfrac{13}{15} + 3\dfrac{7}{15} =$

10. $5\dfrac{13}{21} + \dfrac{11}{21} =$

11. $3\dfrac{14}{25} + 7\dfrac{16}{25} =$

12. $11\dfrac{13}{20} + 3\dfrac{11}{20} =$

13. $9\dfrac{11}{15} + 3\dfrac{14}{15} =$

14. $8\dfrac{13}{20} + 2\dfrac{17}{20} =$

15. $8\dfrac{7}{15} + \dfrac{11}{15} =$

16. $4\dfrac{7}{18} + 10\dfrac{13}{18} =$

17. $7\dfrac{3}{5} + 1\dfrac{4}{5} =$

18. $9\dfrac{9}{20} + \dfrac{13}{20} =$

19. $10\dfrac{10}{21} + 3\dfrac{19}{21} =$

20. $6\dfrac{17}{27} + 9\dfrac{18}{27} =$

J11. Subtraction with like denominators

Find the missing numbers.

Example:

$$2\frac{1}{4} = (1+1) + \frac{1}{4} = (1 + \frac{4}{4}) + \frac{1}{4} = 1\frac{5}{4}$$

1. $3\frac{1}{3} = 2\frac{}{3}$

2. $7\frac{3}{4} = 6\frac{}{4}$

3. $5\frac{3}{7} = 4\frac{}{7}$

4. $1 = \frac{}{8}$

5. $4\frac{3}{6} = 3\frac{}{6}$

6. $5\frac{2}{8} = 4\frac{}{8}$

7. $7\frac{7}{10} = 6\frac{}{10}$

8. $4\frac{3}{9} = 3\frac{}{9}$

9. $5 = 4\frac{}{7}$

10. $7\frac{3}{6} = 6\frac{}{6}$

11. $10\frac{3}{12} = 9\frac{}{12}$

12. $4\frac{4}{15} = 3\frac{}{15}$

13. $1\frac{4}{10} = \frac{}{10}$

14. $8\frac{3}{16} = 7\frac{}{16}$

15. $9\frac{5}{11} = 8\frac{}{11}$

16. $1\frac{7}{12} = \frac{}{12}$

17. $10\frac{4}{7} = 9\frac{}{7}$

18. $8\frac{1}{6} = 7\frac{}{6}$

19. $6\frac{5}{12} = 5\frac{}{12}$

20. $2 = 1\frac{}{5}$

Name _____ Date _____

Subtract. Write each difference in simplest form.

Example: 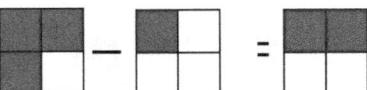 $\dfrac{3}{4} - \dfrac{1}{4} = \dfrac{3-1}{4} = \dfrac{2}{4} = \dfrac{1}{2}$

1. $\dfrac{2}{3} - \dfrac{1}{3} =$ 2. $\dfrac{5}{6} - \dfrac{2}{6} =$

3. $\dfrac{5}{8} - \dfrac{3}{8} =$ 4. $\dfrac{5}{7} - \dfrac{2}{7} =$

5. $\dfrac{7}{10} - \dfrac{3}{10} =$ 6. $\dfrac{8}{9} - \dfrac{2}{9} =$

7. $\dfrac{7}{12} - \dfrac{1}{12} =$ 8. $\dfrac{9}{10} - \dfrac{7}{10} =$

9. $\dfrac{7}{8} - \dfrac{3}{8} =$ 10. $\dfrac{8}{9} - \dfrac{5}{9} =$

11. $\dfrac{7}{12} - \dfrac{5}{12} =$ 12. $\dfrac{13}{18} - \dfrac{5}{18} =$

13. $\dfrac{11}{16} - \dfrac{5}{16} =$ 14. $\dfrac{11}{15} - \dfrac{8}{15} =$

15. $\dfrac{17}{24} - \dfrac{5}{24} =$ 16. $\dfrac{16}{21} - \dfrac{8}{21} =$

17. $\dfrac{16}{27} - \dfrac{5}{27} - \dfrac{4}{27} =$ 18. $\dfrac{13}{18} - \dfrac{5}{18} - \dfrac{2}{18} =$

19. $\dfrac{15}{18} - \dfrac{7}{18} - \dfrac{5}{18} =$ 20. $\dfrac{16}{21} - \dfrac{7}{21} - \dfrac{6}{21} =$

21. $\dfrac{17}{24} - \dfrac{6}{24} - \dfrac{7}{24} =$ 22. $\dfrac{12}{15} - \dfrac{5}{15} - \dfrac{4}{15} =$

Name _____ Date _____

Subtract. Write each difference in simplest form.

Example: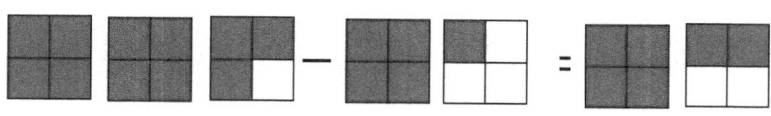

$$2\frac{3}{4} - 1\frac{1}{4} = (2-1) + (\frac{3}{4} - \frac{1}{4}) = 1 + \frac{2}{4} = 1 + \frac{1}{2} = 1\frac{1}{2}$$

1. $3\frac{3}{4} - 1\frac{1}{4} =$
2. $4\frac{5}{6} - 4\frac{1}{6} =$

3. $6\frac{7}{8} - 2\frac{2}{8} =$
4. $7\frac{4}{5} - 2\frac{4}{5} =$

5. $6\frac{7}{9} - 2\frac{5}{9} =$
6. $3\frac{2}{6} - 2 =$

7. $7\frac{7}{10} - 4\frac{2}{10} =$
8. $7\frac{7}{10} - 4\frac{2}{10} =$

9. $6\frac{5}{8} - \frac{3}{8} =$
10. $9\frac{2}{5} - 5\frac{1}{5} =$

11. $7\frac{7}{10} - 7\frac{1}{10} =$
12. $3\frac{4}{5} - 1\frac{1}{5} =$

13. $6\frac{4}{7} - 6 =$
14. $8\frac{2}{3} - \frac{1}{3} =$

15. $9\frac{2}{8} - 7 =$
16. $9\frac{5}{9} - 2\frac{2}{9} =$

17. $8\frac{5}{6} - 4\frac{5}{6} =$
18. $11\frac{10}{12} - 5\frac{7}{12} =$

19. $8\frac{7}{15} - 5\frac{2}{15} =$
20. $8\frac{19}{25} - 3\frac{4}{25} =$

Name _____ Date _____

Subtract. Write each difference in simplest form.

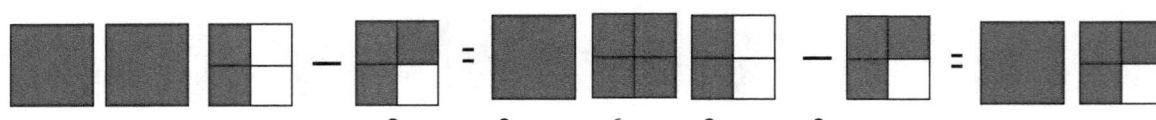

$2\dfrac{2}{4} - \dfrac{3}{4} = 1\dfrac{6}{4} - \dfrac{3}{4} = 1\dfrac{3}{4}$

1. $3\dfrac{1}{3} - 1\dfrac{2}{3} =$

2. $7\dfrac{1}{5} - 2\dfrac{3}{5} =$

3. $5\dfrac{1}{4} - 1\dfrac{3}{4} =$

4. $6 - 2\dfrac{5}{6} =$

5. $7\dfrac{1}{6} - 1\dfrac{5}{6} =$

6. $8\dfrac{1}{7} - \dfrac{3}{7} =$

7. $4\dfrac{2}{8} - 1\dfrac{7}{8} =$

8. $6\dfrac{2}{9} - 4\dfrac{8}{9} =$

9. $5\dfrac{3}{10} - 2\dfrac{7}{10} =$

10. $10\dfrac{2}{10} - \dfrac{9}{10} =$

11. $5 - 2\dfrac{1}{6} =$

12. $7\dfrac{5}{12} - 6\dfrac{11}{12} =$

13. $5\dfrac{4}{15} - \dfrac{11}{15} =$

14. $12\dfrac{5}{9} - 1\dfrac{7}{9} =$

15. $9\dfrac{8}{21} - 7\dfrac{17}{21} =$

16. $8\dfrac{7}{24} - 3\dfrac{17}{24} =$

17. $7 - \dfrac{8}{9} =$

18. $7\dfrac{5}{24} - \dfrac{19}{24} =$

19. $9\dfrac{7}{15} - 2\dfrac{11}{15} =$

20. $5 - 2\dfrac{7}{13} =$

J12. Multiplication of fractions

Example: $\dfrac{1}{3} \times \dfrac{5}{8} = \dfrac{1 \times 5}{3 \times 8} = \dfrac{5}{24}$

1. $\dfrac{3}{5} \times \dfrac{3}{8} =$

2. $\dfrac{2}{7} \times \dfrac{1}{6} =$

3. $\dfrac{1}{4} \times \dfrac{3}{5} =$

4. $\dfrac{3}{8} \times \dfrac{5}{7} =$

5. $\dfrac{3}{7} \times \dfrac{2}{5} =$

6. $\dfrac{5}{9} \times \dfrac{2}{3} =$

7. $\dfrac{1}{2} \times \dfrac{3}{4} =$

8. $\dfrac{5}{6} \times \dfrac{1}{4} =$

9. $\dfrac{7}{9} \times \dfrac{1}{2} =$

10. $\dfrac{4}{7} \times \dfrac{5}{9} =$

11. $\dfrac{3}{5} \times \dfrac{7}{8} =$

12. $\dfrac{3}{10} \times \dfrac{3}{4} =$

13. $\dfrac{2}{5} \times \dfrac{8}{9} =$

14. $\dfrac{1}{6} \times \dfrac{5}{7} =$

15. $\dfrac{4}{9} \times \dfrac{2}{5} =$

16. $\dfrac{3}{8} \times \dfrac{3}{5} =$

17. $\dfrac{6}{7} \times \dfrac{5}{8} =$

18. $\dfrac{5}{12} \times \dfrac{3}{5} =$

Name _____ Date _____

Multiply fractions by cancellation.

Example: $\dfrac{2}{5} \times \dfrac{5}{8} = \dfrac{\cancel{2}^1}{\cancel{5}_1} \times \dfrac{\cancel{5}^1}{\cancel{8}_4} = \dfrac{1 \times 1}{1 \times 4} = \dfrac{1}{4}$

1. $\dfrac{2}{3} \times \dfrac{3}{8} =$

2. $\dfrac{3}{5} \times \dfrac{5}{6} =$

3. $\dfrac{3}{7} \times \dfrac{5}{6} =$

4. $\dfrac{7}{8} \times \dfrac{4}{9} =$

5. $\dfrac{3}{7} \times \dfrac{7}{6} =$

6. $\dfrac{5}{9} \times \dfrac{3}{10} =$

7. $\dfrac{5}{6} \times \dfrac{3}{15} =$

8. $\dfrac{7}{12} \times \dfrac{3}{8} =$

9. $\dfrac{9}{16} \times \dfrac{8}{15} =$

10. $\dfrac{7}{12} \times \dfrac{4}{7} =$

11. $\dfrac{5}{9} \times \dfrac{3}{10} =$

12. $\dfrac{3}{15} \times \dfrac{5}{12} =$

Name _____   Date _____

13. $\dfrac{6}{20} \times \dfrac{5}{9} =$
14. $\dfrac{9}{14} \times \dfrac{7}{12} =$

15. $\dfrac{9}{12} \times \dfrac{4}{6} =$
16. $\dfrac{15}{20} \times \dfrac{5}{9} =$

17. $\dfrac{3}{20} \times \dfrac{10}{12} =$
18. $\dfrac{2}{9} \times \dfrac{18}{24} =$

19. $\dfrac{12}{30} \times \dfrac{24}{36} =$
20. $\dfrac{4}{9} \times \dfrac{27}{18} =$

21. $\dfrac{10}{25} \times \dfrac{18}{20} =$
22. $\dfrac{10}{30} \times \dfrac{3}{4} =$

23. $\dfrac{5}{9} \times \dfrac{10}{50} =$
24. $\dfrac{20}{4} \times \dfrac{3}{30} =$

25. $\dfrac{20}{12} \times \dfrac{9}{60} =$
26. $\dfrac{14}{40} \times \dfrac{30}{56} =$

27. $\dfrac{8}{9} \times \dfrac{15}{16} =$

28. $\dfrac{6}{24} \times \dfrac{5}{25} =$

29. $\dfrac{4}{12} \times \dfrac{3}{15} =$

30. $\dfrac{6}{18} \times \dfrac{4}{8} =$

31. $\dfrac{12}{49} \times \dfrac{14}{24} =$

32. $\dfrac{8}{15} \times \dfrac{10}{16} =$

33. $\dfrac{13}{36} \times \dfrac{12}{26} =$

34. $\dfrac{3}{28} \times \dfrac{14}{15} =$

35. $\dfrac{35}{16} \times \dfrac{4}{42} =$

36. $\dfrac{12}{35} \times \dfrac{14}{18} =$

37. $\dfrac{14}{36} \times \dfrac{12}{21} =$

38. $\dfrac{9}{30} \times \dfrac{20}{27} =$

39. $\dfrac{9}{32} \times \dfrac{8}{27} =$

40. $\dfrac{30}{40} \times \dfrac{2}{5} =$

Name _____ Date _____

Multiply fractions and whole numbers.

Example:

$$3\frac{1}{6} \times 9 = \frac{19}{\cancel{6}_2} \times \frac{\cancel{9}^3}{1} = \frac{19 \times 3}{2 \times 1} = \frac{57}{2} = 28\frac{1}{2}$$

1. $\dfrac{1}{2} \times 4$

2. $6 \times \dfrac{1}{3}$

3. $\dfrac{3}{4} \times 8$

4. $9 \times \dfrac{2}{3}$

5. $\dfrac{2}{9} \times 4$

6. $8 \times \dfrac{3}{5}$

7. $\dfrac{2}{7} \times 21$

8. $12 \times \dfrac{5}{9}$

9. $\dfrac{13}{25} \times 5$

10. $12 \times \dfrac{7}{15}$

Name _____ Date _____

11. $\dfrac{7}{12} \times 18$

12. $20 \times \dfrac{18}{30}$

13. $\dfrac{8}{11} \times 33$

14. $16 \times \dfrac{9}{18}$

15. $\dfrac{16}{30} \times 20$

16. $10 \times \dfrac{15}{20}$

17. $\dfrac{15}{33} \times 22$

18. $77 \times \dfrac{27}{55}$

19. $\dfrac{18}{55} \times 44$

20. $66 \times \dfrac{18}{22}$

21. $\dfrac{63}{80} \times 50$

22. $90 \times \dfrac{36}{80}$

Name _____   Date _____

Find the missing numbers.

1. $\dfrac{1}{2} \times \dfrac{2}{1} = 1$

2. $\dfrac{1}{3} \times \underline{} = 1$

3. $\dfrac{8}{3} \times \underline{} = 1$

4. $\dfrac{5}{2} \times \underline{} = 1$

5. $\underline{} \times \dfrac{6}{5} = 1$

6. $\underline{} \times \dfrac{4}{3} = 1$

7. $1\dfrac{1}{2} \times \underline{} = 1$

8. $\underline{} \times 3\dfrac{2}{7} = 1$

9. $5 \times \underline{} = 1$

10. $\underline{} \times \dfrac{1}{9} = 1$

11. $1 \times \underline{} = 1$

12. $\underline{} \times 8 = 1$

Write the reciprocals of the following fractions.

1. $\dfrac{3}{7}$, ____

2. $\dfrac{1}{9}$, ____

3. $\dfrac{5}{2}$, ____

4. 3 , ____

5. $2\dfrac{1}{4}$, ____

6. $\dfrac{1}{6}$, ____

7. 8 , ____

8. $5\dfrac{1}{2}$, ____

9. $2\dfrac{7}{10}$, ____

10. $3\dfrac{7}{9}$, ____

11. $1\dfrac{5}{8}$, ____

12. $10\dfrac{2}{3}$, ____

J13. Division of fractions

Example:

$$\frac{5}{8} \div \frac{1}{6} = \frac{5}{8} \times \frac{6}{1} = \frac{5}{\cancel{8}_4} \times \frac{\cancel{6}^3}{1} = \frac{5 \times 3}{4 \times 1} = \frac{15}{4} = 3\frac{3}{4}$$

1. $\dfrac{1}{4} \div \dfrac{2}{5} =$ 2. $\dfrac{3}{7} \div \dfrac{6}{11} =$

3. $\dfrac{8}{9} \div \dfrac{2}{3} =$ 4. $\dfrac{1}{6} \div \dfrac{7}{12} =$

5. $\dfrac{2}{3} \div \dfrac{5}{6} =$ 6. $\dfrac{7}{12} \div \dfrac{2}{9} =$

7. $\dfrac{8}{15} \div \dfrac{10}{9} =$ 8. $\dfrac{5}{14} \div \dfrac{10}{21} =$

9. $\dfrac{9}{16} \div \dfrac{5}{12} =$ 10. $\dfrac{9}{10} \div \dfrac{6}{25} =$

11. $\dfrac{12}{35} \div \dfrac{9}{14} =$ 12. $\dfrac{7}{11} \div \dfrac{21}{22} =$

Name _____ Date _____

13. $\dfrac{5}{18} \div \dfrac{8}{15} =$

14. $\dfrac{7}{9} \div \dfrac{7}{12} =$

15. $\dfrac{6}{14} \div \dfrac{3}{7} =$

16. $\dfrac{2}{15} \div \dfrac{7}{12} =$

17. $\dfrac{15}{28} \div \dfrac{3}{14} =$

18. $\dfrac{15}{22} \div \dfrac{5}{11} =$

19. $\dfrac{7}{10} \div \dfrac{12}{20} =$

20. $\dfrac{8}{15} \div \dfrac{12}{25} =$

21. $\dfrac{15}{24} \div \dfrac{5}{18} =$

22. $\dfrac{4}{7} \div \dfrac{2}{9} =$

23. $\dfrac{3}{7} \div \dfrac{3}{14} =$

24. $\dfrac{5}{12} \div \dfrac{5}{6} =$

25. $\dfrac{16}{27} \div \dfrac{5}{12} =$

26. $\dfrac{8}{15} \div \dfrac{7}{30} =$

Name _____   Date _____

Divide with whole numbers.

Example:

$\dfrac{2}{7} \div 2 = \dfrac{\cancel{2}^{1}}{7} \times \dfrac{1}{\cancel{2}_{1}} = \dfrac{1}{7}$ $3 \div \dfrac{1}{4} = 3 \times \dfrac{4}{1} = \dfrac{3 \times 4}{1} = 12$

1. $\dfrac{1}{2} \div 2 =$

2. $2 \div \dfrac{1}{2} =$

3. $1 \div 5 =$

4. $\dfrac{1}{5} \div 4 =$

5. $4 \div \dfrac{4}{7} =$

6. $\dfrac{5}{8} \div 12 =$

7. $\dfrac{2}{9} \div 4 =$

8. $1 \div \dfrac{5}{6} =$

9. $\dfrac{7}{8} \div 1 =$

10. $\dfrac{7}{12} \div 14 =$

11. $3\dfrac{1}{5} \div 8 =$

12. $4\dfrac{2}{3} \div 7 =$

Name _____   Date _____

13. $1\dfrac{5}{7} \div 4 =$

14. $3\dfrac{1}{8} \div 15 =$

15. $3\dfrac{3}{5} \div 6 =$

16. $3\dfrac{4}{7} \div 5 =$

17. $6 \div 1\dfrac{1}{4} =$

18. $7 \div 2\dfrac{1}{3} =$

19. $6 \div 1\dfrac{1}{5} =$

20. $3 \div 2\dfrac{1}{7} =$

21. $5 \div 4\dfrac{1}{6} =$

22. $10 \div 2\dfrac{2}{9} =$

23. $2\dfrac{1}{7} \div 5 =$

24. $2\dfrac{3}{11} \div 5 =$

25. $8\dfrac{3}{4} \div 21 =$

26. $7\dfrac{1}{5} \div 6 =$

J14. Problem solving

Write a fraction in lowest form for each question.

1. There are 10 dimes in one dollar. 3 dimes are what fraction of a dollar?

2. There are 12 inches in one foot. 8 inches are what fraction of a foot?

3. There are 60 minutes in one hour. 37 minutes are what fraction of an hour?

4. Janet spent $8 on food, $20 on cloths with $15 left. What fraction of her money was spent on cloths?

5. Rachel has 12 blue marbles, 15 red marbles, and 20 green marbles. What fraction of her marbles is red?

6. Rachel had some free time before go to bed. She spent 1 hour riding bicycles, 30 minutes reading books, and 40 minutes watching TV. What fraction of her free time did she spend on watching TV?

7. Andrew went to a chess tournament. He participates 35 matches and lost 5. What fraction of the matches did he win?

Name _____ Date _____

8. Lisa took a math contest with 60 questions. She made 5 of the questions wrong. What fraction of the questions did she get right?

9. Benny had $1\frac{1}{2}$ pounds of apples. Julia gave $2\frac{1}{3}$ pounds of apples to Benny. How many pounds of apples does Benny have now?

10. A wood is $4\frac{1}{8}$ feet long. A bamboo stick is $\frac{5}{7}$ feet longer than the wood. How long is the bamboo stick?

11. Steven is $40\frac{5}{12}$ pounds. Nick is $5\frac{3}{8}$ pounds heavier than Steven. What is Nick's weight?

12. Linda has $6\frac{4}{5}$ feet of ribbon. Cindy has $12\frac{3}{7}$ feet of ribbon. If connect their ribbons together, how long will be the ribbon?

13. Jeff and Jason took turns to drive a car. Jeff drove $22\frac{26}{35}$ miles, Jason drove $17\frac{9}{20}$ miles. How long did they drove altogether?

Name _____ Date _____

Subtraction of fraction

1. A watermelon weighs $9\frac{7}{12}$ pounds. A honey dew weighs $1\frac{3}{8}$ pounds. How many pounds heavier is the watermelon than the honey dew?

2. A pizza weighs $2\frac{1}{8}$ pounds. Joe ate $\frac{6}{7}$ pounds. How much pizza was left?

3. Vivien spent $\frac{2}{5}$ of her money on food, $\frac{1}{4}$ of her money on clothing. What fraction of her money was left?

4. George weighed $146\frac{1}{4}$ pounds. He went on diet and lost $5\frac{7}{9}$ pounds. How many pounds does he weigh now?

5. Jason is $1\frac{3}{5}$ meters tall. Jonathan is $\frac{5}{12}$ meters shorter than Jason. How tall is Jonathan?

Addition and Subtraction of fractions

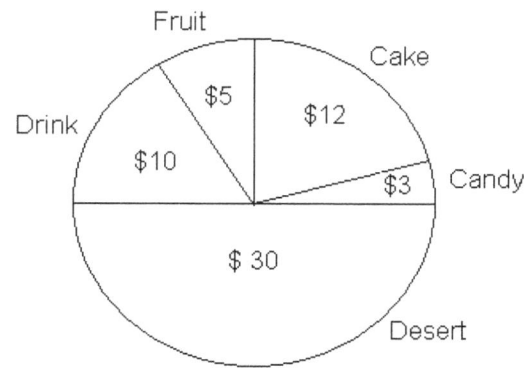

Jecica's expense for a bithday party

4. How much did the birthday party cost her?

5. What fraction of the total is each kind?

Drink _____ Fruit _____ Cake _____
Candy _____ Desert _____

6. What fraction did she spend on desert and cake?

7. What fraction did she spend on drink and candy?

8. How much more did she spend on desert than on fruit in fraction?

Name _____ Date _____

Multiplication of fractions

Example

Benjamin gave $\frac{1}{4}$ of $32 to Michael. How much does Michael have? How much does Benjamin have left?

    Michael has __$ 8__
    I have __$ 24__ left.

$8			

1. Dylan gave $\frac{1}{5}$ of 200 chocolate bars to Edward.
   Edward had _____ chocolate bars.
   Dylan had _____ chocolate bars left.

2. Simon had 20 books and he gave $\frac{1}{4}$ of them to Carmon.
   Carmon had _____ books.
   Simon has _____ books left

3. Hanna spent $\frac{1}{3}$ of her allowance, which is $ 6 on snack. How much does she have now?
   Now She only has $ _____ left.

4. After Simon gave $\frac{1}{3}$ of candies to Christina, he had 18 candies left. How many candies did he have at the beginning?
   He had _____ candies.

5. Tom gave $\frac{1}{5}$ of his marbles to Iris and still had 20 left. How many marbles did he have at the beginning?
   Tom got _____ marbles.

6 Hanna gave $\frac{1}{4}$ of her stickers to Jack. Jack got 5 stickers. How many stickers did Hanna have left?
   Hanna had _____ stickers left.

5			

7 Mina gave $\frac{1}{6}$ of her allowance to Tony. Tony got $ 8. How much did Mina have left?
   Mina had $ _____ left.

8					

Name _____   Date _____

8 Jeff cut $\frac{1}{12}$ of wood off. The small piece is 2 feet long. How long is the wood now?

The wood is _____ feet long now. | 2 | | | | | | | | | | | |

9 Shirley gave $\frac{1}{6}$ of her allowance to Sherry. Sherry got $7. How much did Shirley have left?

Shirley had $ _____ left. | 7 | | | | | |

10 Taylor gave $\frac{1}{3}$ his marbles to John. John got 6 marbles. How many marbles did Taylor have left?

Taylor had _____ marbles left. | 6 | | |

11 Tom had 35 cards. He gave $\frac{1}{7}$ to Sam and he lost $\frac{1}{5}$. How many cards did he have left?

Tom lost _____ cards.

He had _____ left.

12 Smith has 64 gums. He gives $\frac{1}{4}$ to Dylan and $\frac{1}{2}$ to Mabel. How many gums does Smith have now?

Smith gives _____ gums to Dylan.

Smith gives _____ gums to Mabel.

Now Smith has _____ gums.

13 Jay has 60 video games. He gives $\frac{1}{12}$ to John and $\frac{1}{5}$ to Jason. He sells $\frac{1}{2}$ of the games to his friends. How many games does he have now?

He sells _____ games to her friends.

He now has _____ games.

Name _____ Date _____

Multiplication of fractions

1. There were 30 students in a class. On Friday, $\frac{1}{5}$ of students were absent. How many students attended class on Friday?

2. Lisa makes $12 an hour. If she works $6\frac{1}{4}$ hours a day, how much does she make on a day?

3. 84 students signed up for summer school. $\frac{1}{7}$ of them failed to make it. How many students joined the summer school?

4. Out of 12 subjects, John got $\frac{5}{6}$ of them A's. How many subjects did he get A's?

5. Mrs. Cook bought $3\frac{1}{5}$ pounds of beef steak at $6.50 per pound. How much did she pay for the beef steak?

6. Apples are sold at $1.80 per pound. How much will it cost for $3\frac{2}{5}$ pounds?

7. Steve bought 36 apples. He ate $\frac{2}{9}$ of them and gave $\frac{1}{4}$ of them to Ann. How many apples did he have at last?

8. Sam had $3\frac{2}{9}$ free hours before going to bed. He spent $\frac{1}{4}$ of the time playing chess, $\frac{1}{3}$ of the time doing his project. How long were left for watching TV?

Division of fractions

1. $\dfrac{3}{7}$ of a number is $4\dfrac{1}{3}$. What is this number?

2. A ribbon measures $6\dfrac{2}{5}$ m long. How many pieces can $1\dfrac{3}{5}$ m long ribbon be cut from it?

3. How many $\dfrac{3}{8}$ are there in $9\dfrac{3}{4}$?

4. Fix a piece of wire of $7\dfrac{3}{5}$ m long into a square. What is the side length of the square?

5. Peter bought $5\dfrac{7}{12}$ pounds of apples for $21. How much is one pound of apples cost?

6. Jocelyn has a ribbon with $6\dfrac{3}{8}$ m long to share with her five friends. If they share it equally, how long of the ribbon can each girl get?

7. A snail is climbing up a tree of $8\dfrac{2}{5}$ feet tall. If the snail climbs $2\dfrac{1}{3}$ feet a day, how long will it take the snail to climb up the top of the tree?

Name _____   Date _____

Addition, Subtraction, Multiplication, and Division

1. I spent $\frac{1}{3}$ of my allowance to buy a video game and saved the rest. What fraction of my allowance was saved?

16. Sam read $\frac{1}{5}$ of his book on Monday and $\frac{1}{3}$ of his book on Tuesday. What fraction of his book was not read?

17. A bottle of milk was $\frac{4}{5}$ full. I drank half of it. What fraction of the milk was left in the bottle?

18. After painting a room for 3 hours, Jim only completed $\frac{3}{8}$ of it. What fraction of the room was not painted?

19. Find the perimeter of the triangle with sides measuring $2\frac{2}{7}$ cm, $4\frac{1}{3}$ cm and $3\frac{1}{2}$ cm.

20. Stanley gave $\frac{1}{4}$ of his cards to Tom and $\frac{2}{5}$ of his cards to John. What fraction of his cards was left?

Name _____ Date _____

1. Windy jogged $3\frac{5}{6}$ miles on Friday, $4\frac{3}{4}$ miles on Saturday, and $2\frac{2}{3}$ miles on Sunday. How long did she jogged all together in three days?

2. There are 28 students in a class. $\frac{6}{7}$ of the students have been to Science World. How many students have been to Science World?

3. Janet earns $2700 a month. At the end of the year, she is given $\frac{4}{9}$ month's bonus. How much bonus does she get?

4. May has 45 apples. If she eats $\frac{2}{15}$ of them every day for 6 days, how many apples will be left after 6 days?

5. Sam has 80 pages of paper. If he uses $\frac{3}{16}$ of the paper for a project every day for 5 days, how many pages of paper will be left after the project?

6. Iris has 30 coins in her wallet. If $\frac{1}{6}$ of them are pennies, $\frac{2}{5}$ of them are dimes, and the rest are quarters, what fraction of the coins are quarters?

1. Rachel's dog weighs 35 pounds and her cat weighs $\frac{7}{10}$ as much as the dog. How much does her cat weigh?

2. Daniel lives $8\frac{1}{5}$ miles away from school. Susan lives $1\frac{5}{8}$ times as far from school as Daniel does. How far does Susan live from school?

3. A frog jumps $1\frac{5}{9}$ feet up a well every day. If the well is $12\frac{2}{3}$ feet deep, how many days later will the frog get out of the well?

4. How many pieces of ribbon can $\frac{4}{5}$ feet long can be cut from $7\frac{1}{5}$ feet?

5. Steve drove 60 miles in $1\frac{1}{2}$ hours. How many miles did he drive in one hour?

6. Hanna earns $4500 a month. She spends $\frac{1}{3}$ of her income on food and clothes $\frac{1}{10}$, of it on leisure and saves the rest. How much is saved?

K. Percentages

Percent means 'out of 100'.

1.
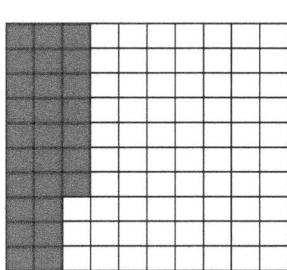
There are 27 black squares and there are 100 squares in all. 27 % of the squares are grey.

2.
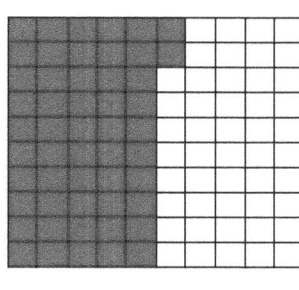
_____ of the squares are grey.

3.
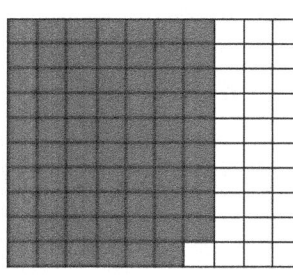
_____ of the squares are grey.

4.
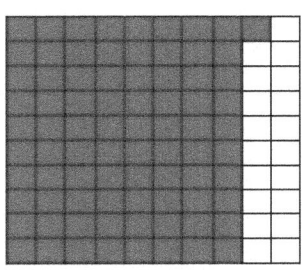
_____ of the squares are grey.

5.
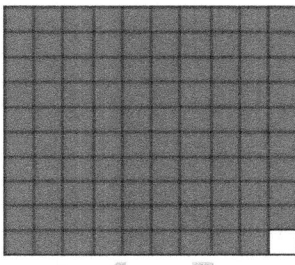
_____ of the squares are grey.

6.
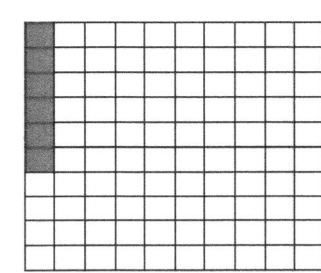
_____ of the squares are grey.

Shade the area

1.

25 % of the squares are black

2.

37 % of the squares are black

3.
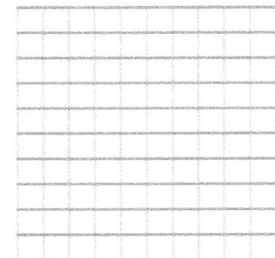
1 % of the squares are black

Estimate to label points for 25%, 50% and 75% of each line segment.

1.

0 % •————————•————————•————————•————————• 100%

2.

0 %————————————————————————————• 100 %

Estimate to label points for 20 %, 40 %, 60 % and 80 % of each line segment.

3. •————————————————————————————————————•
    0 %   100%

4. •——————————————————————————•
    0 %   100 %

Use the information on each line segment. Label the 100 % point. Extend the line if necessary.

5. •—————————•
    0%   25%

6. •———————•
    0%   10%

7. •—————————•
    0%   20%

Solve

1. I got 91 out of 100 questions correct. What percent mark do I get?

2. There is 20 g protein in 100g cookie. What percent of the cookie is protein?

3. Out of 100 students, 60 like tennis. What percent of the students like tennis?

4. Linda has 100 books. 45 of them are in English, 40 are in Spanish. The rest are in French.
   a. What percent of the books are in English?

   b. What percent of the books are in Spanish?

   c. What percent of the books are in French?

5. Out of 100 hats, there are 25 red hats, 35 blue hats and 40 yellow hats.
   a. What percent of the hats are either red or blue?

   b. What percent of the hats are neither red nor blue?

Name _____   Date _____

Express the shaded area in percentage.

1.
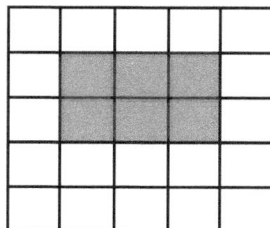

2.
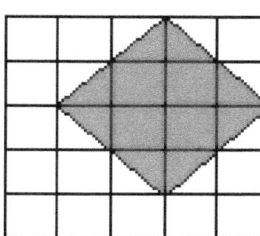

3.
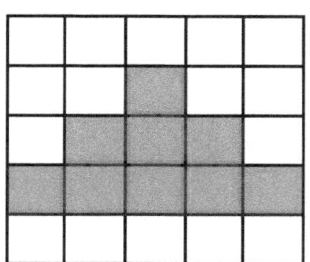

4.
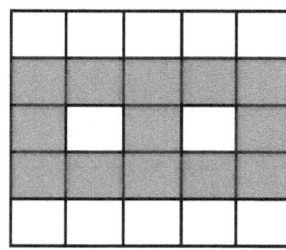

5.
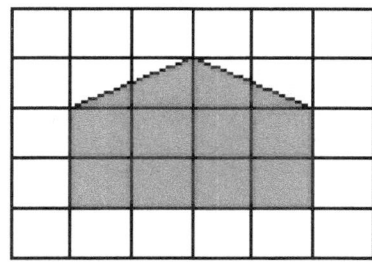

6.
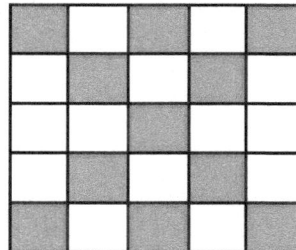

7.
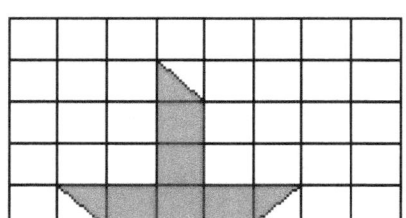

8.
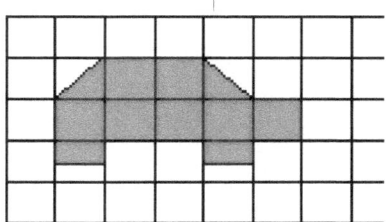

309

Name _____ Date _____

K1. Percentages to decimals

Drop the percent sign and move the decimal point 2 places to the left.

Example: 36.5% = 0.365

1. 23.5 % = _____   2. 34.6 % = _____   3. 54.7 % = _____

4. 4.8 % = _____   5. 6.3 % = _____   6. 3.7 % = _____

7. 60 % = _____   8. 50 % = _____   9. 80 % = _____

10. 2 % = _____   11. 6 % = _____   12. 9 % = _____

13. 3.5 % = _____   14. 5.2 % = _____   15. 9.7 % = _____

16. 142 % = _____   17. 364 % = _____   18. 705 % = _____

19. 3.2 % = _____   20. 25 % = _____   21. 1.34 % = _____

22. 82.7 % = _____   23. 1.36 % = _____   24. 142 % = _____

25. 1.3 % = _____   26. 0.8 % = _____   27. 100 % = _____

28. 12 % = _____   29. 47.3 % = _____   30. 2.3 % = _____

31. 500 % = _____   32. 47.2 % = _____   33. 4 % = _____

34. 1000 % = _____   35. 40.2 % = _____   36. 0.9 % = _____

37. 2000 % = _____   38. 0.7 % = _____   39. 10.2 % = _____

Name _____ Date _____

K2. Decimals to percentages

Move the decimal points 2 places to the right and add the percentage sign at the end.
 Example: 2.35 = 235%

1. 0.36 = _____   2. 0.62 = _____   3. 0.78 = _____

4. 4.51 = _____   5. 9.35 = _____   6. 2.64 = _____

7. 4.2 = _____   8. 9.3 = _____   9. 8.5 = _____

10. 0.2 = _____   11. 0.7 = _____   12. 0.4 = _____

13. 0.01 = _____   14. 0.08 = _____   15. 0.05 = _____

16. 3.81 = _____   17. 0.25 = _____   18. 7 = _____

19. 10 = _____   20. 0.09 = _____   21. 2.9 = _____

22. 0.74 = _____   23. 9.53 = _____   24. 0.006 = _____

25. 15 = _____   26. 0.08 = _____   27. 6.9 = _____

Put in   >,   = OR   <   to make each statement true.

1. 0.16 ____ 1.6%   2. 3.20 ____ 32%

3. 0.47 ____ 47%   4. 3.56 ____ 35.6%

5. 10 ____ 100%   6. 3.56% ____ 3.56

7. 0.78 ____ 780%   8. 2% ____ 0.25

9. 5 ____ 50%   10. 2.85 ____ 0.28%

311

K3. Fractions to percentages

If the denominator can be changed to 100, then change it to 100.

Example: $\dfrac{2}{5} = \dfrac{2 \times 20}{5 \times 20} = \dfrac{40}{100} = 40\%$

1. $\dfrac{3}{100} =$ _____

2. $\dfrac{24}{100} =$ _____

3. $\dfrac{3}{25} = \dfrac{}{100} =$ _____

4. $\dfrac{13}{20} = \dfrac{}{100} =$ _____

5. $\dfrac{4}{5} = \dfrac{}{100} =$ _____

6. $\dfrac{1}{2} = \dfrac{}{100} =$ _____

7. $\dfrac{7}{10} = \dfrac{}{100} =$ _____

8. $\dfrac{3}{4} = \dfrac{}{100} =$ _____

9. $\dfrac{48}{200} = \dfrac{}{100} =$ _____

10. $\dfrac{76}{400} = \dfrac{}{100} =$ _____

11. $\dfrac{35}{500} = \dfrac{}{100} =$ _____

12. $\dfrac{27}{50} = \dfrac{}{100} =$ _____

13. $\dfrac{2}{5} = \dfrac{}{100} =$ _____

14. $\dfrac{24}{300} = \dfrac{}{100} =$ _____

15. $\dfrac{1}{4} =$ _____

16. $\dfrac{3}{5} =$ _____

17. $\dfrac{12}{25} =$ _____

18. $\dfrac{39}{50} =$ _____

19. $\dfrac{84}{200} =$ _____

20. $\dfrac{64}{100} =$ _____

21. $\dfrac{17}{20} =$ _____

22. $\dfrac{80}{500} =$ _____

23. $\dfrac{3}{10} =$ _____

24. $\dfrac{9}{25} =$ _____

Name _____ Date _____

Change the following fractions into percentages

Example: $\dfrac{8}{40} = \dfrac{2}{10} = \dfrac{20}{100} = 20\%$

1. $\dfrac{4}{40} = \dfrac{}{100} =$ _____

2. $\dfrac{12}{40} = \dfrac{}{100} =$ _____

3. $\dfrac{24}{80} = \dfrac{}{100} =$ _____

4. $\dfrac{27}{36} = \dfrac{}{100} =$ _____

5. $\dfrac{15}{30} = \dfrac{}{100} =$ _____

6. $\dfrac{14}{35} = \dfrac{}{100} =$ _____

7. $\dfrac{40}{32} = \dfrac{}{100} =$ _____

8. $\dfrac{36}{60} = \dfrac{}{100} =$ _____

9. $\dfrac{44}{40} = \dfrac{}{100} =$ _____

10. $\dfrac{7}{70} = \dfrac{}{100} =$ _____

11. $\dfrac{30}{75} = \dfrac{}{100} =$ _____

12. $\dfrac{72}{60} = \dfrac{}{100} =$ _____

13. $\dfrac{15}{60} = \dfrac{}{100} =$ _____

14. $\dfrac{35}{28} = \dfrac{}{100} =$ _____

15. $\dfrac{45}{18} =$ _____

16. $\dfrac{45}{125} =$ _____

17. $\dfrac{27}{150} =$ _____

18. $\dfrac{65}{250} =$ _____

19. $\dfrac{21}{28} =$ _____

20. $\dfrac{12}{80} =$ _____

21. $\dfrac{56}{70} =$ _____

22. $\dfrac{49}{175} =$ _____

23. $\dfrac{54}{45} =$ _____

24. $\dfrac{33}{66} =$ _____

Name _____ Date _____

Change the following percentages into fractions

To change percentages to fractions, we usually drop the percent sign, use 100 as denominator and the number as numerator. Then reduce the fraction to the lowest term.

Example: $\quad 2.4\% = \dfrac{2.4}{100} = \dfrac{24}{1000} = \dfrac{3}{125}$

1. $25\% = \dfrac{}{100} =$ _____

2. $36\% = \dfrac{}{100} =$ _____

3. $45\% = \dfrac{}{100} =$ _____

4. $28\% = \dfrac{}{100} =$ _____

5. $8\% =$ _____

6. $24\% =$ _____

7. $16\% =$ _____

8. $20\% =$ _____

9. $78\% =$ _____

10. $80\% =$ _____

11. $6.3\% =$ _____

12. $8.7\% =$ _____

13. $19\% =$ _____

14. $64\% =$ _____

15. $32.5\% =$ _____

16. $28.4\% =$ _____

17. $75\% =$ _____

18. $56\% =$ _____

19. $6.8\% =$ _____

20. $8.5\% =$ _____

K4. Fractions, decimals, ratios, and percentages

	Fraction	Ratio	Decimal	Percentage
1.	$\frac{1}{4}$	1 : 4	0.25	25%
2.			0.8	
3.		2 : 5		
4.				30%
5.	$\frac{3}{8}$			
6.		3 : 10		
7.			0.55	
8.				27%
9.		7 : 20		
10.	$\frac{17}{40}$			
11.				24%
12.			0.32	
13.				58%
14.		8 : 25		
15.	$\frac{27}{40}$			

Name _____   Date _____

Application of percentages

Find a percentage of a number (model 1)

Example: 25% of 17 = 0.25 × 17 = 4.25

1. 35 % of 15 =   2. 57 % of 40 =

3. 46 % of 25 =   4. 6% of 29 =

5. 28 % of 60 =   6. 40% of 51 =

7. 29% of 10 =   8. 8 % of 111 =

9. 47 % of 50 =   10. 27 % of 30 =

11. 16% of 32 =   12. 72 % of 9 =

13. 32 % of 12 =   14. 60 % of 17 =

15. 8.4 % of 55 =   16. 15.8 % of 5 =

17. 60 % of 53 =   18. 9.5 % of 23 =

19. $21\frac{1}{2}$ % of 50 =   20. $9\frac{3}{4}$ % of 14 =

21. $6\frac{3}{4}$ % of 15 =   22. $16\frac{2}{5}$ % of 36 =

23. $9\frac{5}{8}$ % of 30 =   24. $17\frac{1}{5}$ % of 45 =

Name _____ Date _____

Problem solving

Example:
60 % of 80 roses in a garden are yellow. How many yellow roses are there in the garden?

$80 \times 60\% = 48$ There are 48 yellow roses in a garden.

1. 20 % of 40 coins in a wallet are dimes. How many dimes are there? _____

2. 40% of 200 marbles in a bag are blue. How many blue marbles are there? _____

3. 35% of 80 people have a black hat. How many people have a black hat? _____

4. Lisa had $50. She spent 60% of it. How much does she have now? _____

5. There are 120 animals in a farm. 25% of them are ducks. How many ducks are there? _____

6. 55% of 60 students in a class know how to play chess. How many students can play chess? _____

7. There were 30 cookies in a box. James ate 20% of the cookies. How many cookies are left? _____

8. In a school of 850 students, 70 % of them are bilinguals. How many students can speak two kinds of languages? _____

9. James took a test of 160 questions. He got 85% of them right. How many questions did he get wrong? _____

10. Ann has 30 hats. 20% of them are white. How many hats are not white? _____

Name _____ Date _____

Find what percentage one number is of another (model 2)

Example: 6 is what percentage of 15? $\dfrac{6}{15} = 0.4 \times 100\% = 40\%$

What percentage of 45 is 9? $\dfrac{9}{45} = 0.2 \times 100\% = 20\%$

1. 35 is what percent of 50? _____

2. 53 is what percent of 100? _____

3. 45 is what percent of 75? _____

4. 84 is what percent of 21? _____

5. 20 is what percent of 25? _____

6. 27 is what percent of 54? _____

7. What percent of 60 is 15? _____

8. What percent of 45 is 9? _____

9. 25 is what percent of 75? _____

10. 35 is what percent of 140? _____

11. 48 is what percent of 80? _____

12. What percent of 40 is 200? _____

13. What percent of 24 is 18? _____

14. What percent of 38 is 95? _____

15. What percent of 64 is 24? _____

16. 72 is what percent of 100? _____

17. 42 is what percent of 84? _____

18. 30 is what percent of 120? _____

Name   Date

K5. Problem solving

Example:
There are 120 pages in a fiction book. Stanley read 45 pages. What percent of the book did he finish?

$$\frac{45}{120} = \frac{15}{40} = 0.375 = 37.5\%$$

1. William hit 4 foul shots out of 16 shots in a game. What percent of his shots are foul shots? _____

2. There are two green marbles in every 10 marbles. What percent of the marbles is green? _____

3. In a chess tournament, Sam won 18 out of 30 games. What percent of the games did he win? _____

4. 3 m was cut off from a 15 m rod. What percent of the wood was cut off? _____

5. A pizza was cut into 8 pieces. Lisa ate 3 pieces. What percent of the pizza was left? _____

6. Linda had 80 cups with coffee to be filled up for a party. She already made 60 cups. What percent of the cups is filled? _____

7. Jim put 8 oranges into a basket of 24 apples. What percent of the fruits in the basket are oranges? _____

8. There are 5 white cars and 10 black cars in a parking lot. There came another white car. What percent of the cars are white cars now? _____

9. Jenny had 20 candies. She ate 3. What percent of the candy was left? _____

Name _____ Date _____

Find the whole given the part and its percentages (Model 3)

Example: 20 % of what number is 80?
80 ÷ 20% = 80 ÷ 0.2 = 400

1. 30 % of what number is 60?
2. 50 % of what number is 65?

3. 20 % of what number is 20?
4. 80 % of what number is 80?

5. 15 % of what number is 30?
6. 60 % of what number is 240?

7. 40 % of what number is 100?
8. 90 is 3 % of what number?

9. 2.4 % of what number is 54?
10. 4.9 is 7 % of what number?

11. $3\frac{1}{2}$ % of what number is 49?
12. $5\frac{5}{6}$ % of what number is 105?

13. $4\frac{1}{3}$ % of what number is 117?
14. $2\frac{7}{10}$ % of what number is 8.1?

15. $10\frac{1}{4}$ % of what number is 20.5?
16. $2\frac{2}{5}$ % of what number is 9.6?

| Name _____ Date _____ |

Problem solving

Example: Ann took 25% candies and had 45 candies left. How many candies were there at the beginning?

1 − 25% = 75%

75% of the total number of candies is 45

The total number of candies is $45 \div 75\% = 45 \div 0.75 = 60$ candies

1. Linda spends 10% of her salary on entertainment every month. If she spent $260 last month on entertainment, what was her salary for last month?

2. 12 students in a class choose orange juice as their favorite drink, which is 40% of the total number of the students in the class. How many students are there in the class?

3. It took Cindy 3 hours to travel 25% of the distance from Detroit to Miami. If she kept the same speed, how long should it take her to drive to Miami?

4. Cindy drove 25% of the distance from Detroit to Miami. If she drove 345 miles already, what is the total distance from Detroit to Miami?

5. Ann bought a shirt at 30% discount and saved $9. What was the original price of the shirt?

6. Ann bought a pair of shoes at 20% discount and saved $12. What is the new price of the pair of shoes?

7. Sean used 80% of his paper and had 36 sheets left. How many sheets of paper did he have at the beginning?

8. Sean used 45% of his paper and had 110 sheets left. How many sheets of paper did he use?

Name _____ Date _____

L. Ratio and proportion

L1. Ratios

A ratio is the relative magnitudes of two quantities.

Fill in the blanks.

# of chicken	# of mouth	# of eyes	# of legs	# of mouths : # of eyes : # of legs
1	1	2	2	1:1:2:2
2				
3				
5				

# of rabbits	# of mouth	# of eyes	# of legs	# of mouths : # of eyes : # of legs
1	1	2	4	1:1:2:4
2				
5				
8				

# of bees	# of mouth	# of eyes	# of legs	# of mouths : # of eyes : # of legs
1	1	2	6	1:1:2:6
3				
6				
9				

# of crabs	# of mouth	# of eyes	# of legs	# of mouths : # of eyes : # of legs
1	1	2	8	1:1:2:8
7				
10				
50				

Name _____   Date _____

Write the following ratios in three ways

There are 3 dogs, 2 cats, 5 sheep, 6 cows, and 4 horses in a farm.

		a to b	a : b	$\frac{a}{b}$
1.	dogs to cats	3 to 2	3 : 2	$\frac{3}{2}$
2.	dogs to sheep			
3.	cows to all animals			
4.	dogs to horses			
5.	horses to cats			
6.	sheep to cats			
7.	all animals to sheep			
8.	Sheep to pets			
9.	cows to horses			
10.	dogs to pets			
11.	pets to livestock			
12.	Livestock to all animals			

Equivalent ratios

If both numbers in a ratio are multiplied or divided by the same number to give another ratio, the ratios are equivalent.

Example: $\frac{5}{10} = \frac{5 \div 5}{10 \div 5} = \frac{1}{2}$ $\frac{3}{6} = \frac{3 \div 3}{6 \div 3} = \frac{1}{2}$

So $\frac{5}{10} = \frac{1}{2} = \frac{3}{6}$ are equivalent. They are equivalent ratios

Decide whether the following pairs of fractions are equal or not. Fill in = OR ≠

1. $\frac{5}{8}$ ___ $\frac{10}{16}$ 2. $\frac{3}{7}$ ___ $\frac{5}{10}$ 3. $\frac{3}{18}$ ___ $\frac{10}{15}$

4. $\frac{5}{15}$ ___ $\frac{18}{30}$ 5. $\frac{6}{11}$ ___ $\frac{12}{22}$ 6. $\frac{7}{9}$ ___ $\frac{21}{27}$

7. $\frac{5}{8}$ ___ $\frac{25}{40}$ 8. $\frac{6}{15}$ ___ $\frac{2}{5}$ 9. $\frac{9}{12}$ ___ $\frac{3}{4}$

10. $\frac{4}{6}$ ___ $\frac{1}{6}$ 11. $\frac{4}{8}$ ___ $\frac{9}{21}$ 12. $\frac{9}{15}$ ___ $\frac{1}{3}$

Find the missing numbers.

1. $\frac{4}{5} = \frac{\_\_}{10}$ 2. $\frac{5}{6} = \frac{\_\_}{36}$ 3. $\frac{15}{45} = \frac{\_\_}{3}$

4. $\frac{4}{9} = \frac{\_\_}{36}$ 5. $\frac{24}{76} = \frac{\_\_}{19}$ 6. $\frac{12}{36} = \frac{\_\_}{3}$

7. $\frac{7}{12} = \frac{\_\_}{60}$ 8. $\frac{7}{15} = \frac{\_\_}{45}$ 9. $\frac{78}{66} = \frac{\_\_}{11}$

10. $\frac{42}{56} = \frac{3}{\_\_}$ 11. $\frac{5}{6} = \frac{50}{\_\_}$ 12. $\frac{51}{63} = \frac{17}{\_\_}$

Name _____ Date _____

Fill in the blanks.

	Verbal Description	a to b	a : b	$\dfrac{a}{b}$ (reduced to the lowest terms)
1.	10 out of 40	10 to 40	10 : 40	$\dfrac{10}{40} = \dfrac{1}{4}$
2.		5 to 15		
3.			24 : 60	
4.				$\dfrac{6}{11}$
5.	10 out of 90			
6.			56 : 88	
7.		22 to 55		
8.				$\dfrac{3}{7}$
9.			14 : 21	
10.		50 to 15		
11.				$\dfrac{9}{11}$
12.	63 out of 18			
13.			16 : 36	
14.	45 out of 30			
15.				$\dfrac{15}{16}$

Name _____ Date _____

We need to change them into the same units to compare.
Example: 1 hours to 20 minutes = 60 minutes to 20 minutes = 60 : 20 = 3: 1

Facts to know

1 m = 1000 mm	1 km = 1000 m	1 cm =10 mm	1 m = 100 cm
1 kg = 100g	1 *l* = 1000 *ml*	$1 = 100 ¢	1 year = 365 days
1 ft = 12 in	1 yd = 3 ft	1 lb = 16 ounces	1 month = 30 days

Write each ratio in its simplest form

1. 20 min to 48 min = _____   2. $ 5 to 10 cents = _____

3. 3 days to 6 hours = _____   4. 2000 g to 3 kg = _____

5. 12 days to April = _____   6. 3 months to 2 years = _____

7. 2 km to 600 m = _____   8. 8 cm to 5 mm = _____

9. 3 cm to 60 mm = _____   10. 5 kg to 400 g = _____

11. 3 hours to 40 min = _____   12. $3 to 50 cents = _____

13. 50 cm to 30 mm = _____   14. 5 months to 3 years = _____

15. 4 days to 2 weeks = _____   16. 6 dimes to 9 pennies = _____

17. 10 ounces to 2 lb _____   18. 3 feet to 20 inches _____

19. 6 yards to 8 feet _____   20. 5 quarters to 6 nickels _____

21. 60 inches to 5 feet _____   22. 4 lb to 5 ounces _____

23. 15 days to July _____   24. 5 feet to 6 yards _____

326

L2. Proportion

A proportion is an equation which shows that two ratios are equal. Two ratios are equal if their cross products are equal.

Example: $\dfrac{3}{7} = \dfrac{6}{14}$ is a proportion because $3 \times 14 = 6 \times 7$

Example: Find x $\dfrac{6}{4} = \dfrac{x}{8}$

$\dfrac{6}{4} = \dfrac{x}{8} \Rightarrow x = 6 \times 8 \div 4 = 12$

1. $\dfrac{x}{8} = \dfrac{7}{4}$ $x =$ 2. $\dfrac{x}{16} = \dfrac{25}{10}$ $x =$

3. $\dfrac{x}{5} = \dfrac{9}{3}$ $x =$ 4. $\dfrac{x}{4} = \dfrac{27}{18}$ $x =$

5. $\dfrac{7}{x} = \dfrac{5}{25}$ $x =$ 6. $\dfrac{12}{x} = \dfrac{21}{35}$ $x =$

7. $\dfrac{6}{x} = \dfrac{7}{56}$ $x =$ 8. $\dfrac{9}{x} = \dfrac{15}{40}$ $x =$

9. $\dfrac{12}{8} = \dfrac{x}{10}$ $x =$ 10. $\dfrac{16}{14} = \dfrac{x}{49}$ $x =$

11. $\dfrac{9}{12} = \dfrac{x}{20}$ $x =$ 12. $\dfrac{15}{9} = \dfrac{x}{21}$ $x =$

13. $\dfrac{3}{10} = \dfrac{18}{x}$ $x =$ 14. $\dfrac{15}{6} = \dfrac{35}{x}$ $x =$

15. $\dfrac{14}{6} = \dfrac{35}{x}$ $x =$ 16. $\dfrac{24}{16} = \dfrac{54}{x}$ $x =$

17. $\dfrac{14}{x} = \dfrac{21}{36}$ $x =$ 18. $\dfrac{25}{x} = \dfrac{35}{49}$ $x =$

19. $\dfrac{30}{25} = \dfrac{x}{20}$ $x =$ 12. $\dfrac{18}{36} = \dfrac{x}{48}$ $x =$

Complete the following table

5 apple pies cost $ 15.   How much do 3, 8, 10, 60, 100 apple pies cost?
  1 apple pie costs $15 ÷ 5 = $ 3
  3 apple pies costs $3 × 3 = $9

Number of pencils	1	8	10	60	100
Cost ($)	3	24	30	180	300

1.

Number of apples	1	2	3	4	5	8	40
Cost ($)		0.50					

2.

hours	1	2	5	10	20	30	40
Kilometers traveled			300				

3.

Number of boxes	1	2	3	4	5	9	20
Number of pencils				48			

4.

Hours worked	1	2	4	5	8	25	40
How much earned($)					80		

5.

Cost ($)	2.50	5.00	10.00	15	25	45	60
Bottles of milk	1						

6.

Kilograms of candy	1	2	3	4	8	20	25
Cost($)				20			

7.

Number of oranges	1	5	7	10	15	30	55
Weight(g)							

Problems Using Proportions

3 apples weigh 1 pound. How many pounds do 15 apples weigh?

Number of apples	weight (lb.)
3	1
15	x

$\frac{3}{15} = \frac{1}{x} \Rightarrow x = 15 \times 1 \div 3 = 5$

So, 15 apples weigh 5 lb.

1. 4 pens cost $11. How much is 16 pens?

Pens	Price
4	11
16	x

2. There are 16 ounces in 1 pound. How many ounces are there in 5 pounds?

Ounces	Pound

3. 4 bottles of apple juice cost $3.50. How much is 6 bottles of apples juice?

Apples Juice	Price

4. Four quarters make one dollar. How many quarters make 10 dollars?

Quarters	Dollar

5. 100 g almond costs $3. How much does 500 g almond cost?

Name _____   Date _____

6. 200 g yogurts cost $1.80. How much does 500 g yogurt cost?

7. 3 apples cost $1.20. How much do 7 apples cost?

8. A recipe for pan cake calls 5 cups of flour and 2 cups of sugar. If Jasmin has 20 cups of flour, how many cups of sugar does she need?

9. A car travels at 55 km/hour. What is the distance it can travel in 3 hour?

10. There are 6 feet in 2 yards. How many yards are there in 15 feet?

11. A traffic light changes its color three times every 4 minutes. How many times does it change its color in one hour?

L3. Unit Price

Which is the better buy?

1. a. $1.5 for 500 mL milk b. $4.8 for 4 L milk

2. a. 50 m^2 floor for $280 b. 100 cm^2 floor for $1.2

3. a. $0.98 for 100 g chocolate b. $12 for 1 kg chocolate

4. a. a dozen eggs for $2.76 b. 3 eggs for $0.66

5. a. $2.50 for 350 mL juice b. $12 for 2 L juice

6. a. $1.36 for 100 g meat b. $72 for 5 kg meat

7. a. 2 m^3 wood for $575 b. 10 dm^3 wood for $10.6

8. a. 3 m lace for $4.56 b. 20 cm lace for $0.5

9. a. $0.29 for 30 seconds phone call b. $6.3 for 10 minutes phone call

10. a. $3.98 for 5 kg rice b. $420 for 2 t rice

11. a. $1.15 for 1 L gas b. $5 000 for 8 kL gas

12. a. $ 450 a month to rent a car b. $ 148 a week to rent a car

13. a. $ 9.68 for 2 kg fish b. $ 0.69 for 100 g fish

14. a. $ 1.00 for 200 mL spring water b. $ 15 for 20 L spring water

15. a. 2.5 m cloths for $ 32.5 b. 12 m cloths for $178

16. a. 30 minutes parking for $1.25 b. 2 hrs. parking for $ 6

17. a. $ 9.68 to travel 100 km b. $ 0.24 to travel 1000 m

18. a. 5 t flour for $ 1480 b. 20 kg flour for $4.8

Name _____   Date _____

L4. Unit Rate

Rate is a quantity measured with respect to another measured quantity.
For example: a car travel at a speed of 60 kilometers per hour: 60 km/h.

Find the unit rate.

1. A car traveled 400 km in 5 hours. _____

2. Ken ran 100 m in 8 seconds. _____

3. Linda walked 2 km in 10 minutes. _____

4. A train traveled 400 km in 16 hours. _____

5. Shirley typed 320 words in 5 minutes. _____

6. Amy read 180 pages in 2 days. _____

7. Kelly received a $192 phone bill for 6 months. _____

8. A plant grew 12 cm in 2 months. _____

9. A jet airplane traveled 75 km in 5 minutes. _____

10. Sam scored 128 hits in 8 games. _____

11. Ken visited 8 countries in 2 years. _____

12. A newborn kitty gained 960 g in 50 days. _____

13. Edward paid $ 1.25 for 5 phone calls. _____

14. Cindy bought 4 m lace for $ 3.96 _____

15. A snail climbed 30 cm up a tree in 8 minutes. _____

16. A frog did 345 jumps in 15 minutes _____

17. A farm produced 4800 eggs in 3 days. _____

18. May made 45 cups of coffee in 90 minutes. _____

19. A rabbit ate 315 carrots in 45 days. _____

Name _____ Date _____

Find the total amount.

1. Edward made 8 phone calls. It costs $0.25 to make each phone call. _____

2. Cindy bought 12 m lace of $ 1.98/m. _____

3. A snail climbed for 3 hours at the speed of 5mm/ min. _____

4. Ken visited 3 countries every year for 8 years. _____

5. A kitty ate 80 g food every day for a month. _____

6. Amy read 150 pages every day for 15 days. _____

7. Kelly paid $25/mon phone bill for 8 months. _____

8. Tim ran 1200 m every day for 12 days. _____

9. Mike walked 2.4 km every day for a month. _____

10. Sam ran 15 minutes at the speed of 200 m/min. _____

11. A plant grew 30 mm/d for 1 month. _____

12. A jet airplane traveled at the speed of 250 m/s for 30 minutes. _____

13. A train traveled 4 hours at the speed of 110 km/h. _____

14. Maggie typed for 25 minutes at the rate of 5 words/min. _____

15. A car traveled 3 hours at the speed of 75 km /h. _____

16. A frog jumped for 1 hour at the rate of 5 jumps/min. _____

17. Steve mowed 4 lawns every week for a month. _____

18. May made pies for 30 minutes at the rate of 5 minutes per pie. _____

19. A rabbit ate 12 carrots every day for 3 months. _____

Name _____   Date _____

Problem Solving

1. The ratio of the number of red marbles to blue marbles in a jar is 2 : 3. If there are 48 red marbles, then how many blue marbles are there?

2. The ration of the number of boys to girls in a chorus is 4 : 7. If there are 88 students in the chorus, how many girls are there?

3. There are 350 audiences in a theater. There are 270 children audiences. Find the ratio of children to adults.

4. 500 *ml* water can fill up 4 cups. How much water is needed to fill up 18 cups?

5. A light blinks 4 times every 15 seconds. How many times does it blink in 3 minutes?

6. There are 45 g of protein in 500 g of breads. How many grams of protein are there in 800 g of bread?

7. A punch requires 300 *ml* of apple juice for every 200 *ml* watermelon juice. If Felix wants to make 2 *l* punch, how many milliliters apple juice does he need?

8. Tony walks 12 steps in 8 m. How many steps does he need to walk 1 kilometer?

9. Kyle gets 85% in his test. He gets 6 questions wrong. How many questions does he answer correctly?

10. Karen makes 8 out 10 in her recent test. If there are 40 questions in her test, how many questions did she not answer correctly?

11. The ratio of the number of dimes to nickels is 3 : 4. If there are 42 coins altogether, how much are these coins worth?

12. The ratio of the number of chickens to rabbits is 2 : 5. Find the ratio of the number of the chicken's legs to rabbit's legs.

M. Measurement

M1. Mass and weight

> 1t = 1000kg = 1 000 000g = 1 000 000 000mg
>
> 1kg = 1000g = 1 000 000mg
>
> 1 g = 1 000 mg

1. Grams and Milligrams.

Example: 1. 6 g = 6 × 1 000 mg = 6 000 mg
            2. 800 mg = 800 ÷ 1000 g = 0.8 g

1. 2 g = _____ mg   2. 6 g = _____ mg   3. 4 g = _____ mg

4. 3 000 mg = _____ g   5. 5 000 mg = _____ g   6. 7 000 mg = _____ g

7. 80 g = _____ mg   8. 6 000 mg = _____ g   9. 12 g = _____ mg

10. 4500 mg = _____ g 11. 810 g = _____ mg   12. 720 mg = _____ g

13. 8.5 g = _____ mg   14. 660 mg = _____ g   15. 6.2 g = _____ mg

16. 360 mg = _____ g   17. 0.7 g = _____ mg   18. 49 mg = _____ g

2. Kilograms and Grams

Example: 1. 5 kg = 5 × 1 000 g = 6 000 g
            2. 900 g = 900 ÷ 1000 kg = 0.9 kg

1. 1 kg = _____ g   2. 8 kg = _____ g   3. 5 kg = _____ g

4. 2 000 g = _____ kg 5. 7 000 g = _____ kg 6. 76 000 g = _____ kg

7. 72 kg = _____ g   8. 86 000 g = _____ kg 9. 80 kg = _____ g

10. 42 000 g = _____ kg 11. 89 kg = _____ g 12. 91 000 g = _____ kg

13. 2.5 kg = _____ g   14. 670 g = _____ kg   15. 8.6 kg = _____ g

16. 450 g = _____ kg   17. 0.84 kg = _____ G 18. 460 g = _____ kg

Name _____ Date _____

1. Tons and Kilograms.

Example: 1. 4 t = __4 × 1 000__ kg = __4 000__ kg
           2. 700 kg = __700 ÷ 1000__ kg = __0.7__ kg

1. 1 t = _____ kg   2. 5 t = _____ kg   3. 8 t = _____ kg

4. 5 000 kg = _____ t   5. 3 000 kg = _____ t   6. 8 000 kg = _____ t

7. 10 t = _____ kg   8. 12 000 kg = _____ t   9. 53 t = _____ kg

10. 620 kg = _____ t   11. 62 t = _____ kg   12. 7 200 kg = _____ t

13. 6.7 t = _____ kg   14. 1020 kg = _____ t   15. 8.2 t = _____ kg

16. 3600 kg = _____ t   17. 0.52 t = _____ kg   18. 480 kg = _____ t

2. Fill in the following blanks.

1. 3000 mg = _____ g   2. 2.8 g = _____ mg   3. 37 mg = _____ g

4. 5 t = _____ kg   5. 20 t = _____ kg   6. 3.8 t = _____ kg

7. 31 000 g = _____ kg   8. 4.3 kg = _____ g   9. 910 g = _____ kg

10. 5.25 g = _____ kg   11. 4250 mg = _____ g   12. 0.2 g = _____ mg

13. 46 mg = _____ g   14. 5.2 g = _____ mg   15. 3090 mg = _____ g

16. 305 kg = _____ t   17. 3.4 t = _____ kg   18. 20 kg = _____ t

19. 2.05 mg = _____ g   20. 0.42 g = _____ mg   21. 59 mg = _____ g

22. 3800 kg = _____ t   23. 21.5 t = _____ kg   24. 9200 kg = _____ t

25. 36.6 kg = _____ g   26. 350 g = _____ kg   27. 35.1 kg = _____ g

28. 5.05 kg = _____ t   29. 0.053 t = _____ kg   30. 47.2 kg = _____ t

31. 0.051 t = _____ kg   32. 1450 kg = _____ t   33. 3.61 t = _____ kg

A drop of water has a mass of about 50mg. 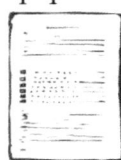	A piece of paper is about 2 g. 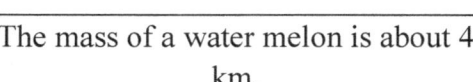
The mass of an apple is about 300 g. 	The mass of a water melon is about 4 km. 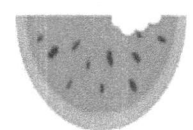
A cow is about 600 kg. 	The weight of a whale is about 30 t. 

Circle the best unit.

1. the mass of an orange   a. 200 g   b. 200 mg   c. 200 kg

2. a box of crackers is about   a. 1 g   b. 1 kg   c. 1 t

3. the mass of a penny   a. 2 mg   b. 2 g   c. 2 kg

4. an elephant is about   a. 5 g   b. 5 kg   c. 5t

5. The weight of a mosquito is about   a. 2 mg   b. 2 g   c. 2 kg

6. A new born baby is about   a. 3 g   b. 3 kg   c. 3 t

7. A crab is about   a. 1 g   b. 1 kg   c. 1 mg

8. A cucumber is about   a. 200 g   b. 200 mg   c. 200 kg

9. The mass of a loaf of bread   a. 500 g   b. 5 kg   c. 5 g

10. the mass of an eraser   a. 20 g   b. 1 kg   c. 30 mg

Name _____   Date _____

M2. Length

> 1km = 1000m = 100 000 cm = 1 000 000 mm
> 1m = 100 cm = 1000 mm
> 1 cm = 10 mm

1. Centimeters and Millimeters

Example   1. 2cm = <u>2×10</u> mm = <u>20</u> mm

2. 6 mm = <u>6 ÷10</u> cm = <u>0.6</u> cm

1. 4 cm = _____ mm
2. 3 cm = _____ mm
3. 38 cm = _____ mm
4. 50 mm = _____ cm
5. 80 mm = _____ cm
6. 300 mm = _____ cm
7. 10 cm = _____ mm
8. 500 mm = _____ cm
9. 18 cm = _____ mm
10. 70 mm = _____ cm
11. 36 cm = _____ mm
12. 300 mm = _____ cm
13. 3.2 cm = _____ mm
14. 450 mm = _____ cm
15. 5.3 cm = _____ mm
16. 5.6 mm = _____ cm
17. 8.4 cm = _____ mm
18. 4.9 mm = _____ cm

2. Meters and Centimeters

Example   1. 4.8 m = <u>4.8×100</u> cm = <u>480</u> cm

2. 8 cm = <u>8 ÷100</u> m = <u>0.08</u> m

1. 2 m = _____ cm
2. 10m = _____ cm
3. 900 cm = _____ m
4. 910 cm = _____ m
5. 51 m = _____ m
6. 200 cm = _____ m
7. 400 cm = _____ m
8. 18 m _____ cm
9. 300 cm = _____ m
10. 280 cm = _____ m
11. 330 cm = _____ m
12. 560 cm = _____ m
13. 4.6 m = _____ cm
14. 50 m = _____ cm
15. 2.1 m = _____ cm
16. 630 cm = _____ m
17. 3.9 m = _____ cm
18. 640 cm = _____ m

Name _____ Date _____

3. Meters and Millimeters

Example   1. 5 m = $\underline{5 \times 1000}$ mm = $\underline{5000}$ mm

2. 8 mm = $\underline{8 \div 1000}$ m = $\underline{0.008}$ m

1. 3 m = _____ mm
2. 4 m = _____ mm
3. 51 m = _____ mm
4. 6000 mm = _____ m
5. 1000 mm = _____ m
6. 5000 mm = _____ m
7. 70 m = _____ mm
8. 800 mm = _____ m
9. 61 m = _____ mm
10. 5000 mm = _____ m
11. 25 m = _____ mm
12. 9300 mm = _____ m
13. 1.6 m = _____ mm
14. 2800 mm = _____ m
15. 2.4 m = _____ mm
16. 420 mm = _____ m
17. 0.9 m = _____ mm
18. 19 mm = _____ m

4. Kilometers and meters

Example   1. 7 km = $\underline{7 \times 1000}$ m = $\underline{7000}$ m

2. 3 m = $\underline{3 \div 1000}$ km = $\underline{0.003}$ km

1. 1 km = _____ m
2. 3 km = _____ m
3. 27 km = _____ m
4. 6000 m = _____ km
5. 8000 m = _____ km
6. 4 km = _____ m
7. 8600 m = _____ km
8. 4800 m = _____ km
9. 87 km = _____ m
10. 8500 m = _____ km
11. 9900 m = _____ km
12. 2300 m = _____ km
13. 5.7 km = _____ m
14. 72 km = _____ m
15. 5.8 km = _____ m
16. 7800 m = _____ km
17. 8.8 km = _____ m
18. 330 m = _____ km

5. Fill in the following blank.

1.   5 km = _____ m = _____ cm = _____ mm

2.   6 000 000 mm = _____ cm = _____ m = _____ km

Name _____   Date _____

The thickness of a dollar coin is about 2 mm. 	The length of a new pencil is about 20 cm. 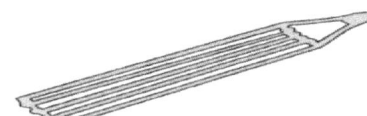
The height of a normal door is about 2 m. 	The length of modern marathon is about 42 km. 

Circle the best unit.

1. the length of a table   a. 2 m   b. 20 m   c. 2 km

2. the thickness of a dime   a. 1 mm   b. 1 cm   c. 100 cm

3. the diameter of an apple   a. 10 mm   b. 10 cm   c. 10 m

4. the height of Simon Mountain   a. 3000 mm   b. 3000 cm   c. 3000 m

5. the distance from City Vancouver to Hope   a. 150 m   b. 150 km   c. 150 mm

6. the length of standard swimming pool   a. 50 m   b. 50 cm   c. 50 km

7. In 1 hour, a car can travel a distance of   a. 60 m   b. 60 km   c. 60 mm

8. The world men triple jump records   a. 18.29 cm   b. 18.29 m   c. 18.29 km

9. The length of an ant   a. 10 mm   b. 10 cm   c. 10 m

10. the length of a car   a. 5 cm   b. 5 m   c. 5 mm

M3. Area

$$1 km^2 = 1\,000\,000 m^2 = 10\,000\,000\,000\ cm^2$$
$$1 m^2 = 10\,000\ cm^2$$

1. Square meters and square centimeters

Example   1. $5.9\ m^2 =$ __5.9 × 10 000__ $cm^2 =$ __59 000__ cm^2

2. $580\ cm^2 =$ __580 ÷ 10 000__ $m^2 =$ __0.058__ m^2

1. $9\ m^2 =$ _____ cm^2 2. $64\ m^2 =$ _____ cm^2

3. $50\,000\ cm^2 =$ _____ m^2 4. $9000\ cm^2 =$ _____ m^2

5. $20\ m^2 =$ _____ cm^2 6. $36\,000\ cm^2 =$ _____ m^2

7. $9\,500\ cm^2 =$ _____ m^2 8. $4\,500\ cm^2 =$ _____ m^2

9. $0.45\ m^2 =$ _____ cm^2 10. $2680\ cm^2 =$ _____ m^2

11. $6300\ cm^2 =$ _____ m^2 12. $4.9\ m^2 =$ _____ cm^2

2. Square kilometers and square meters.

Example   1. $3\ km^2 =$ __3 × 1 000 000__ $m^2 =$ __3 000 000__ m^2

2. $800\ m^2 =$ __800 ÷ 1 000 000__ $km^2 =$ __0.008__ km^2

1. $6\ km^2 =$ _____ m^2 2. $0.4\ km^2 =$ _____ m^2

3. $70\,000\ m^2 =$ _____ km^2 4. $5000\ m^2 =$ _____ km^2

5. $56\,000\ m^2 =$ _____ km^2 6. $4800\ m^2 =$ _____ km^2

7. $51200\ m^2 =$ _____ km^2 8. $6900\ m^2 =$ _____ km^2

9. $0.027\ km^2 =$ _____ m^2 10. $0.72\ km^2 =$ _____ m^2

11. $17500\ m^2 =$ _____ km^2 12. $8.55\ km^2 =$ _____ m^2

Name _____ Date _____

The area of a human nail is about 2 cm². 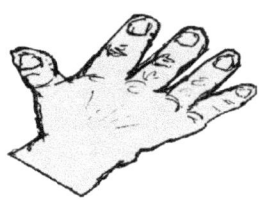	A book cover has an area of about 550 cm². 
The top area of a table is about 1 m². 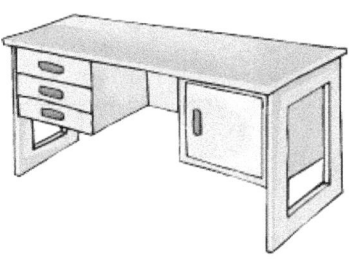	Vancouver has an area of about 3000 km². 

Circle the best unit.

1. A classroom has an area of about   a. 60 cm²   b. 60 m²   c. 60 km²

2. A computer screen has an area of about   a. 750 cm²   b. 750 m²   c. 750 km²

3. The area of a basketball court is about   a. 450 cm²   b. 450 m²   c. 450 km²

4. A human hand may cover an area of   a. 200 cm²   b. 200 m²   c. 200 km²

5. Lake Baikal has an area of   a. 30000 cm²   b. 30000 m²   c. 30000 km²

6. The area of a window may be   a. 2 cm²   b. 2 m²   c. 2 km²

7. A chess board may have an area of   a. 2500 cm²   b. 2500 m²   c. 2500 km²

8. The area of Michigan lake is about   a. 58000 cm²   b. 58000 m²   c. 58000 km²

9. A calculator may cover an area of about   a. 150 cm²   b. 150 m²   c. 150 km²

10. A bed may cover an area of   a. 3 cm²   b. 3 m²   c. 3 mm

M4. Volume

$$1 \text{ kL} = 1\,000 \text{ L} = 1\,000\,000 \text{ mL}$$
$$1 \text{ L} = 1\,000 \text{ mL}$$

1. Litres and Millilitres.

Example:
1. $3 \text{ L} = \underline{3 \times 1000} \text{ mL} = \underline{3\,000 \text{ mL}}$
2. $500 \text{ mL} = \underline{500 \div 1000} \text{ L} = \underline{0.5 \text{ L}}$

1. 5 L = _____ mL
2. 2 L = _____ mL
3. 8000 mL = _____ L
4. 5800 mL = _____ L
5. 3700 mL = _____ L
6. 300 mL = _____ L
7. 480 mL = _____ L
8. 37 L = _____ mL
9. 3.7 L = _____ mL
10. 480 mL = _____ L
11. 8800 mL = _____ L
12. 6.5 L = _____ mL

2. Kilolitres and Litres.

Example:
1. $1 \text{ KL} = \underline{1 \times 1000} \text{ L} = \underline{1\,000 \text{ L}}$
2. $700 \text{ L} = \underline{700 \div 1000} \text{ kL} = \underline{0.7 \text{ kL}}$

1. 5 kL = _____ L
2. 7 kL = _____ L
3. 7300 L = _____ kL
4. 3000 L = _____ kL
5. 100 L = _____ kL
6. 5500 L = _____ kL
7. 37 kL = _____ L
10. 230 L = _____ kL
9. 280 L = _____ kL
12. 1.7 kL = _____ L
11. 3.5 kL = _____ L
14. 3800 L = _____ kL

Name _____ Date _____

M5. Capacity

$$1 \text{ m}^3 = 1\,000 \text{ dm}^3 = 1\,000\,000 \text{ cm}^3$$
$$1 \text{ dm}^3 = 1\,000 \text{ cm}^3$$

3. Cubic decimetres and cubic centimeters.

Example:
1. $5 \text{ dm}^3 = \underline{5 \times 1000} \text{ cm}^3 = \underline{5\,000 \text{ cm}^3}$
2. $800 \text{ cm}^3 = \underline{800 \div 1000} \text{ dm}^3 = \underline{0.8 \text{ dm}^3}$

1. $40 \text{ dm}^3 =$ _____ cm^3 2. $8 \text{ dm}^3 =$ _____ cm^3

3. $43000 \text{ cm}^3 =$ _____ dm^3 4. $7000 \text{ cm}^3 =$ _____ dm^3

5. $280 \text{ cm}^3 =$ _____ dm^3 6. $8300 \text{ cm}^3 =$ _____ dm^3

7. $827 \text{ cm}^3 =$ _____ dm^3 8. $470 \text{ cm}^3 =$ _____ dm^3

9. $7.6 \text{ dm}^3 =$ _____ cm^3 10. $8.3 \text{ dm}^3 =$ _____ cm^3

11. $370 \text{ cm}^3 =$ _____ dm^3 11. $7800 \text{ cm}^3 =$ _____ dm^3

4. Cubic metres and cubic decimetres.

Example:
1. $1 \text{ m}^3 = \underline{1 \times 1000} \text{ dm}^3 = \underline{1\,000 \text{ dm}^3}$
2. $300 \text{ dm}^3 = \underline{300 \div 1000} \text{ m}^3 = \underline{0.3 \text{ m}^3}$

1. $8 \text{ m}^3 =$ _____ dm^3 2. $40 \text{ m}^3 =$ _____ dm^3

4. $7000 \text{ dm}^3 =$ _____ m^3 5. $43000 \text{ dm}^3 =$ _____ m^3

7. $5300 \text{ dm}^3 =$ _____ m^3 8. $280 \text{ dm}^3 =$ _____ m^3

10. $470 \text{ dm}^3 =$ _____ m^3 11. $827 \text{ dm}^3 =$ _____ m^3

13. $5.3 \text{ m}^3 =$ _____ dm^3 14. $7.6 \text{ m}^3 =$ _____ dm^3

16. $8700 \text{ dm}^3 =$ _____ m^3 17. $370 \text{ dm}^3 =$ _____ m^3

Name	Date

Capacity and Volume

Capacity is the amount that can be contained. Capacity is usually measured in L, mL, and kL.

Volume is the amount of space occupied by an object. Volume is usually measured in cm^3, dm^3 and m^3.

$$1 \text{ kL} = 1 \text{ m}^3 = 1\,000 \text{ dm}^3 = 1\,000\,000 \text{ cm}^3$$

$$1 \text{ L} = 1 \text{ dm}^3 = 1\,000 \text{ cm}^3$$

$$1 \text{ mL} = 1 \text{ cm}^3$$

1. 4 mL _____ cm^3
2. 9 kL = _____ m^3
3. 9800 L = _____ cm^3
4. 8000 L = _____ m^3
5. 900 kL = _____ dm^3
6. 5300 mL = _____ dm^3
7. 33 L = _____ dm^3
8. 780 kL = _____ dm^3
9. 780 L = _____ m^3
10. 5.3 mL = _____ dm^3
11. 6.9 L = _____ cm^3
12. 9800 kL = _____ m^3

$$1 \text{ m}^3 = 1 \text{ kL} = 1\,000 \text{ L} = 1\,000\,000 \text{ mL}$$

$$1 \text{ dm}^3 = 1 \text{ L} = 1000 \text{ mL}$$

$$1 \text{ cm}^3 = 1 \text{ mL}$$

1. 4 m^3 = _____ L
2. 70 dm^3 = _____ L
3. 9800 cm^3 = _____ L
4. 73000 dm^3 = _____ L
5. 800 dm^3 = _____ kL
6. 490 cm^3 = _____ mL
7. 33 m^3 = _____ L
8. 947 dm^3 = _____ kL
9. 780 cm^3 = _____ mL
10. 8.6 m^3 = _____ L
11. 6.9 m^3 = _____ mL
12. 380 cm^3 = _____ kL

Name _____   Date _____

The capacity of a small bottle of medicine is about 5 mL. 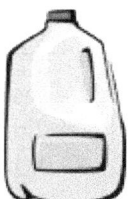	A can of cola is about 350 mL. 
A big bottle can hold 4 litres of milk.	A standard swimming pool can hold up to 3 000 m³ water. 

Circle the best unit.

1.	A can of juice is about	a. 300 mL	b. 300 L	c. 300 kL
2.	Jessica took cough syrup of about	a. 5 mL	b. 5 L	c. 1 L
3.	A car tank can contain gas of	a. 20 mL	b. 2 L	c. 20 L
4.	The volume of a 1 m cube is	a. 1 m³	b. 1 dm³	c. 1 cm³
5.	A kettle may hold	a. 2 mL	b. 2 L	c. 200 L
6.	A bath tub may contain	a. 1 mL	b. 1 L	c. 1 kL
7.	A small bedroom may have a capacity of	a. 50 m³	b. 50 dm³	c. 50 cm³
8.	The volume of a volleyball is about	a. 10 cm³	b. 10 dm³	c. 10 m³
9.	The volume of a tennis is about	a. 30 cm³	b. 30 dm³	c. 30 m³
10.	A cup may hold water of	a. 200 mL	b. 20 L	c. 20 kL

M6. The Metric System

Weight

Metric unit of mass	ton	kilogram	gram	milligram
Symbol	t	kg	g	mg
Value	1 000 000	1000 g	1 g	0.001 g

Length

Length	kilometre	metre	decimetre	centimetre	millimetre
Symbol	km	m	dm	cm	Mm
Value	1 000 m	1 m	0.1 m	0.01 m	0.001 m

Area

Area	Square kilometre	Square metre	Square centimetre
Symbol	km^2	m^2	cm^2
Value	$0.000\ 001\ km^2$	$1\ m^2$	$10\ 000\ cm^2$

Volume

Area	cubic metre	cubic decimetre	cubic centimetre
Symbol	m^3	dm^3	cm^3
Value	$1\ m^3$	$1\ 000\ dm^3$	$1\ 000\ 000\ cm^3$

Capacity

Metric unit of capacity	kilolitre	litre	millilitre
Symbol	kL	L	mL
Value	1000 L	1 L	0.001 L

Name _____ Date _____

Converting Units in Metric System

Example:

1. 51 kg = <u>51 × 1000</u> g = <u>51 000</u> g

2. 28 L = <u>28 × 1000</u> mL = <u>28 000</u> mL

3. 35 m = <u>35 ÷ 100</u> km = <u>0.35</u> km

4. 4200 cm^2 = <u>4200 ÷ 10 000</u> m^2 = <u>0.42</u> m^2

5. 3.6 m^3 = <u>3.6 × 1 000</u> dm^3 = <u>3600</u> dm^3

Fill in the missing numbers

1. 45 kg = _____ g
2. 19 L = _____ mL
3. 360 cm = _____ m
4. 1638 ml = _____ L
5. 27 L = _____ mL
6. 4321 m = _____ km
7. 320 mL = _____ L
8. 1430 g = _____ kg
9. 580 m = _____ km
10. 42 m^2 = _____ cm^2
11. 1390 g = _____ kg
12. 20 L = _____ mL
13. 3590 g = _____ kg
14. 3600 g = _____ kg
15. 12 dm^3 = _____ cm^3
16. 25.1 mm = _____ cm
17. 2.8 kg = _____ t
18. 361.4 mL = _____ L
19. 3425 mm = _____ m
20. 0.32 L = _____ mL
21. 0.73 m^2 = _____ cm^2
22. 2.5 m^3 = _____ dm^3
23. 126.4 ml = _____ L
24. 47.9 g = _____ t
25. 45.9 mm = _____ cm
26. 640 cm^2 = _____ m^2
27. 42 km = _____ cm
28. 6.8 kg = _____ g

Name _____ Date _____

Fill in the missing numbers

1. 560 mm² = _____ m²   2. 85.6 mm = _____ m

3. 410 kg = _____ g   4. 263 m = _____ km

5. 630 mL = _____ L   6. 25 kg = _____ g

7. 3460 m² = _____ km²   8. 17 cm = _____ m

9. 57 m² = _____ cm²   10. 0.45 L = _____ mL

11. 8050 m = _____ km   12. 0.75 km = _____ cm

13. 470 m = _____ mm   14. 9.7 g = _____ kg

15. 8.9 kg = _____ t   16. 7.2 dm³ = _____ cm³

17. 608 cm = _____ m   18. 205 cm = _____ m

19. 0.35 L = _____ mL   20. 84 mm² = _____ cm²

21. 4900 g = _____ kg   22. 30 L = _____ kL

23. 6.8 dm³ = _____ cm³   24. 9.6 g = _____ kg

25. 0.83 kg = _____ g   26. 63.4 m² = _____ km²

27. 5720 cm = _____ km   28. 0.75 cm = _____ mm

29. 65.8 L = _____ kL   30. 5.6 cm = _____ Mm

31. 8.4 m² = _____ cm²   32. 3450 g = _____ t

33. 78.9 g = _____ kg   34. 2 dm³ = _____ cm³

35. 870 dm³ = _____ m³   36. 35.6 kg = _____ t

37. 49.6 mm = _____ m   38. 0.067 kg = _____ g

39. 89 mm = _____ m   40. 520 cm = _____ m

Name _____ Date _____

M7. Weight (British units)

The **tonne** (SI symbol: **t**) or **metric ton** (American) is equivalent to approximately 2 204.6 pounds, 1.10 tons (US)

1 ton = 2000 pounds	1 pound = 16 ounces

1. 45 pounds = _____ ounces
2. 1.5 tons = _____ pounds
3. 2.7 tons = _____ pounds
4. 48 ounces = _____ pounds
5. 0.25 tones = _____ pounds
6. 128 pounds = _____ tons
7. 0.01 tones = _____ ounces
8. 488 pounds = _____ tons
9. 4 ounces = _____ pounds
10. 1 ounces = _____ pounds
11. 60 ounces = _____ pounds
12. 400 ounces = _____ tons
13. 0.29 tones = _____ pounds
14. 0.025 tones = _____ ounces
15. 3.5 pounds = _____ ounces
16. 90 ounces = _____ pounds

Find the missing numbers.

1. 59 ounces = _____ pounds _____ ounces
2. 8 019 pounds = _____ tons _____ pounds
3. 89 ounces = _____ pounds _____ ounces
4. 6.5 pounds = _____ pounds _____ ounces
5. 9.25 pounds = _____ pounds _____ ounces
6. 50 000 ounces = _____ tons _____ pounds _____ ounces
7. 0.004 25 tons = _____ pounds _____ ounces
8. 0.005 375 tons = _____ pounds _____ ounces
9. 721 000 ounces = _____ tones _____ pounds _____ ounces
10. 320 520 ounces = _____ tones _____ pounds _____ ounces

Name _____ Date _____

M8. Length (British Units)

1 miles =1760 yard	1 yard = 3 feet	1 foot = 12 inches

1. 0.5 miles = _____ yards   42 feet = _____ yards
3. 1 yards = _____ inches   0.6 feet = _____ inches
5. 30 inches = _____ feet   0.3 yards = _____ inches
7. 0.02 miles = _____ yards   1 100 yards = _____ miles
9. 63 inches = _____ yards   2.5 yards = _____ inches
11. 3.5 feet = _____ inches   18 inches = _____ yards

Find the missing numbers.

1. 35 feet = _____ yards _____ feet
2. 28 inches = _____ feet _____ inches
3. 136 inches = _____ yards _____ feet _____ inches
4. 89 inches = _____ yards _____ feet _____ inches
5. 110 inches = _____ yards _____ feet _____ inches

Find the missing numbers.

1. 17 feet = 4 yards + _____ feet
2. 88 inches = 5 Feet + _____ inches
3. 29 feet = 7 yards + _____ feet
4. 97 inches = 2 yards + 2 feet + _____ inches
5. 185 inches = 4 yards + _____ feet + 17 inches
6. 165 inches = 3 yards + _____ feet + 21 inches

N. Plane Figures

N1. Directions

The little kitty got lost. Tell her where she should go.

1. If the kitty wants to find the shoe, she should go _____.

2. If she feels hungry, she should go _____ to buy a burger.

3. She can go _____ to shopping Mall to buy a cap for herself.

4. If she wants to go home, she should go _____.

5. The church is on the _____ of the shopping mall.

6. The shopping mall is on the _____ of the church.

7. The bus is on the _____ of the house.

8. The farm is on the _____ of the house.

9. The house is on the _____ of the farm.

10. The dog is on the _____ of the burger store.

11. If the bus drives to the church, it should go _____.

12. If the bus heads to the farm, it should go _____.

13. The dog misses his friends in the farm, he should go _____.

14. The dog goes east two blocks, then turn north one block, he can find a _____.

Name _____   Date _____

Connect in order.

1. A (1, 1) B (1, 6) C (4, 3)

   D (7, 6) E (7, 1)

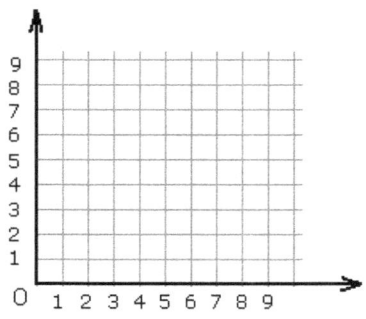

2. A (7, 5) B (2, 5)   C (2, 8)

   D (7, 8) E (7, 2)   F (2, 2)

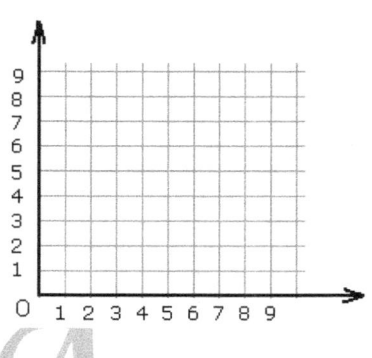

3. A (5, 2) B (3, 5) C (7, 5)

   D (5, 2) E (9, 2) F (5, 8)

   G (1, 2)   H (5, 2)

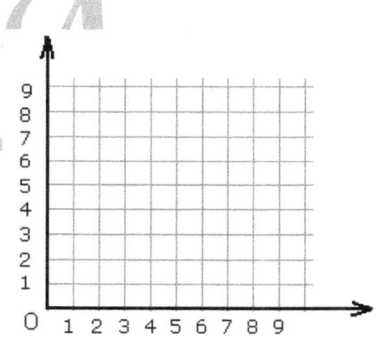

4. A (2, 8) B (3, 8) C (3, 7)

   D (4, 7) E (4, 8) F (5, 8)

   G (5, 7) H (6, 7) I (6, 8)

   J (7, 8 K (7, 6) L (6, 6)

   M (6, 2) N (7, 2) O (7, 1)

   P (2, 1) Q (2, 2) R (3, 2)

   S (3, 6) T (2, 6) U (2, 8)

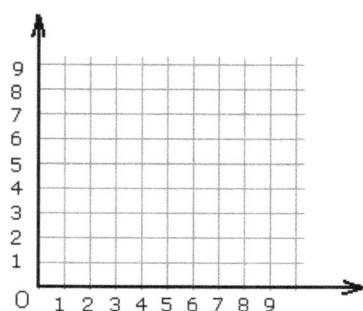

354

Name _____ Date _____

N2. Lines

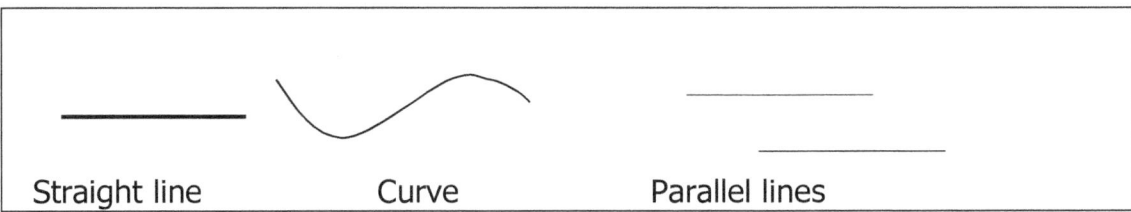

1. Matching.

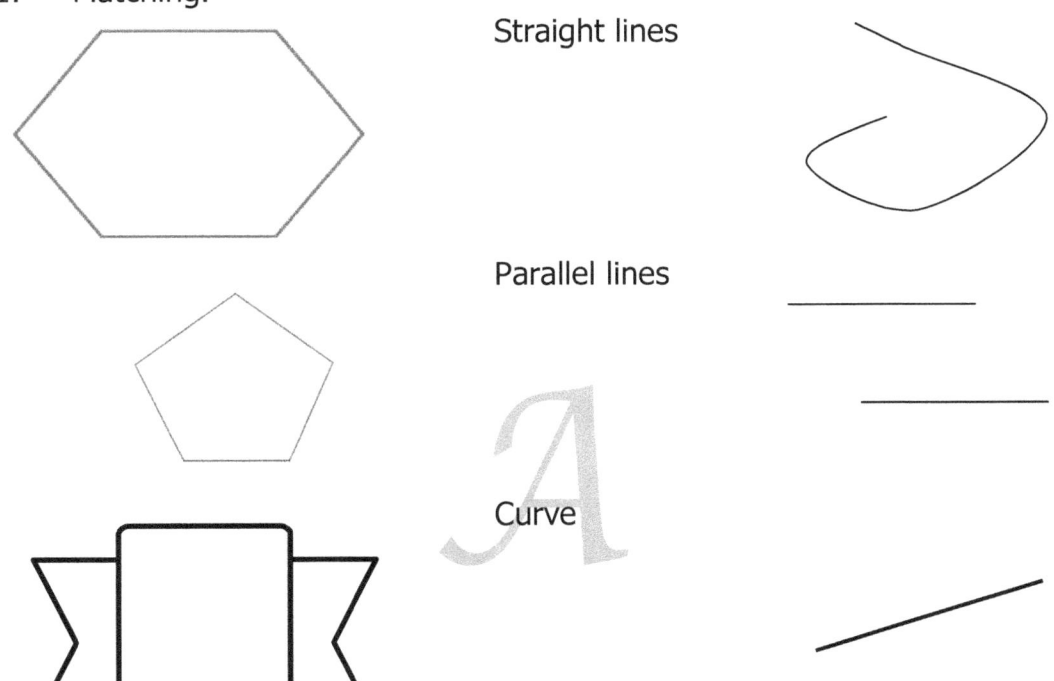

2. Write the name of the following lines.

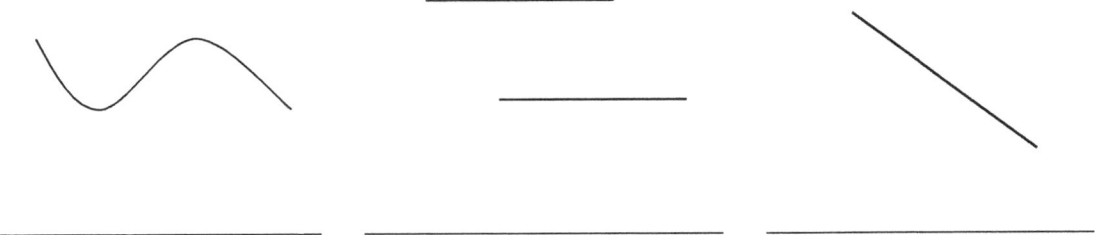

355

Name _____ Date _____

3. What kind of lines does each picture have?

	Straight line	Curve	Parallel lines
bell			
ruler			
star			
mushroom			

4. Draw line(s) through the following dots.

Straight line	Parallel lines	Curve
. B . A	. C . D	. . E F

Name _____ Date _____

Name of lines

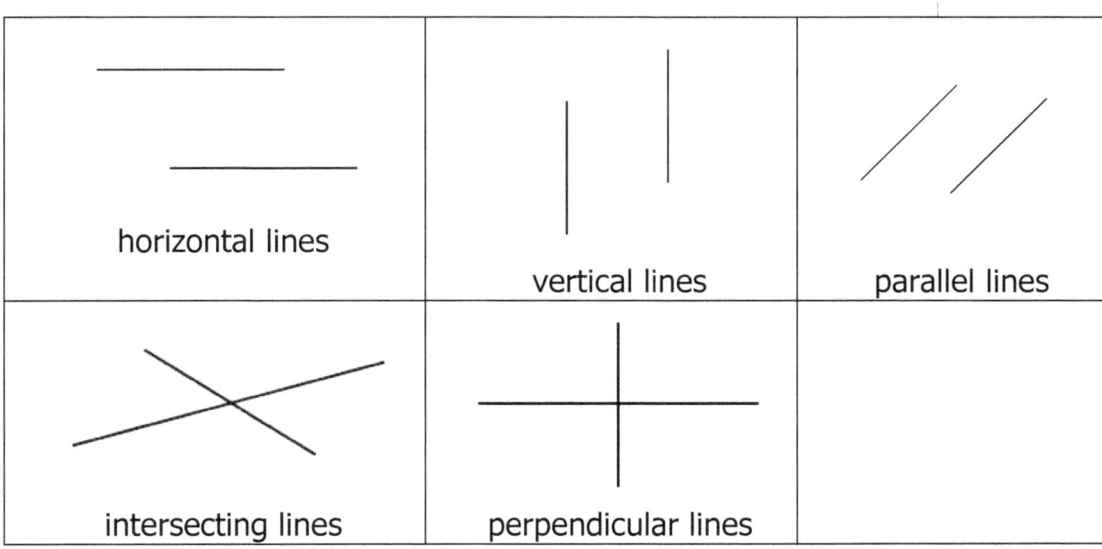

What types of lines can you find in each figure?

	horizontal lines	vertical lines	parallel lines	intersecting lines	perpendicular lines
⊞					
∦					
✕					
✳					

N3. Angles

An angle is formed when two rays meet with a common endpoint. An angle with a measure of 90 degrees is a right angle.

1. Arrange the following angles in order from the largest to the smallest. Put in 1, 2, and 3 to show.

a.

b.

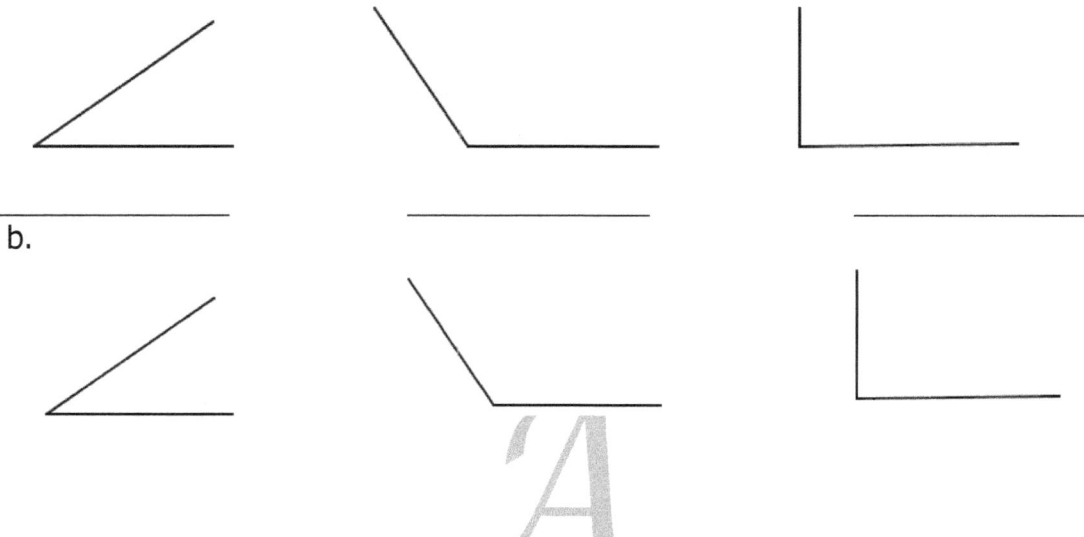

2. Find the number of right angles of the following figures.

   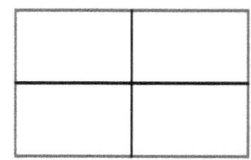   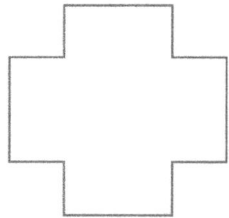

_____   _____   _____

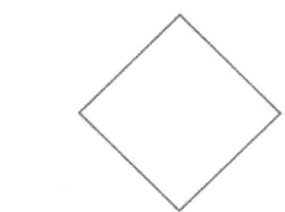   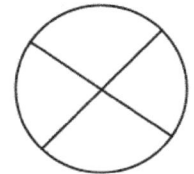   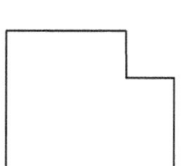

_____   _____   _____

Name _____   Date _____

Measure the following angles.

1.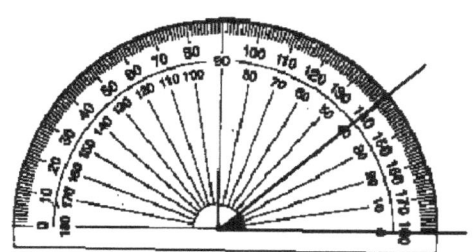

2.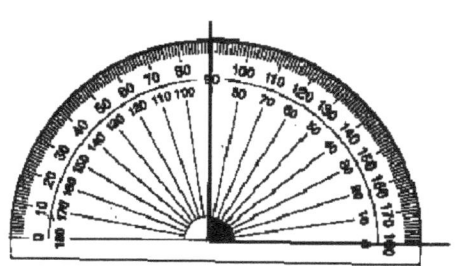

3.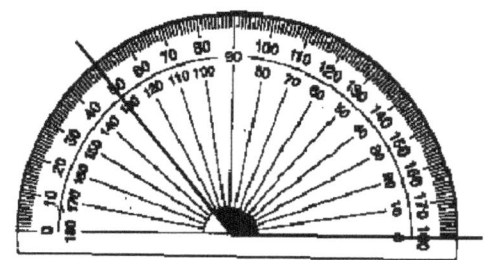

4.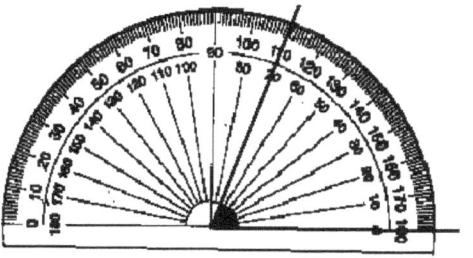

5.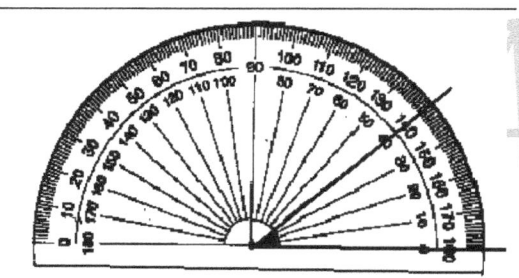

6.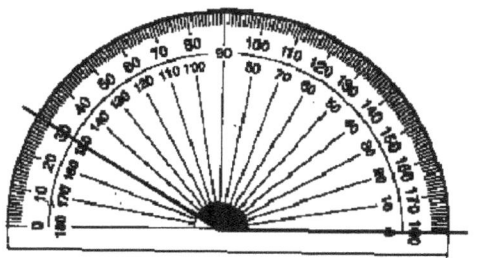

7.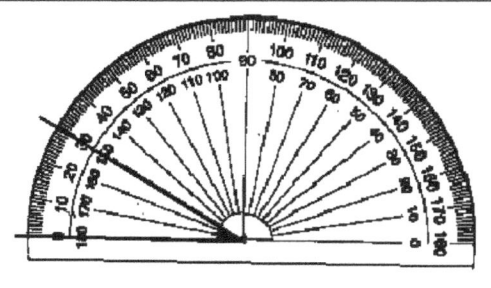

8.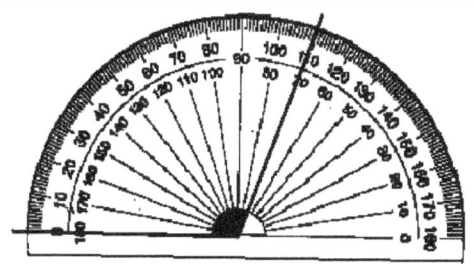

Name _____   Date _____

Measure the following angles.

9.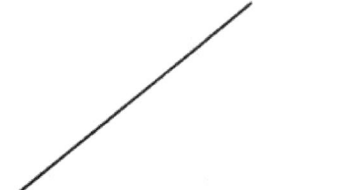

10.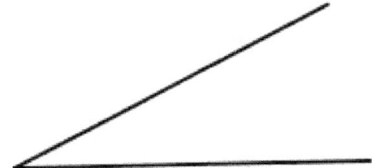

11.

12.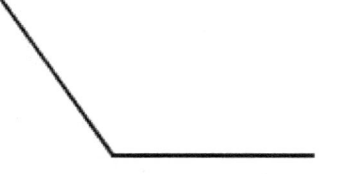

13.

14.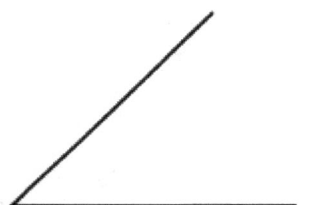

15.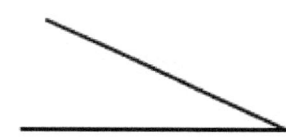

16.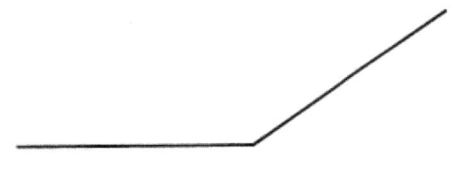

N4. Shapes

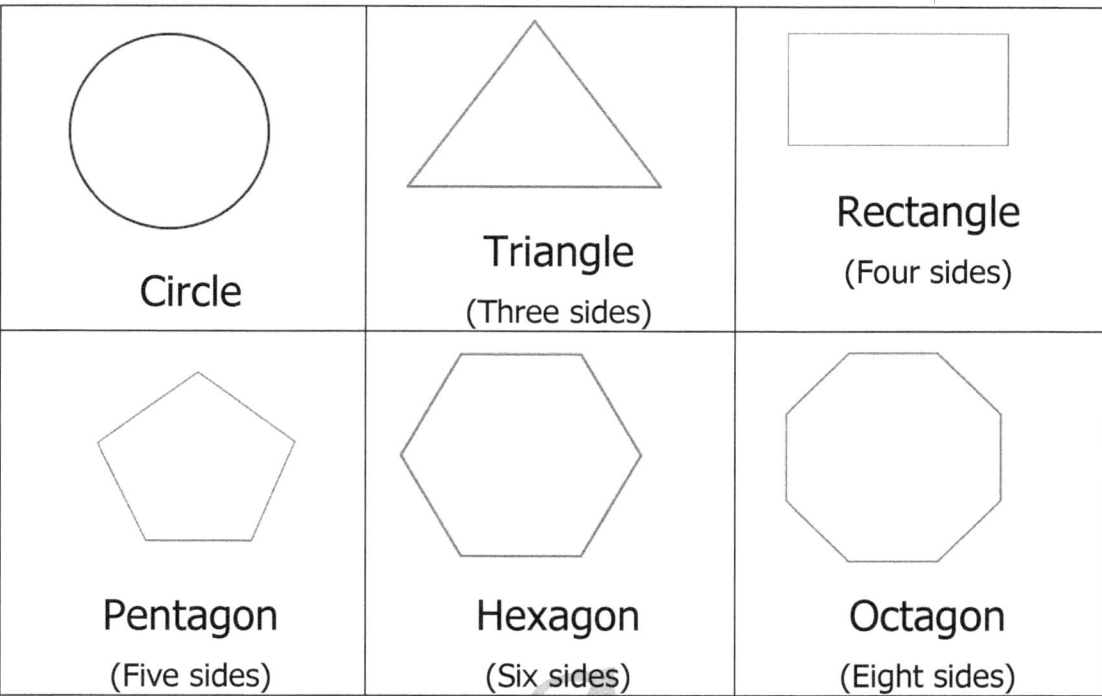

What kinds of shapes can you find in each figure?

	Circle	Triangle	Rectangle	Pentagon	Hexagon	Octagon

Name _____ Date _____

N5. Triangle

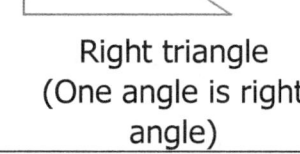 Right triangle (One angle is right angle)	 Isosceles triangle (Two equal sides)	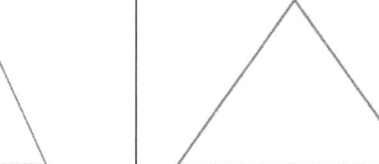 Equilateral triangle (Three equal sides)
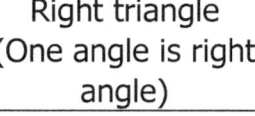 Isosceles right triangle (One right angle with two equal sides)	 Scalene triangle (No equal sides)	

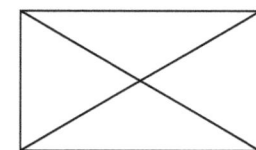

1. There are _____ right triangles.

2. There are _____ isosceles triangles.

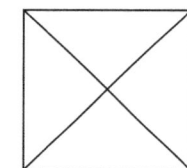

1. There are _____ isosceles right triangles.

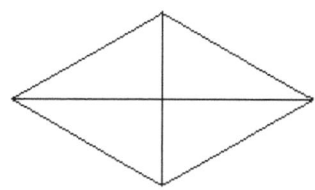

1. There are _____ right triangles.

2. There are _____ isosceles triangles.

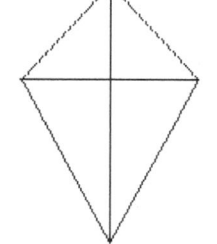

1. There are _____ right triangles.

2. There are _____ isosceles triangles.

Name _____   Date _____

N6. Quadrilaterals

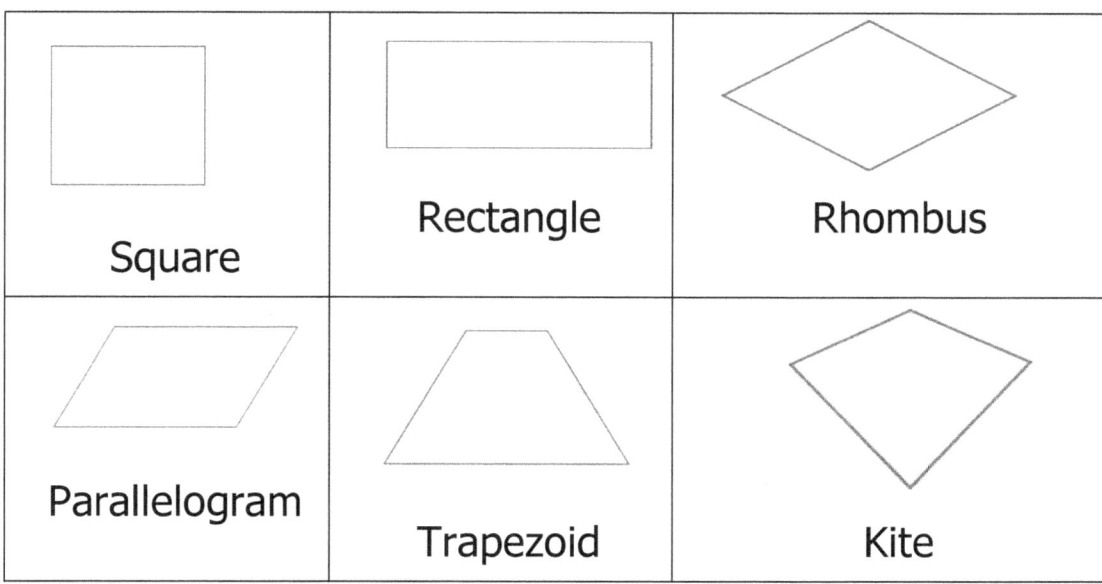

1. How many different rectangles are there?

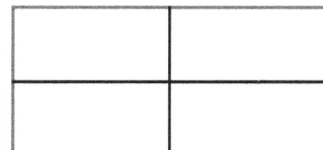

2. How many different triangles are there?

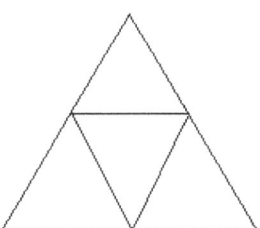

3. How many different squares are there?

Name _____ Date _____

4. Match.

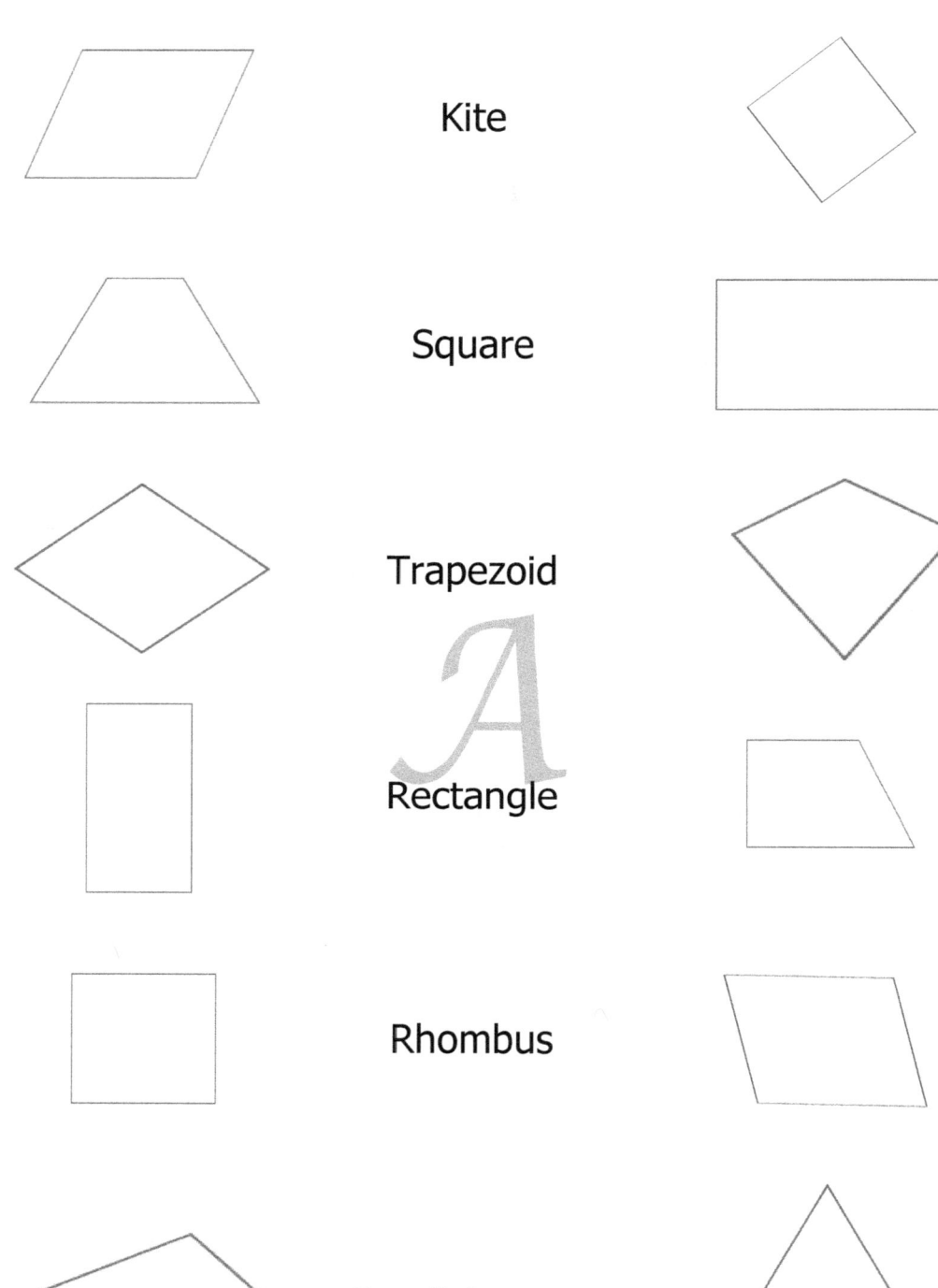

Name _____   Date _____

Shapes

The figure shown below is Chinese Tangram. It is made up seven pieces. Observe carefully and fill in the blanks.

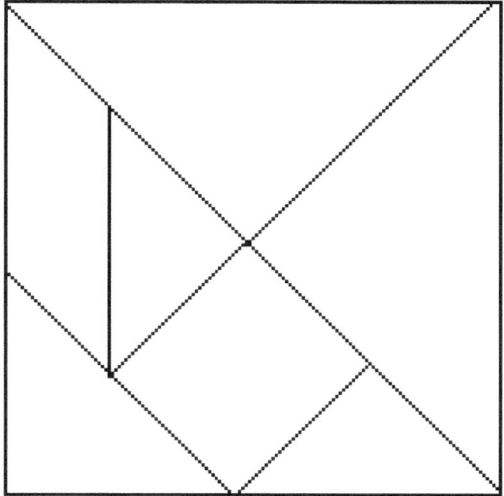

1. There are _____ triangles in the graph.

2. There are _____ squares in the graph.

3. There are (is) _____ parallelogram(s) in the graph.

4. There are _____ trapezoids in the graph.

Name _____   Date _____

Complete the following chart to show the properties of each quadrilateral.

	Name	# of parallel sides	# of equal sides	# of equal angles
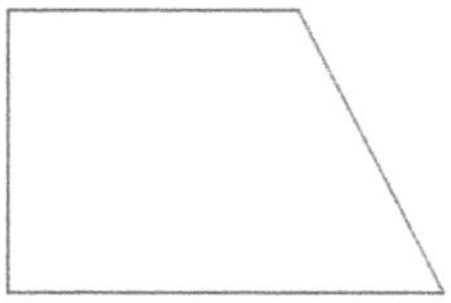				
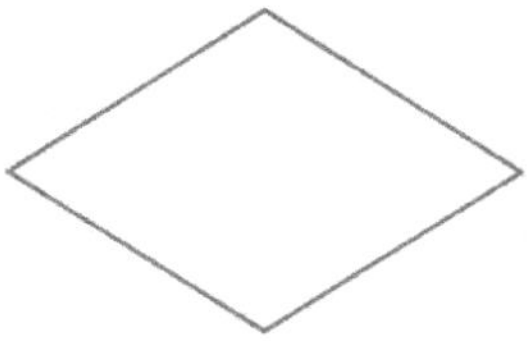				
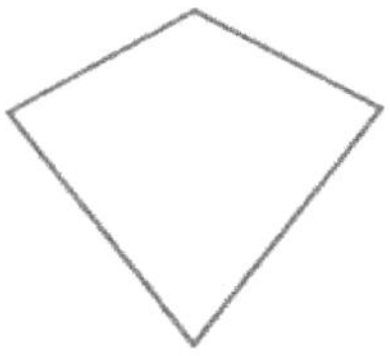				
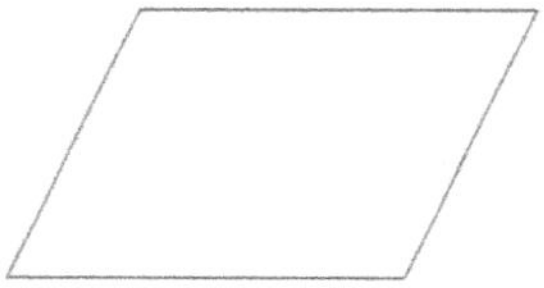				
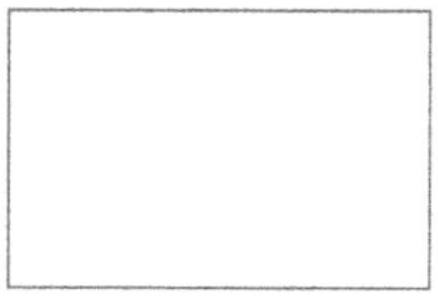				
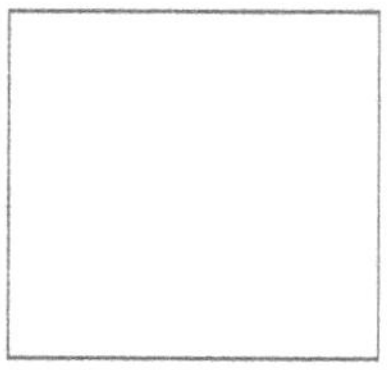				

Name _____   Date _____

Draw the quadrilateral according each description.

2 pairs of parallel sides and 2 pairs of equal sides	2 pairs of parallel sides and 4 equal sides
4 right angles and 2 pairs of equal sides	4 right angles and 4 equal sides
2 pairs of opposite equal sides and 2 pairs of opposite equal angles	2 pairs of adjacent equal sides and 1 pairs of opposite equal angles
1 pair of parallel sides and no equal sides	2 pairs of opposite equal angles and 4 equal sides

N7. Slide

Horizontal slide

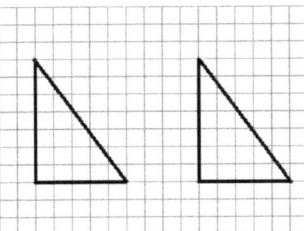

Vertical slide

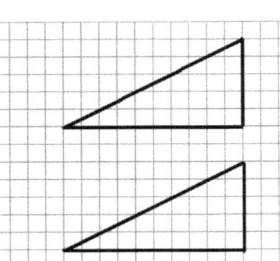

Diagonal slide

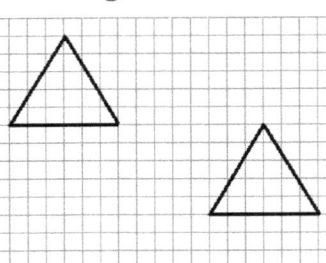

Indicate whether each slide a horizontal, a vertical, or a diagonal slide.

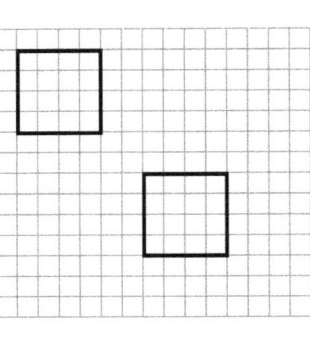

_____

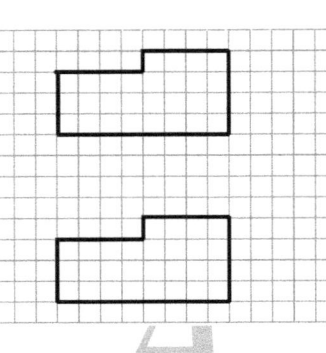

_____

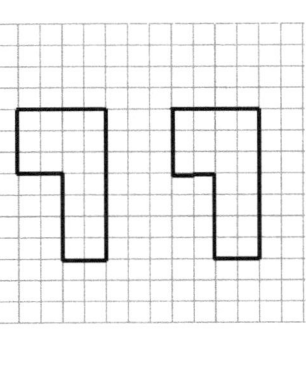

_____

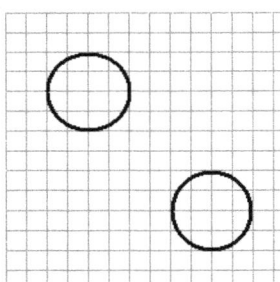

_____

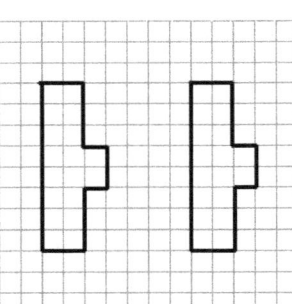

_____

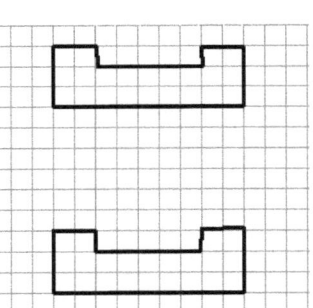

_____

N8. Turn

Point C is a turn centre. Figure A turns from A to B around C,

A quarter turn clockwise or three quarter turn counter clockwise	Half turn	Three quarter turn clockwise or a quarter turn counter clockwise
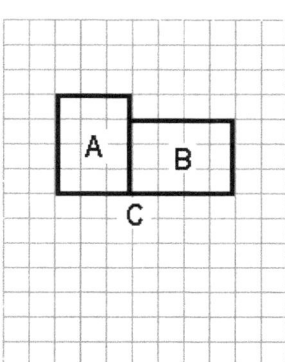	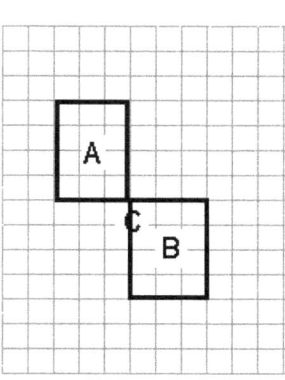	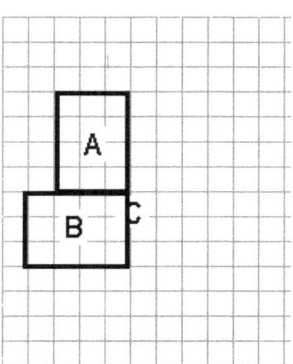

Each figure turns from A to B. Indicate whether each turn is a quarter turn, half turn, or a three quarter turn clockwise about point O.

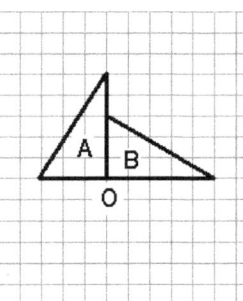 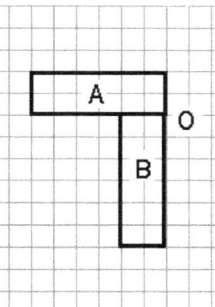 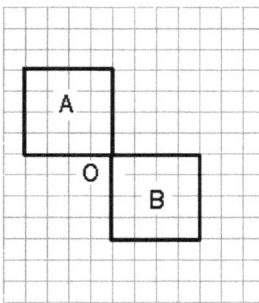

_____ _____ _____

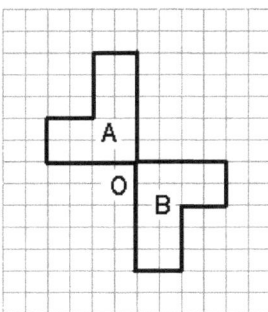 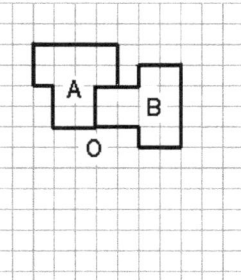 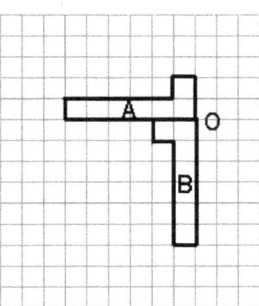

_____ _____ _____

N9. Reflection

Draw the other half of each symmetrical shape.

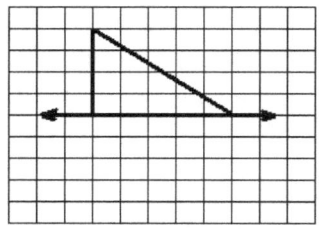 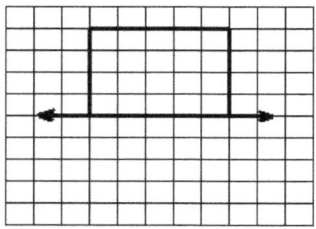 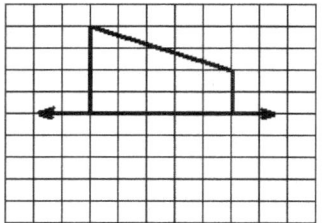

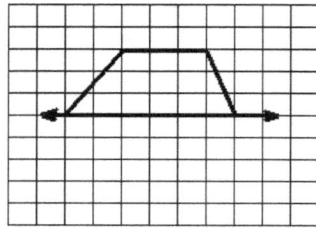 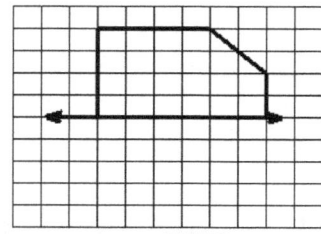 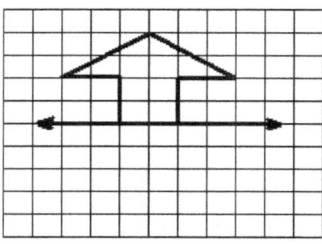

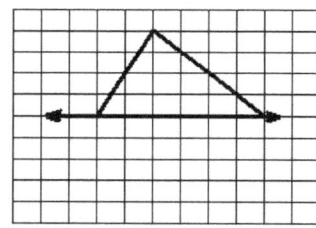 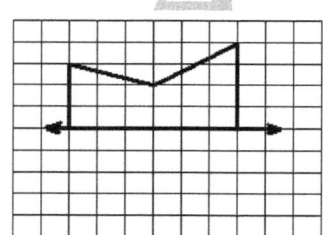 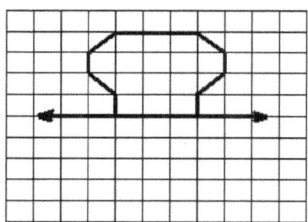

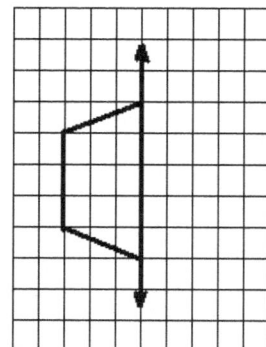 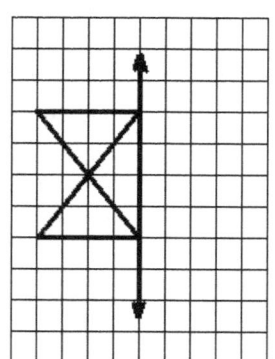 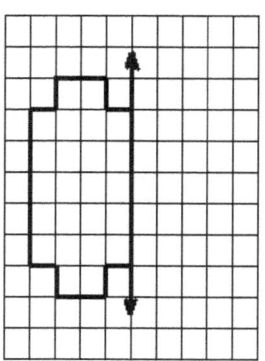

Name _____   Date _____

N10. Symmetry lines

Find all the lines of symmetry for each of the following figures.

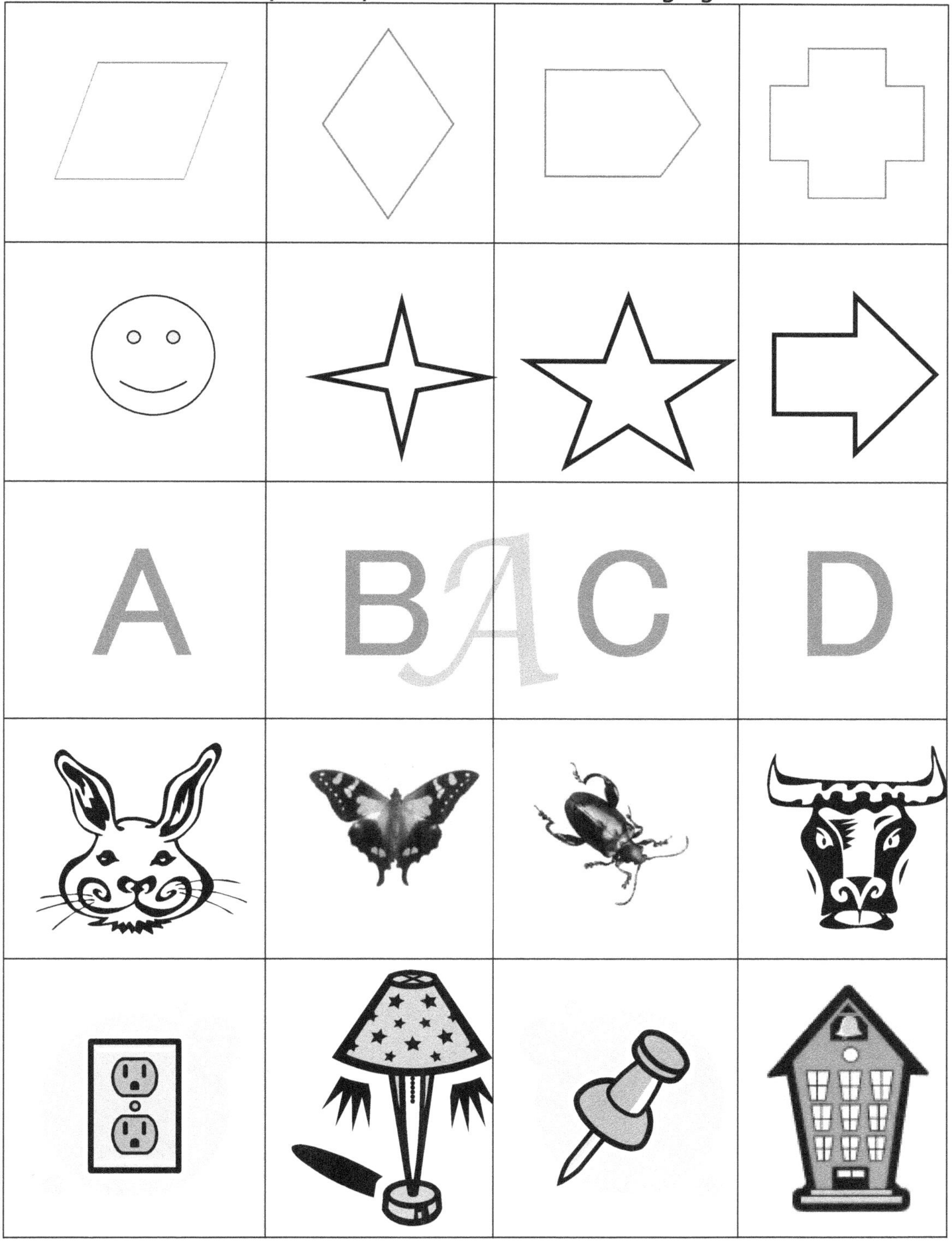

371

Name _____ Date _____

Decide whether each figure is a slide, a turn, or a reflection of figure A.

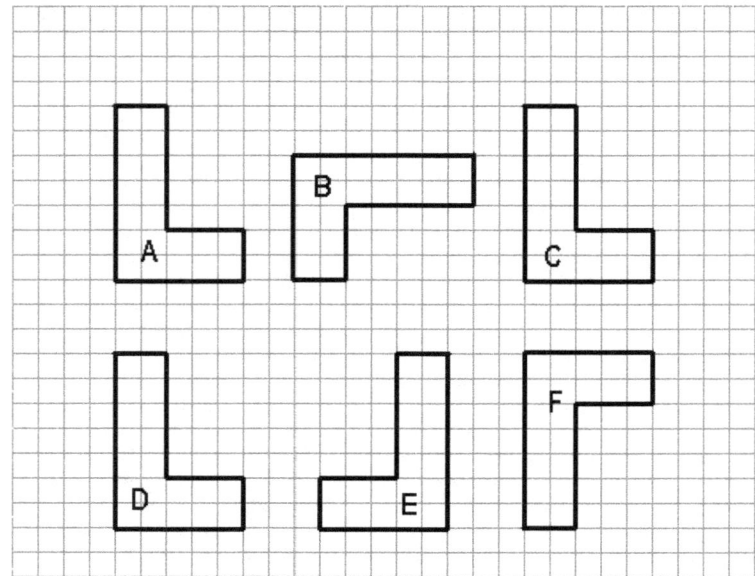

1. Figure B is a _____ of figure A.

2. Figure C is a _____ of figure A.

3. Figure D is a _____ of figure A.

4. Figure E is a _____ of figure D.

5. Figure F is a _____ of figure E.

N11. Congruent figures

If figures have the same size and same shape, then these figures are congruent.
Example:

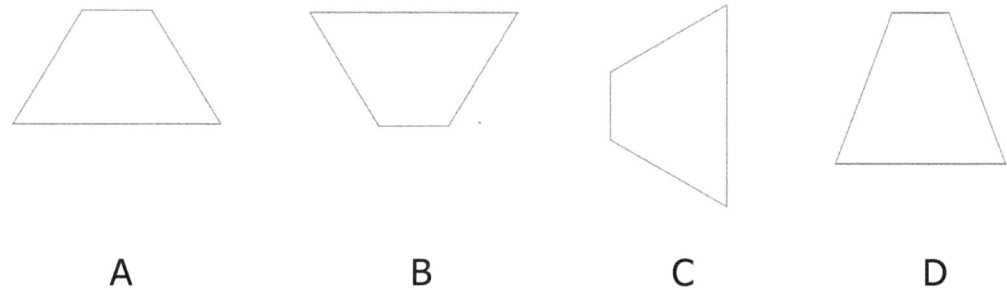

Figure A, B, and C are congruent because they have the same size and same shape.
Figure D is not congruent to A, B, or C, because they have different sizes.

Find all the pairs of congruent figures

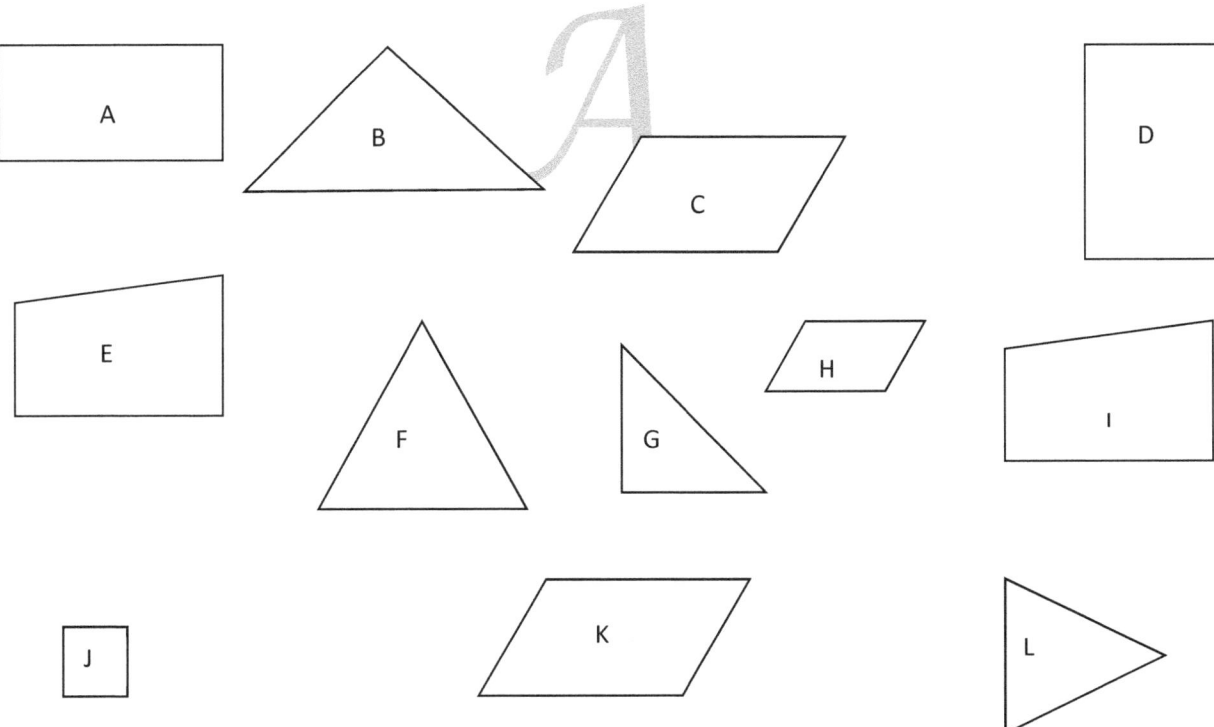

Name _____ Date _____

Divide the following figures into 2 congruent parts.

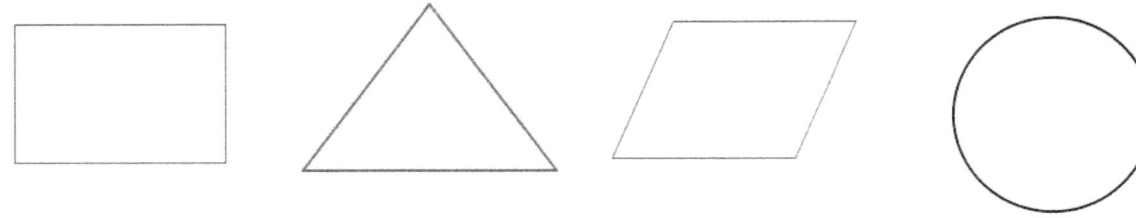

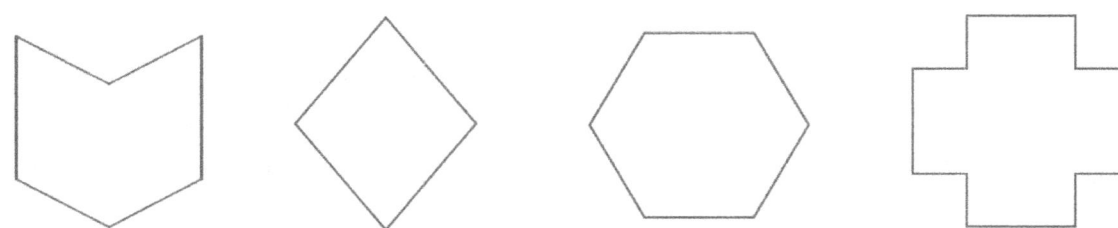

Divide the following figures into 4 congruent parts.

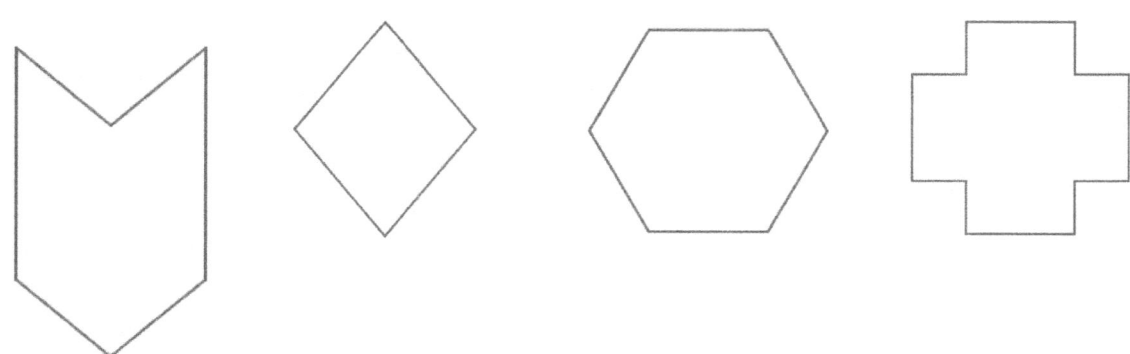

374

Name ________________ Date ________________

Find the figure that is congruent to the figure on the left.

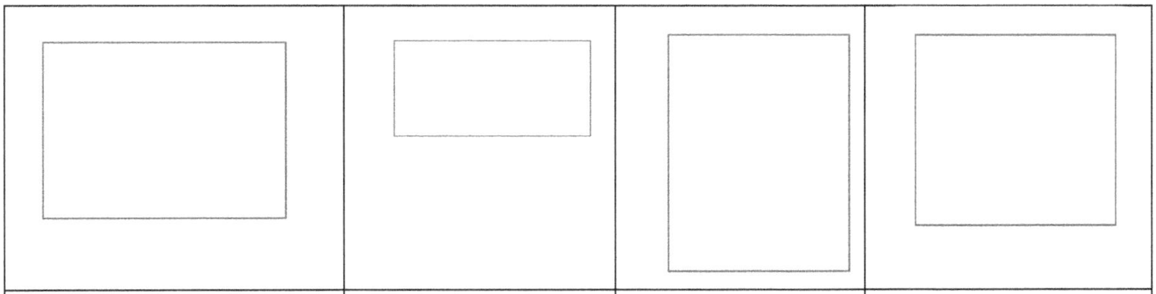

A B C

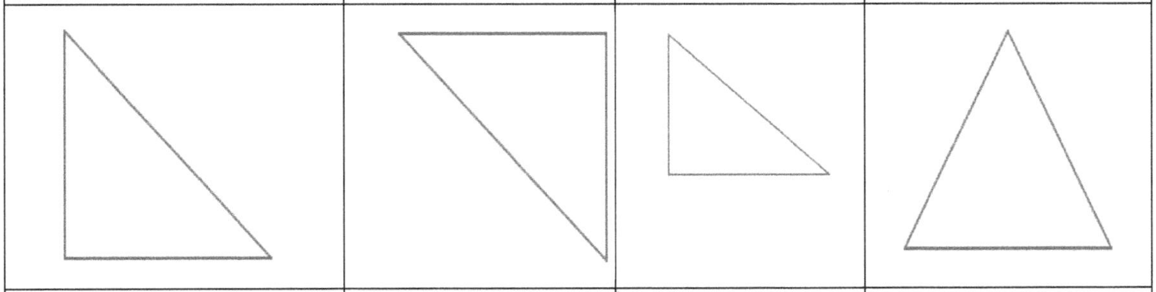

A B C

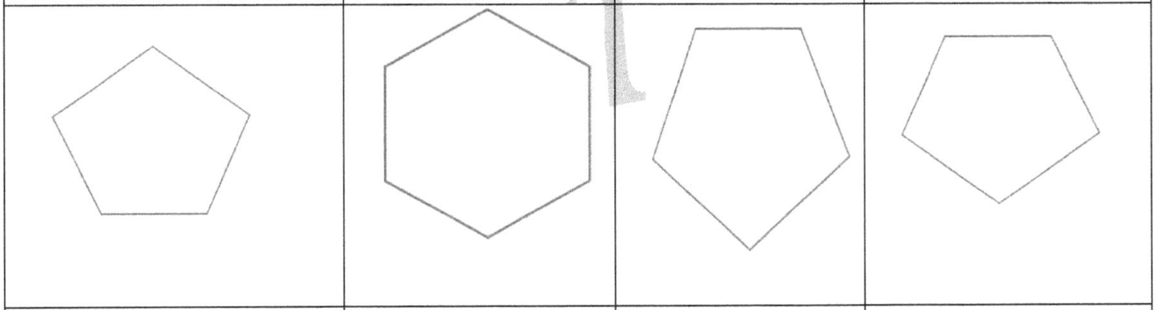

A B C

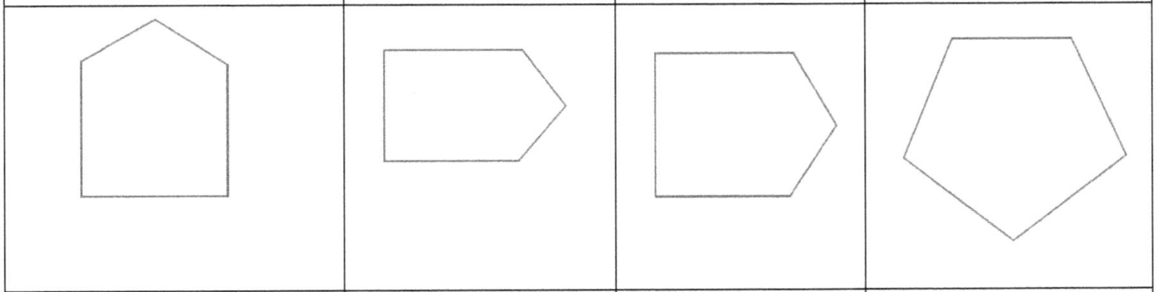

A B C

Name ______________ Date ______________

N12. Similar figures

If all the figures have the same shape but different sizes, then these figures are similar.

Find the figure that is similar to the figure on the left.

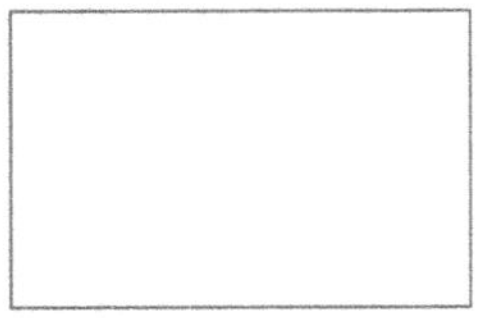		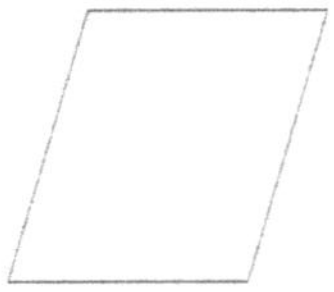	
	A	B	C
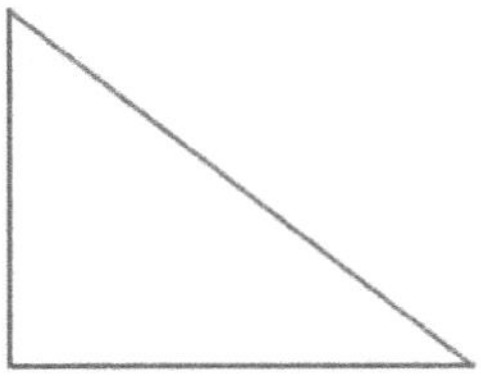	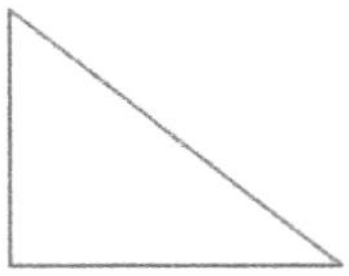	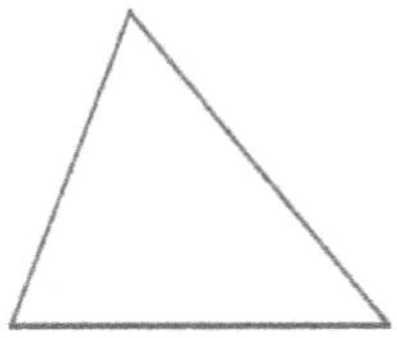	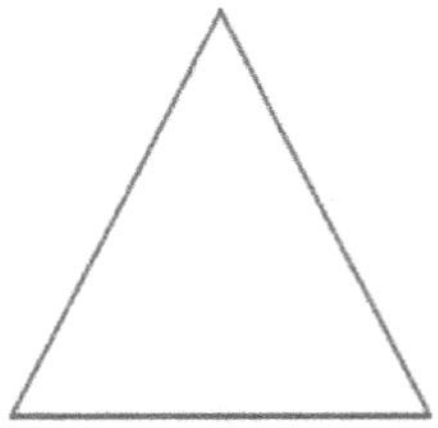
	A	B	C
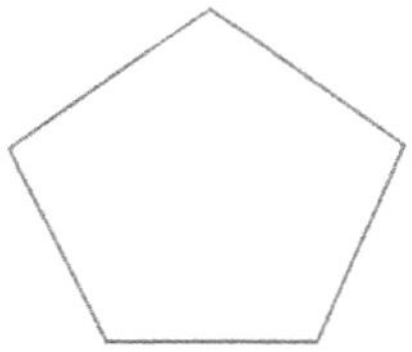	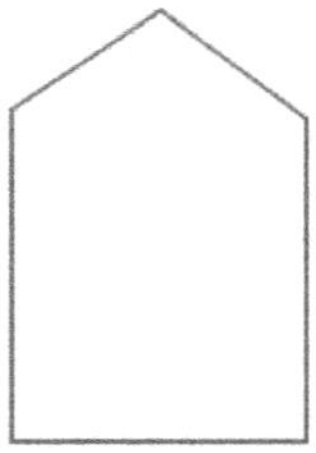	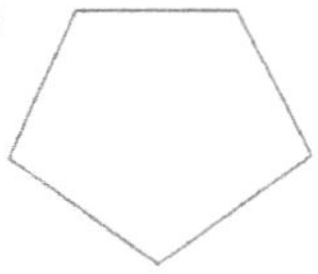	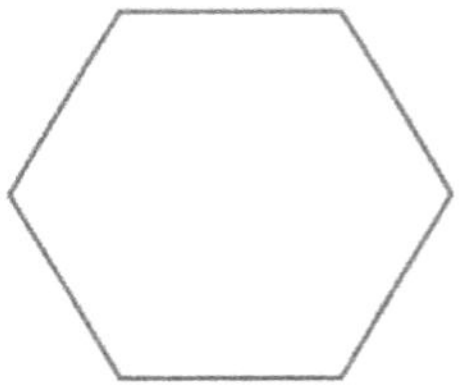
	A	B	C
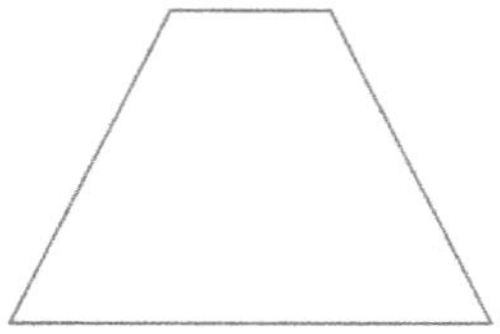	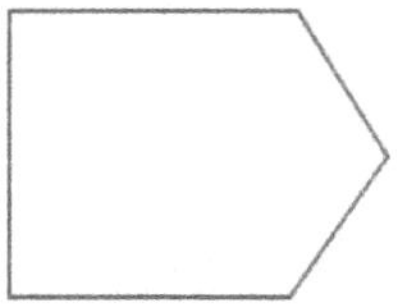	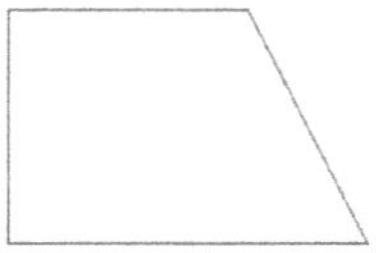	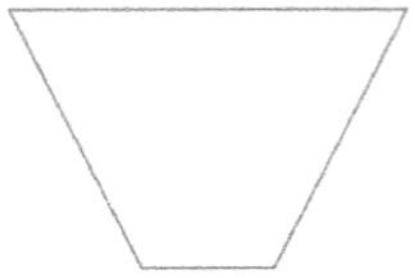
	A	B	C

Name _____ Date _____

O. Perimeter and Area

O1. Perimeter

Perimeter is the distance around the figure.

1. Draw the perimeter of the following figure with a colour pen.

 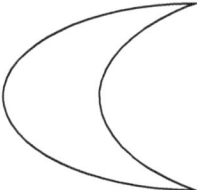

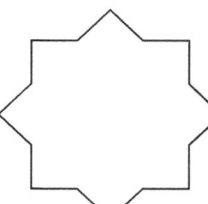 

2. The side of each small square is 1 cm. Find the perimeters of the following shapes.

1.

_____ cm

2.
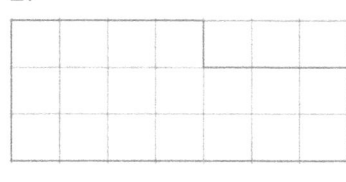
_____ cm

3.
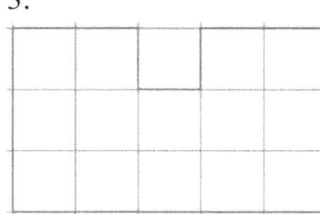
_____ cm

4.
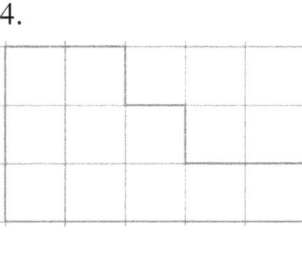
_____ cm

5.

_____ cm

6.
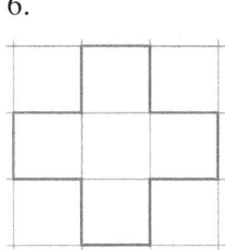
_____ cm

377

Perimeter

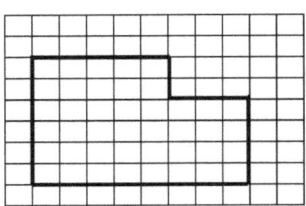
Perimeter =

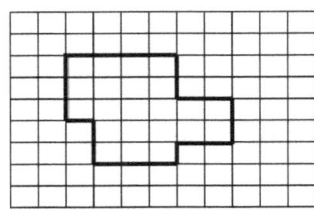
Perimeter =

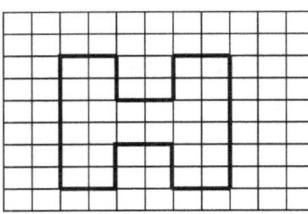
Perimeter =

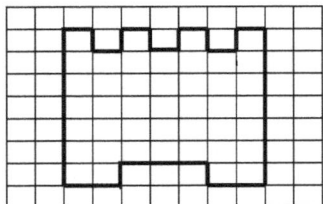
Perimeter =

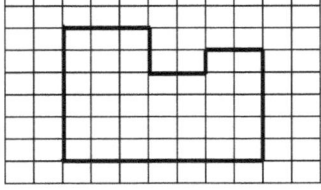
Perimeter =

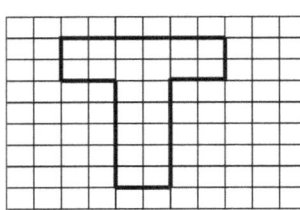
Perimeter =

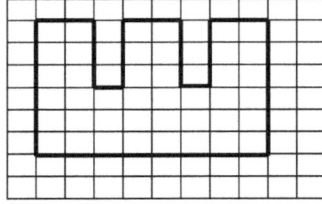
Perimeter =

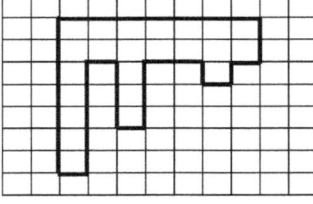
Perimeter =

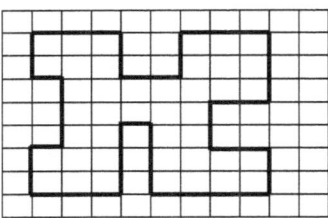
Perimeter =

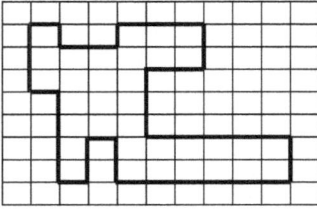
Perimeter =

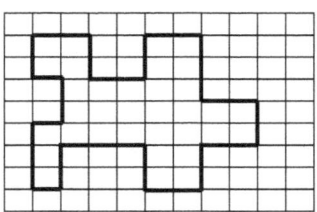
Perimeter =

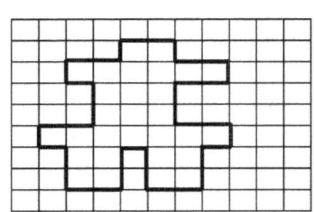
Perimeter =

Name _____   Date _____

Measure the lengths of each side, then find the perimeter of each figure.

Perimeter
=____cm+____cm+____cm+____cm
=

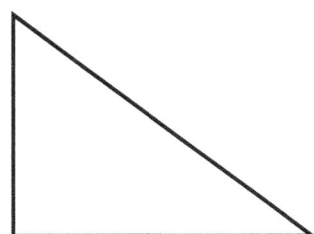

Perimeter
=____cm+____cm+____cm
=

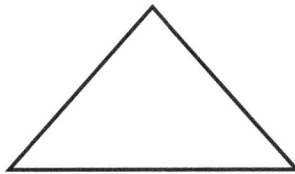

Perimeter
=____cm+____cm+____cm
=

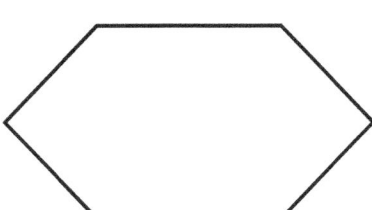

Perimeter =
____cm+____cm+____cm+ ____cm
+____cm+____cm
=

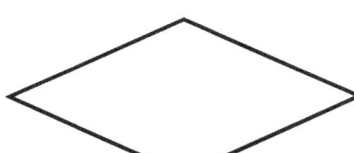

Perimeter
=____cm+____cm+____cm+____cm
=

Perimeter =____cm+____cm+____cm
+____cm+____cm
=

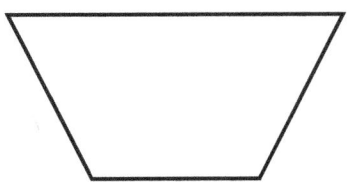

Perimeter=____cm+____cm+____cm
+____cm+____cm
=

Perimeter =____cm+____cm+____cm
+____cm +____cm +____cm
=

Perimeter of a Rectangle

Perimeter of a rectangle = 2 × (Length + Width)

6cm / 4cm
Perimeter = 2×(__ + __) = ___ cm

8cm / 5cm
Perimeter = 2×(__ + __) = ___ cm

12cm / 6cm
Perimeter =

4cm / 1cm
Perimeter =

12cm / 16cm
Perimeter =

14cm / 12cm
Perimeter =

20cm / 25cm
Perimeter =

24cm / 18cm
Perimeter =

Perimeter of a Square

Perimeter of a square = 4 × side Length

Perimeter = 4 × ___ = ____ cm

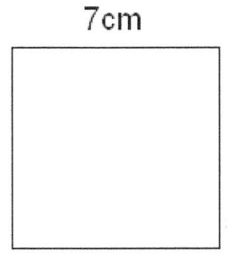

Perimeter = 4 × ___ = ____ cm

Perimeter =

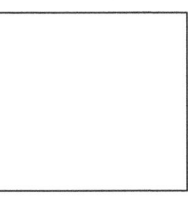

Perimeter =

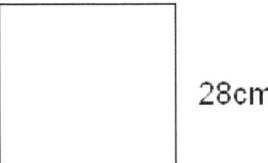

Perimeter =

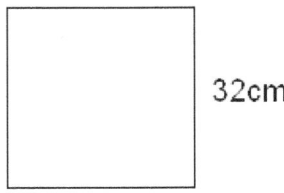

Perimeter =

Perimeter =

Perimeter =

Name _____   Date _____

O2. Area

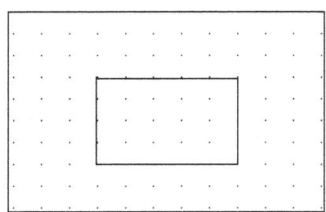
Area =

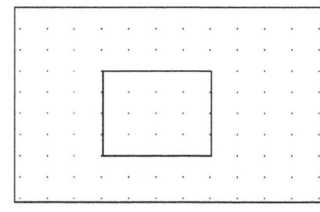
Area =

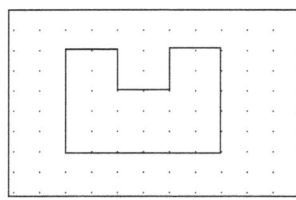
Area =

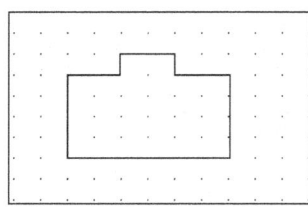
Area =

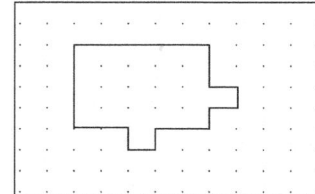
Area =

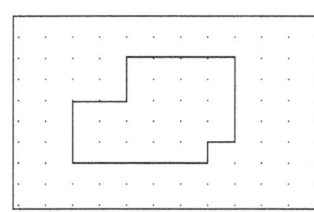
Area =

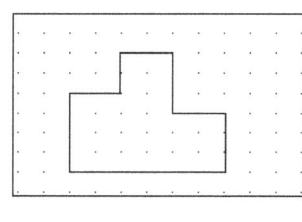
Area =

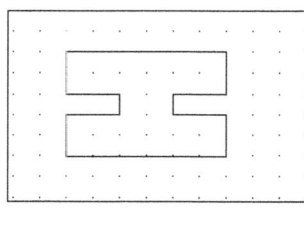
Area =

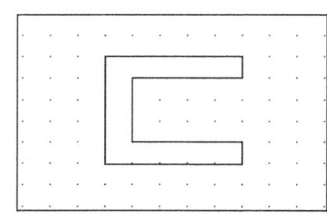
Area =

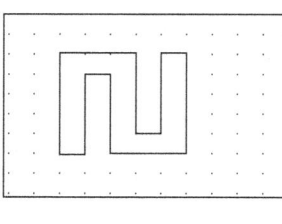
Area =

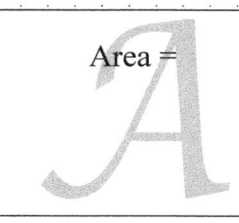
Area =

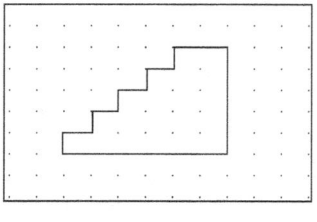
Area =

382

Area

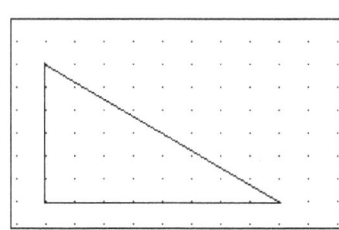

Area =

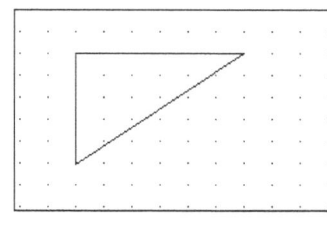

Area =

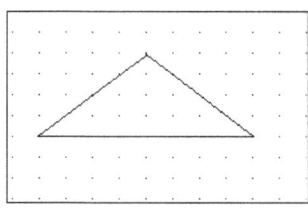

Area =

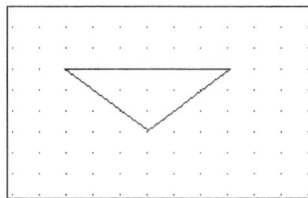

Area =

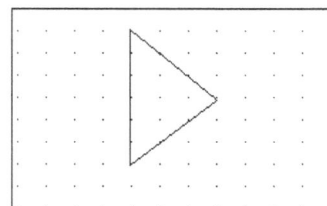

Area =

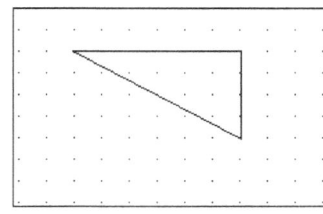

Area =

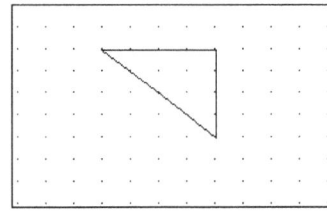

Area =

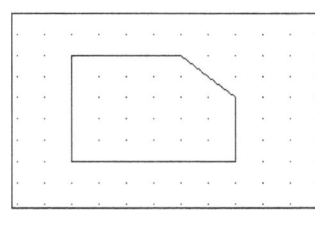

Area =

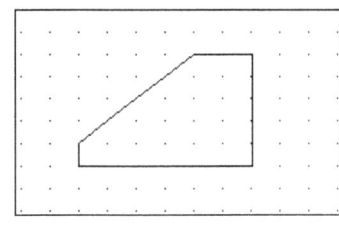

Area =

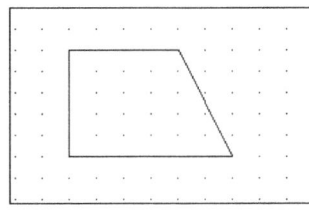

Area =

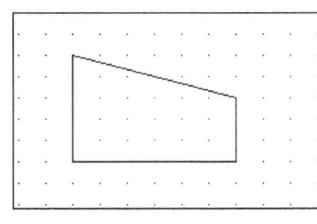

Area =

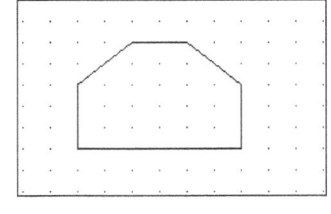

Area =

Name _____ Date _____

Area

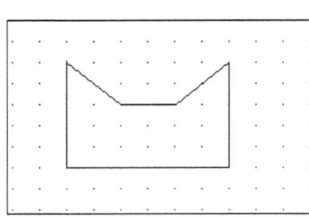

Area =

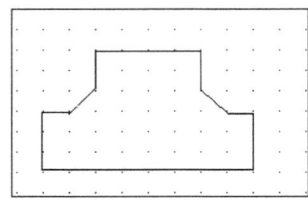

Area =

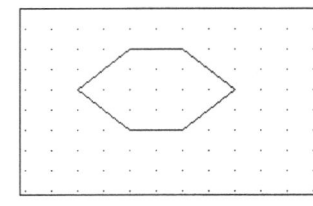

Area =

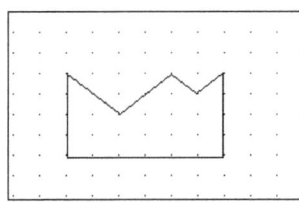

Area =

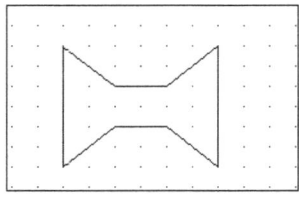

Area =

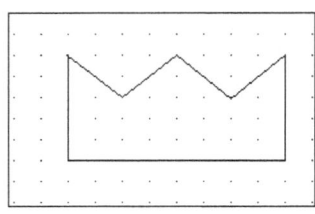

Area =

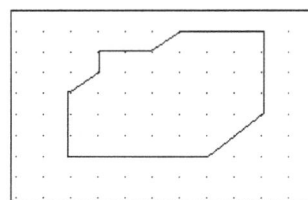

Area =

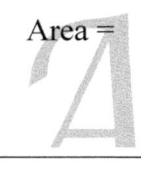

Area =

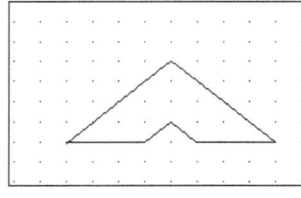

Area =

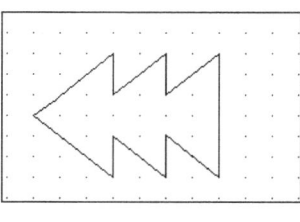

Area =

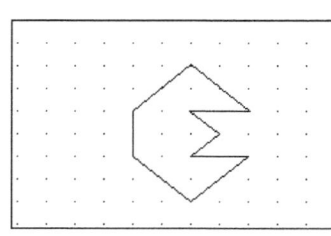

Area =

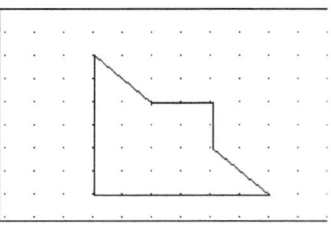

Area =

Name _____ Date _____

Area of a Rectangle

Area of a rectangle = Length × Width

7cm
4cm

13cm
16cm

Area = ___ × ___ = _____ cm^2

Area = ___ × ___ = _____ cm^2

28cm
15cm

24m
22m

Area = cm^2

Area = m^2

16cm
5cm

20m
10m

Area = cm^2

Area = m^2

11cm
25cm

33m
21m

Area = cm^2

Area = m^2

Name _____   Date _____

Find the perimeter and area of each rectangle.

1. 12cm wide, 15cm long

Perimeter = _____cm

Area = _____ cm²

2. 14cm wide, 20cm long

Perimeter = _____cm

Area = _____ cm²

3. 24cm wide, 36cm long

Perimeter = _____

Area = _____

4. 31cm wide, 40cm long

Perimeter = _____

Area = _____

5. 32m wide, 45m long

Perimeter = _____

Area = _____

6. 100m wide, 120m long

Perimeter = _____

Area = _____

7. 15km wide, 30km long

Perimeter = _____

Area = _____

8. 40km wide, 140km long

Perimeter = _____

Area = _____

9. 400cm wide, 500cm long

Perimeter = _____

Area = _____

10. 72km wide, 150km long

Perimeter = _____

Area = _____

Name _____   Date _____

Area of a square

| Area of a square = side Length × side length |

6cm
[square]

12cm
[square]

Area = ___ × ___ = _____ cm²

Area = ___ × ___ = _____ cm²

15m
[square]

[square] 25cm

Area = m²

Area = cm²

[square] 18m

[square] 28cm

Area = m²

Area = cm²

33m
[square]

42cm
[square]

Area = m²

Area = cm²

Name _____   Date _____

Find the perimeter and area of each square.

1. Side length 20cm

Perimeter = _____ cm

Area = _____ cm^2

2. Side length 50cm

Perimeter = _____ cm

Area = _____ cm^2

3. Side length 13cm

Perimeter = _____

Area = _____

4. Side length 48m

Perimeter = _____

Area = _____

5. Side length 63km

Perimeter = _____

Area = _____

6. Side length 36km

Perimeter = _____

Area = _____

7. Side length 28cm

Perimeter = _____

Area = _____

8. Side length 32m

Perimeter = _____

Area = _____

9. Side length 37km

Perimeter = _____

Area = _____

10. Side length 93km

Perimeter = _____

Area = _____

Name _____ Date _____

O3. Area and perimeter

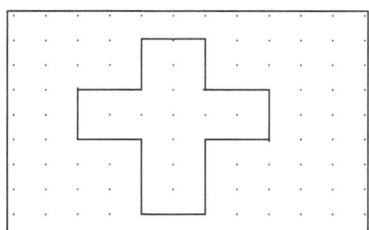

Perimeter _____ units
Area _____ units²

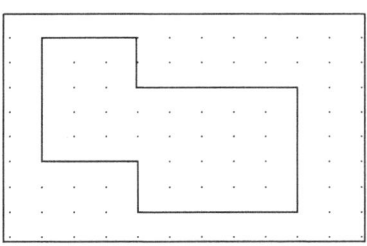

Perimeter _____ units
Area _____ units²

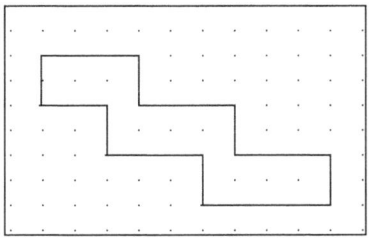

Perimeter _____ units
Area _____ units²

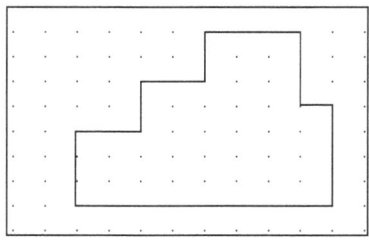

Perimeter _____ units
Area _____ units²

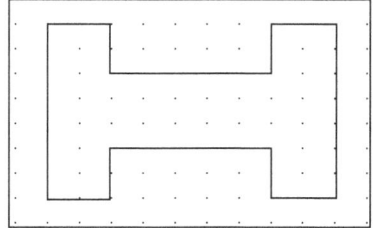

Perimeter _____ units
Area _____ units²

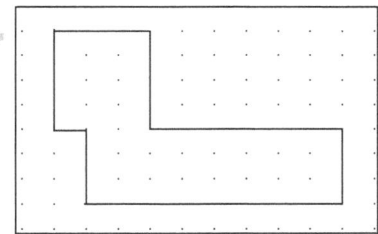

Perimeter _____ units
Area _____ units²

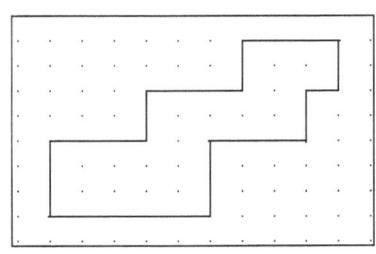

Perimeter _____ units
Area _____ units²

Name _____ Date _____

Fill in the missing value of each rectangle.

	Length	Width	Perimeter	Area
1.	8	4		
2.	12	7		
3.	8		24	
4.		6	30	
5.	8			56
6.		5		65
7.			20	24
8.			48	80

Fill in the missing values of each square.

	Side length	Perimeter	Area
1.	4		
2.	7		
3.		36	
4.		48	
5.			49
6.			81

Name _____   Date _____

Area and Perimeter

1. Averill Garden is in the shape of a rectangle measuring 30m by 40m. The owner wants to fence the Garden, how many meters of fence does he need to buy?

2. Mystery City is in the shape of a square. The length of each side is 180km. There is a road around the city. How long is the road?

3. A field is in the shape of a triangle. The total distance around the field is 480m. What is the length of the missing side?

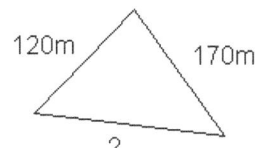

4. Janet walks her dog around a block 4 times a day. The block is 240m long and 320m wide. What is the total distance does she walk with her dog every day?

5. A table is 120cm long and 60cm wide. Lucy wants to cover the table with a table cloth. At least how much cloth does she need?

6. Nick wants to floor his bedroom. His bedroom is 15m long and 11m wide. How many square meters of wood panel does he need?

Name _____ Date _____

7. A basketball court measures 40m by 20m. What is the perimeter of the court?

   What is the area of the court?

8. A volleyball court measures 18m by 9m. What is the perimeter of the court?

   What is the area of the court?

9. The distance around a tennis court is 100m. It is 30 meters long. What is the width of the court?

10. A bear pen is 9m long. If its area is 108m². What is the width of the court?

    What is the perimeter of the court?

11. Linda wants to build a fence for her backyard against the wall of her house. The wall is 12m long. If she needs 30m fence. What is the width of her backyard?

    What is the area of her backyard?

12. Lois wants to fence his rectangular garden against the river. No fence is needed along the river. The area of the garden is 240m². The length along the river is 40m. What is the width of his garden?

    What is the total length of his fence?

P. Solids

P1. Name of solids

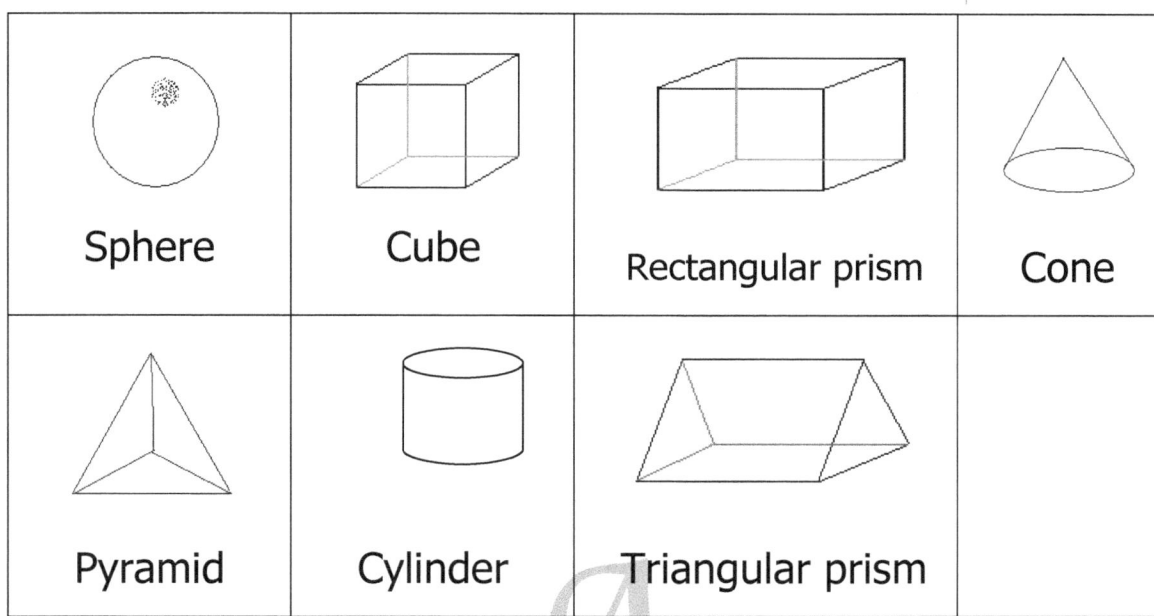

Write the names of the following solids.

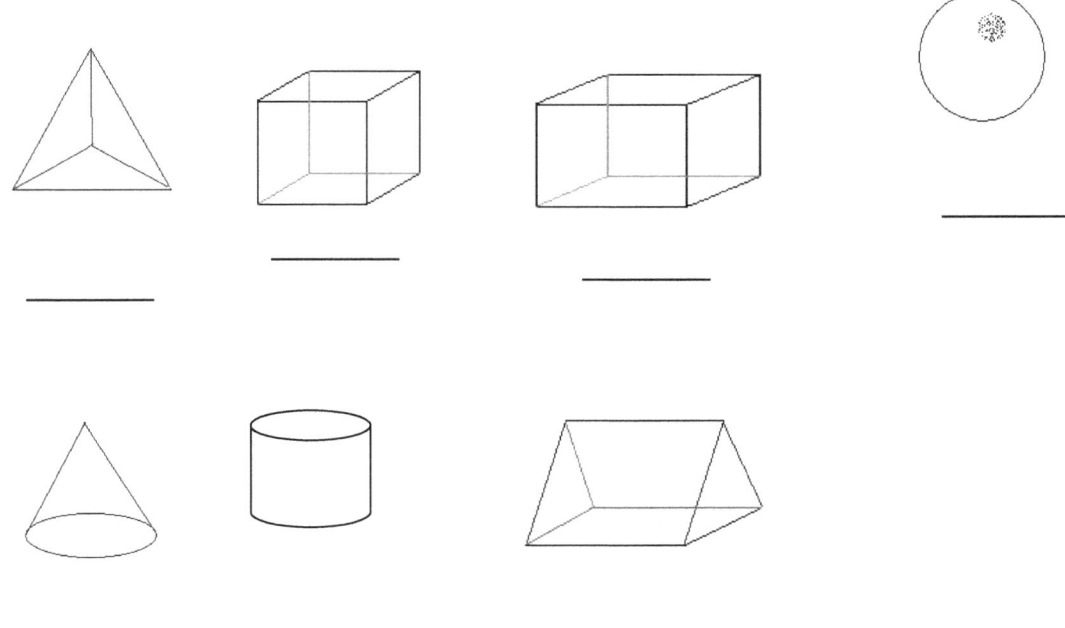

P2. Pyramids or prisms

Prism is a solid figure whose bases have the same size and shape and are parallel to one another, joined by parallelogram faces. 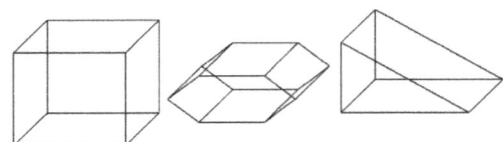	Pyramid is a solid figure whose polygonal bases are bounded by triangular faces which meet at a vertex 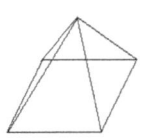 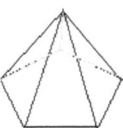 
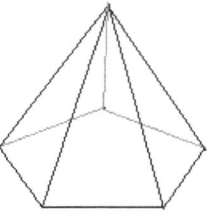 a. pyramid b. prism	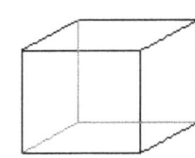 a. pyramid b. prism
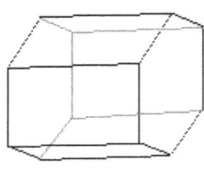 a. pyramid b. prism	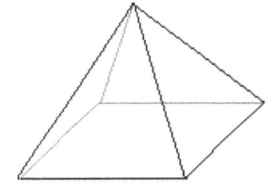 a. pyramid b. prism
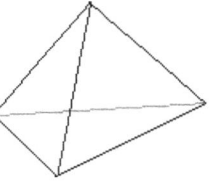 a. pyramid b. prism	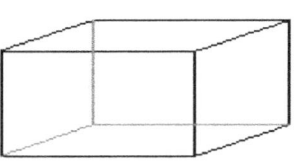 a. pyramid b. prism
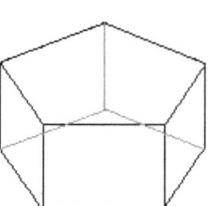 a. pyramid b. prism	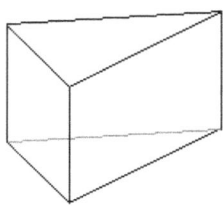 a. pyramid b. prism

Name _____ Date _____

1. Matching.

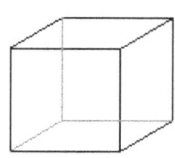   **Triangular Prism**

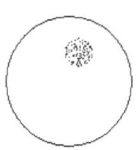   **Pyramid**

   **Cube**

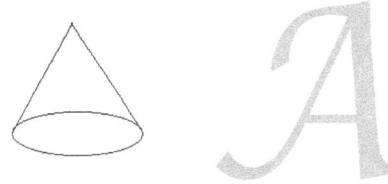   **Rectangular prism**

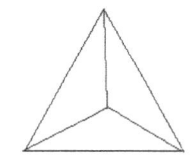   **Cone**

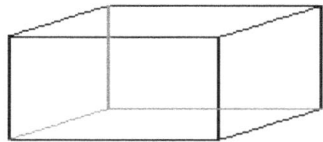   **Sphere**

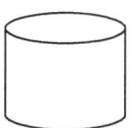   **Cylinder**

Name _____ Date _____

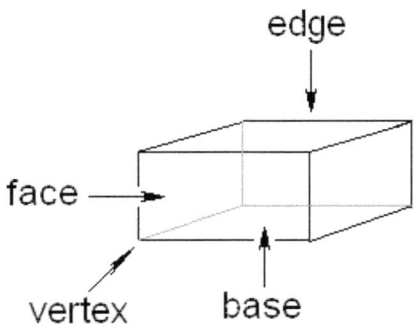

Complete the following chart.

Shape	Name	Number of faces	Number of edges	Number of vertices
(cube)				
(triangular prism)				
(triangular pyramid)				
(rectangular prism)				
(pentagonal prism)				

Matching each solid with their tracing faces.

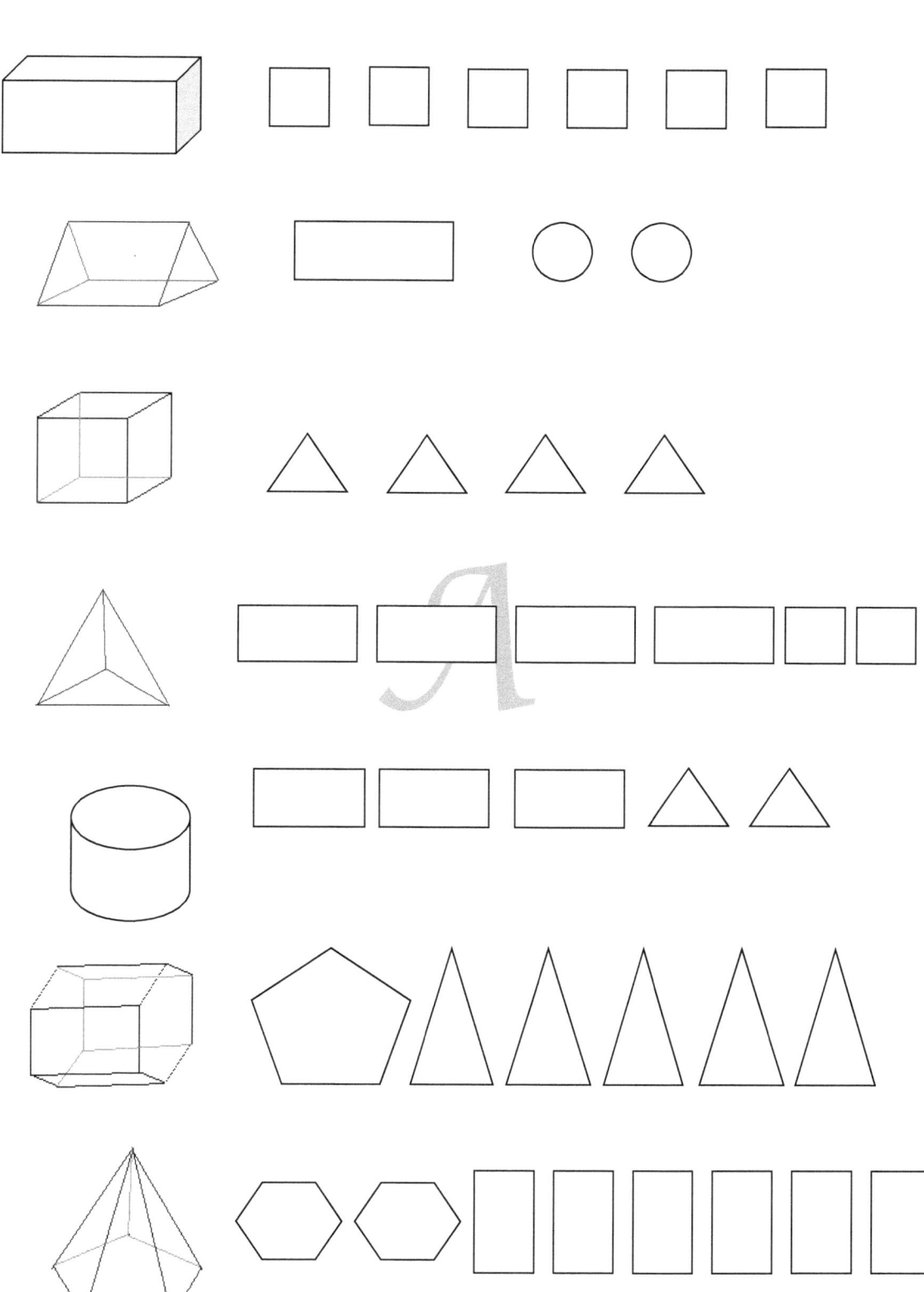

P3. Faces of solids

1. 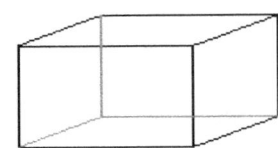   6 rectangular faces

2. 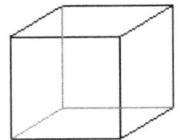   6 _____ faces

3. 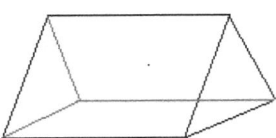   ____ triangular faces and 3 _____ faces

4. 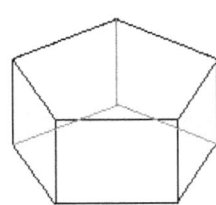   ____ pentagonal faces and 5 _____ faces

5. 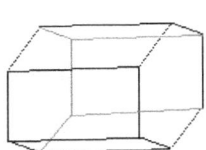   ____ hexagonal faces and 6 _____ faces

6. 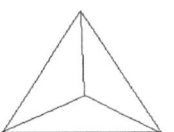   4 _____ faces

7. 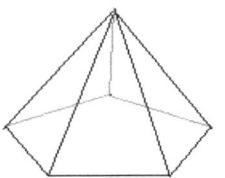   ____ triangular faces and 1 _____ face

8. 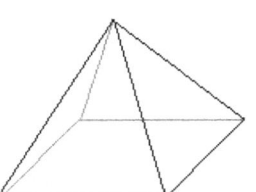   ____ triangular faces and 1 _____ face

Name _____ Date _____

P4. Nets of boxes

1. Circle the net which can be folded to each solid?

1.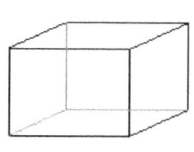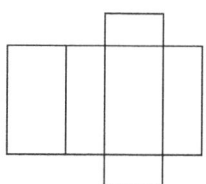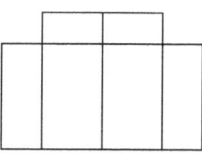

                                     A   B   C

2.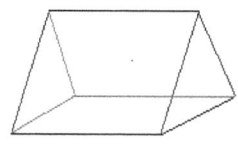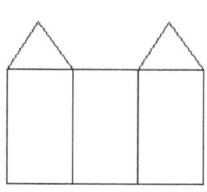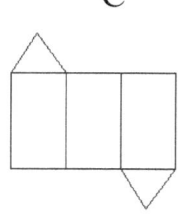

                                     A   B   C

3.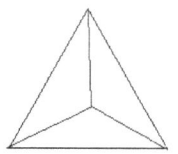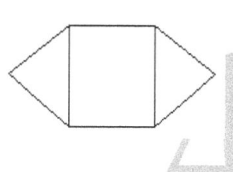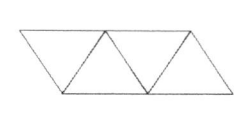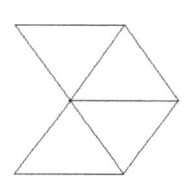

                                     A   B   C

4.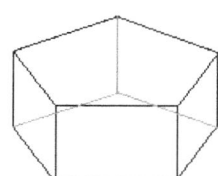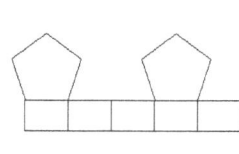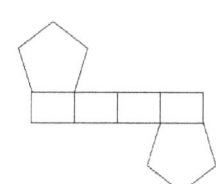

                                     A   B   C

5.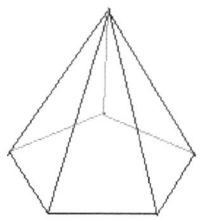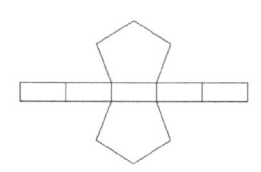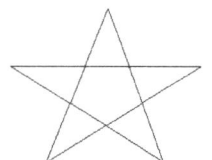

                                     A   B   C

Name _____   Date _____

1. Circle the nets that can be folded to boxes.

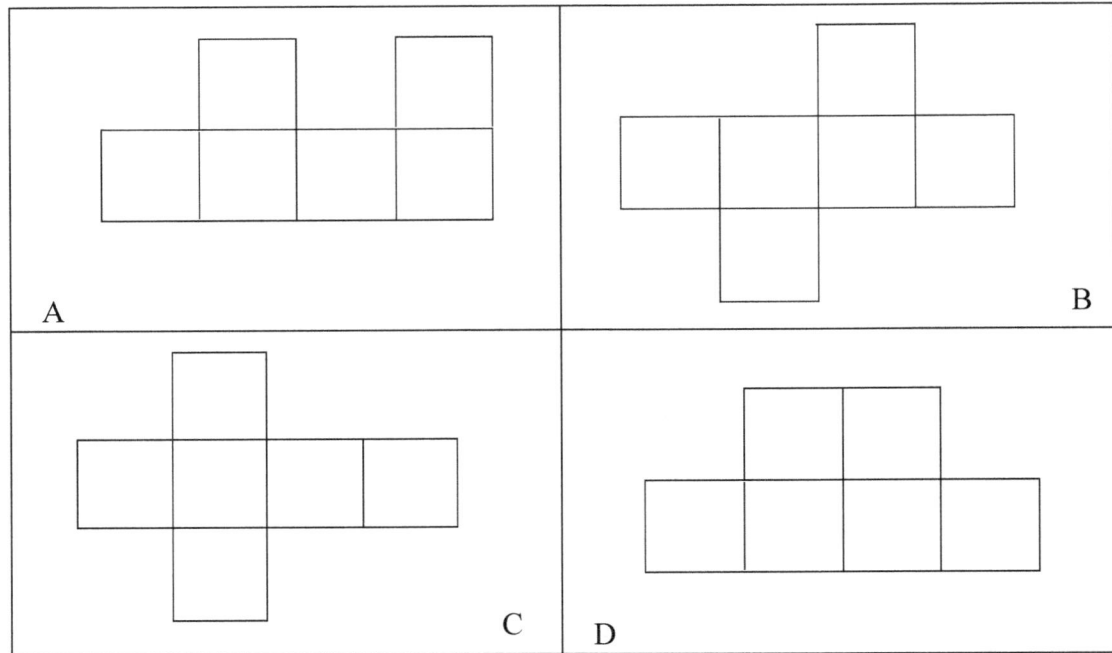

2. The following net make up the cube.

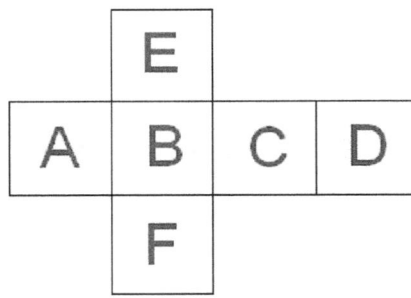
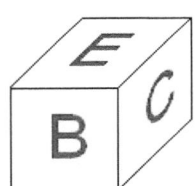

1. Which letter is on the base?

2. Which letter is opposite the letter "B"?

3. Which letter is opposite the letter "C"?

P5. Skeletons

A model showing only edges and vertices

Skeleton	Name	Number of vertices	number of edges for each base	Number of edges for side
	Triangular pyramid	4	3 equal edges	3 equal edges
	Rectangular prism	4	2 pairs of equal edges	4 equal edges

Name _____   Date _____

Q. Graphs

Q1. Tally table

Complete the following chart and answer the following questions.

1. **Favourite Snack**

Snack	Number	Tally
Cookie	7	|||| ||
Chip	3	|||
Fries	5	||||
Ice cream	9	
Popcorn	4	

1. How many people chose cookie as their favourite snack?

2. How many people chose either chips or fries?

3. How many people chose either fries or ice cream?

4. How many people answered the survey?

2. **Favourite Color**

Color	Number	Tally
Red		||||
Blue		|||| |||
Green		|||
Yellow		|||| ||||
Purple		||

1. How many people chose blue as their favourite color?

2. How many people chose either green or red?

3. How many more people chose yellow than purple?

4. List the color in the order of their popularity?

402

Name _____   Date _____

3.   Favourite Food

Food	Number	Tally
Pizzas	15	
Hamburgers	8	
Sandwiches	13	
Pasta	7	
Sushi	6	

1. How many people chose pasta as their favourite food?

2. How many people chose either pizzas or Sandwiches?

3. How many fewer people choose sandwich than sushi?

4. How many people were surveyed?

5. How many people didn't choose hamburger as their favourite food?

4.   Favourite Drinks

Drinks	Number	Tally
Juice		︎𝍷𝍷𝍷𝍷𝍷 𝍷𝍷𝍷𝍷𝍷 IIII
Lemonade		𝍷𝍷𝍷𝍷𝍷 II
Punch		𝍷𝍷𝍷𝍷𝍷 𝍷𝍷𝍷𝍷𝍷
Tea		III
Coke		𝍷𝍷𝍷𝍷𝍷 II

1. How many people chose coke as their favourite drink?

2. How many people chose either punch or juice?

3. How many people answered the survey?

4. List the drink in order from least votes to most votes.

Name _____ Date _____

5.   Clubs

Clubs	Number	Tally
Drawing	9	
Chess	15	
Dancing	8	
Skiing	6	
Swimming	11	

1. What club is the most popular club?

2. If three more people chose dancing club, how many people would have chosen dancing club?

3. How many more people chose swimming club than chose skiing club?

4. How many people didn't choose swimming club as their favourite club?

6.   Sales

Sales	Number	Tally
Shirts	5	
Sweaters	2	
Jackets	7	
Coats	3	
Blouses	8	

1. How many shirts were sold?

2. How many more blouses were sold than sweaters?

3. If 3 more jackets were sold, how many jackets would have been sold?

4. How many items were sold in total?

5. List the sales from the most sold to least sold.

Q2. Line plots

1.

Books read

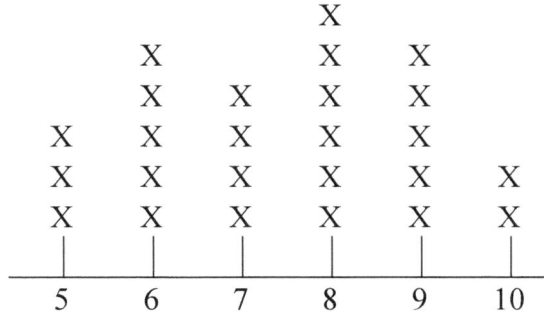

1. How many students read exactly six books?

2. How many students read at least nine books?

3. How many students read less than seven books?

4. How many students were surveyed?

2.

Points scored

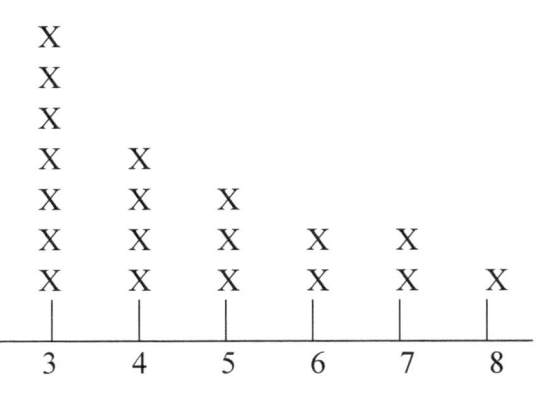

1. What was the most common number of points most of the teams scored?

2. How many points did the champion team score?

3. What are the total points of all the teams combined?

3.

Games won

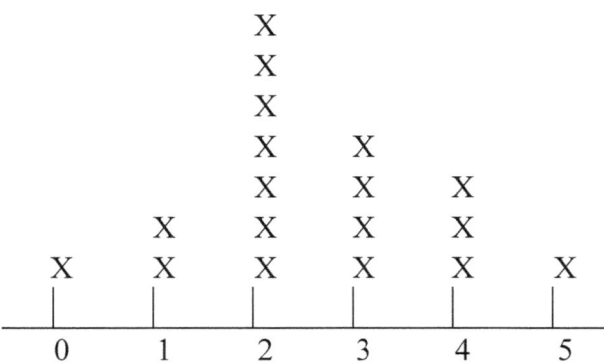

4.

Days used to finish a project

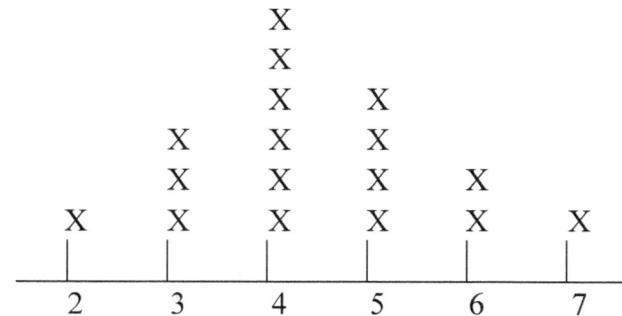

1. How many people joined the event?

2. How many people won at least four games?

3. How many people lost all the games?

4. How many games did the champion win?

1. How many students are there in the class?

2. How many students use exactly 5 days to finish the project?

3. How many students finished their projects more than four days?

4. How many students finished their projects within three days?

5. This is a survey about the number of pets a student keep Draw a line plot according the following information.

Family	Number of pets
Tom	2
James	4
John	3
Michael	6
Jimmy	3
Jenny	5
Laura	7
Cindy	3
Andy	5
Victor	4
David	3
Serena	6
Grace	3
Alex	5
Ann	3
Kelly	6
Christine	4
Jason	2

6. A dart competition was hold. Draw a line plot according the following information.

Three students scored five points.
Four students scored six points.
Eight students scored seven points.
Six students scored eight points.
Seven students scored nine points.
Two students scored ten points.

Q3. Stem-and-leaf plots

1. The following stem-and-leaf graph shows the heights of students in a class. (unit is in cm)

Stem	Leaves
11	8
12	2 4 5 5 9
13	0 8 4 6 6 0 9
14	5 7 3 6 4 6 2 8
15	1 3

1. How many students are 130 cm?

2. How many students are between 130 and 139 cm (inclusive)?

3. How many students are taller than 150cm?

4. How many students are there in the class?

2. The following stem-and-leaf graph shows the scores of the students got in a math test.

Stem	Leaves
5	1
6	2 8 3 6 9 4
7	0 4 7 2 9 5 3 8
8	1 6 3 0 7 9 5 3
9	2 7 4 1 8
10	0 0

1. How many students failed the test (below 60)?

2. How many students got an "A" (at least 86)?

3. How many students get full marks?

4. How many students are there in the class?

5. More students got sixties or nineties?

Name _____ Date _____

3. This is a record of long-jump of a class. Make a stem-and-leaf graph according the data. Unit is in cm.

104	125	117	121	136
138	107	116	129	109
115	117	125	136	124
109	112	114	126	132
117	127	119	137	125

Stem	Leaves

4. This is a record of sales of different department of a store. Make a stem-and leaf graph according to the data. Unit is in dollar.

63	62	80	54	43
57	66	61	69	71
70	68	42	49	52
36	68	85	64	39
73	74	36	57	48

Stem	Leaves

5. This is a record of the weight of each apple in a basket. Make a stem-and leaf graph according to the data. Unit is in gram.

75	81	68	90	108
82	95	79	112	79
98	83	86	105	103
116	86	78	67	102
79	92	95	86	103
98	107	113	104	107

Stem	Leaves

Name _____ Date _____

Q4. Mean and range

Mean, or average, is the sum of all numbers divided by the number of addends.
Range is the difference between the greatest number and the least number.

Find the mean and range for each set of numbers.

Example: Find mean and range of 4, 7, 2, 8, and 9.
Sum = 4 + 7 + 2 + 8 + 9 = 30
How many numbers? 5

$$\text{Mean} = \frac{sum}{\#\ of\ numbers} = \frac{30}{5} = 6$$

Greatest number = 9
Least number = 2
Range = Greatest number – least number = 9 – 2 = 7

	Numbers	mean	range
1.	5, 16, 7, 10, 12		
2.	6, 13, 9, 8		
3.	3, 15, 8. 12, 9, 13		
4.	5. 12, 3, 8		
5.	10, 15, 16, 9, 5		
6.	8, 11, 15, 12, 7, 13		
7.	24, 18, 19, 16, 13		
8.	18, 22, 25, 23		
9.	11, 16, 9, 22, 12		
10	13, 16, 15, 18, 13		

Find the mean and range on a line plot.

Example: Find the mean and range from the line plot below.

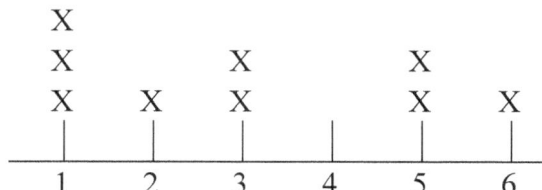

There are 3 of 1, 1 of 2, 2 of 3, 2 of 5 and 1 of 6. So,
Total = 3 × 1 + 1 × 2 + 2 × 3 + 2 × 5 + 1 × 6 = 27
# of numbers = 3 + 1 + 2 + 1 + 2 = 9

Mean = $\dfrac{sum}{\text{\# of numbers}} = \dfrac{27}{9} = 3$

Greatest number = 6
Least number = 1
Range = Greatest number − least number = 6 − 1 = 5

1.

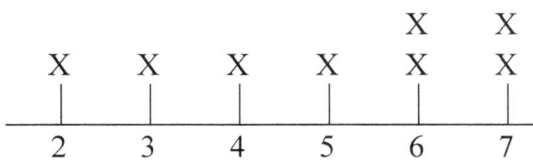

Mean = _____   Range = _____

2.

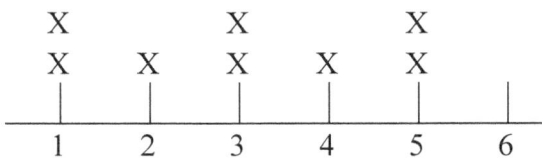

Mean = _____   Range = _____

3.

X
X   X X
X X X X X
| | | | | |
5 6 7 8 9 10

Mean = _____   Range = _____

4.

       X
   X   X X
   X   X X X
| | | | | |
3 4 5 6 7 8

Mean = _____   Range = _____

Name _____   Date _____

Find the mean and range on a stem-and-leaf plot.

Example: Find mean and range from stem-and-leaf plot below.

Stem	Leaves
1	1 4 7
2	0 2 5
3	1

There are 7 numbers in the plot above: 11, 14, 17, 20, 22, 25, and 31.
Total = 11 + 14 + 17 + 20 + 22 + 25 = 140
# of numbers = 7

Mean = $\dfrac{sum}{\# \: of \: numbers} = \dfrac{140}{7} = 20$

Greatest number = 31
Least number = 11
Range = Greatest number – least number = 31 – 11 = 20

1.

Stem	Leaves
2	0
3	3 3 8
4	5 1

Mean = _____   Range = _____

2.

Stem	Leaves
3	1 0 8
4	2 5
5	4

Mean = _____   Range = _____

3.

Stem	Leaves
1	4 2 6 2
2	0
3	3 5 4

Mean = _____   Range = _____

4.

Stem	Leaves
11	2 6
12	3 7 5
13	2 0 7 2 6

Mean = _____   Range = _____

Q5. Pictographs

1.
Favourite Colors

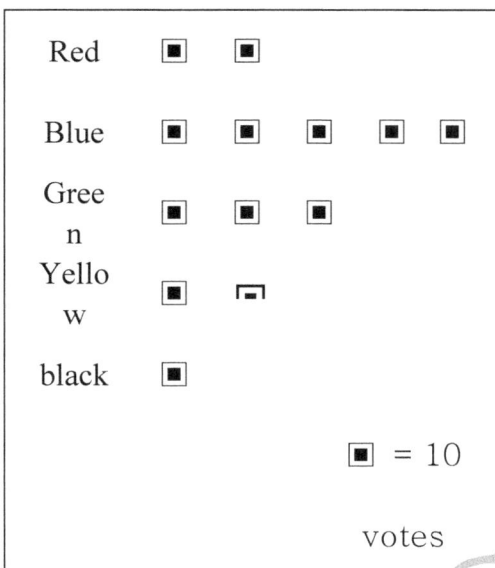

Red	■ ■
Blue	■ ■ ■ ■ ■
Green	■ ■ ■
Yellow	■ ▭
black	■

■ = 10 votes

1. What color is the most popular color?

2. How many students take green as their favourite color?

3. How many students answered the survey?

4. List the popularity form greatest to least.

5. What is the range?

2.
Favourite Games

Soccer	✺ ✺ ✺ ✺
Basketball	✺ ✺
Hockey	✺ ✺ ✺ ✺ ✺
Tennis	✺ ✺
Swimming	✺ ✺ ✺
Skiing	✺

✺ = 8 students

1. What game is the most popular game?

2. How many more students take hockey as their favourite game than basketball?

3. How many students answered the survey?

4. List the popularity form least to greatest.

5. What is the range?

Name _____ Date _____

Make pictographs.

1.

Favourite Food	# of students
Pizzas	15
Sandwiches	20
Pasta	5
Hamburger	10
Sushi	25

Use ♨ to present 5 students

2.

Name of poultry	# of poultry
Chicken	32
Ducks	8
Goose	20
Turkey	12

Use 🕊 to present 4 poultry

3.

Favourite drink	# of students
Coke	9
Juice	12
Tea	3
Water	6
Punch	15

Use 🍸 to present 3 students.

Name _____ Date _____

Q6. Bar graphs

1. Vertical bar graph.

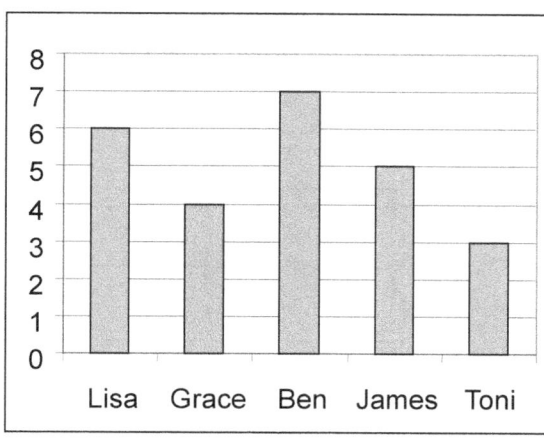

2. Horizontal bar graph.

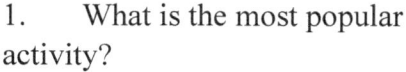

1. Who scored the most points?

2. What are the total points scored?

3. What are the mean points scored?

4. List the name of students according to their points form least to greatest.

5. What is the range?

1. What is the most popular activity?

2. How many more students joined in soccer than tennis?

3. Which activities have at least 7 students joined in?

4. List the activities according to their popularity from greatest to least.

5. What is the range?

Name _____ Date _____

Make a bar graph from each below.

Name	# of chin-ups
John	6
Tom	9
Sam	3
Justin	5
Ben	8

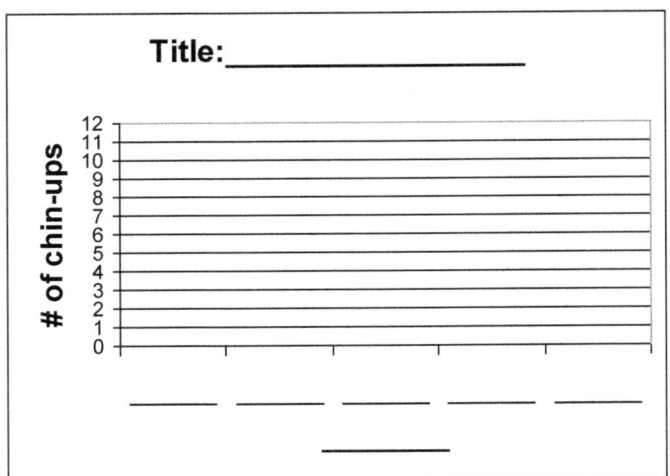

Fruits in a basket	# of fruits
Orange	5
Apple	8
Pear	2
Peach	9
Plum	6

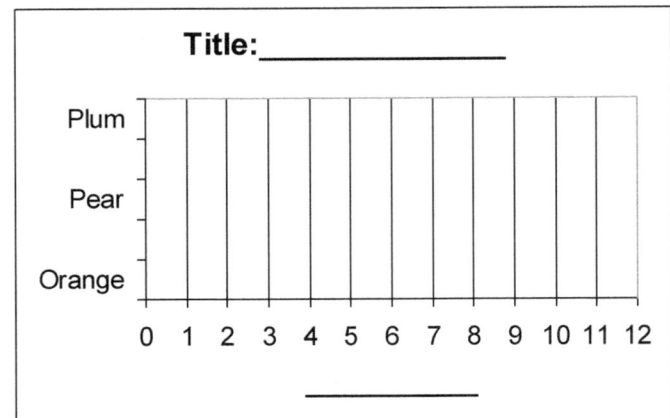

Team	# of games won
Tiger	5
Hunter	8
Eagle	13
Giant	10
Hurricane	9

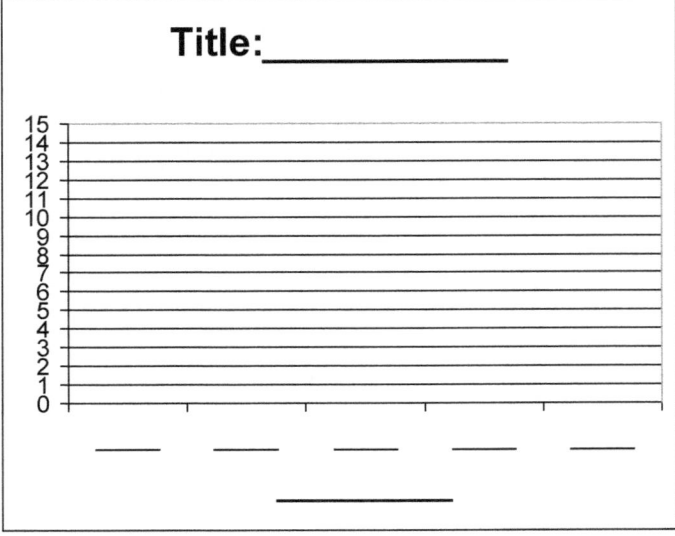

Q7. Circle graphs

1. This circle graph shows the proportion of the pets in a house.

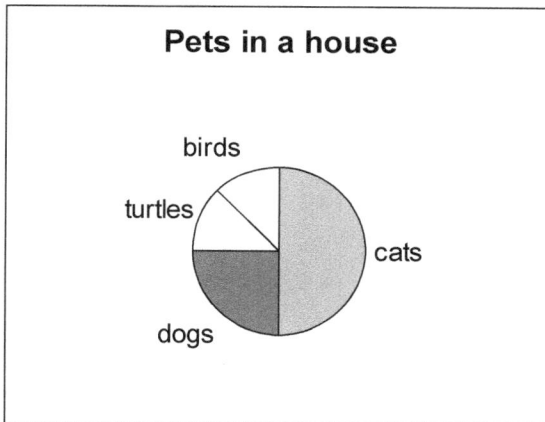

1. What fraction of the pets are cats?

2. What fraction of the pets are dogs?

3. Which two kinds of pets represent $\frac{1}{4}$ of the pets?

4. What is the most number of pets?

2. This circle graph shows the votes of the students in a class on their favourite drinks.

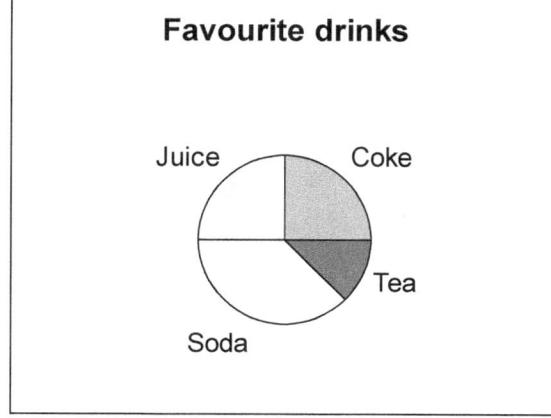

1. What fraction of the class chose juice as their favourite drink?

2. What fraction of the class chose soda as their favourite drink?

3. More students like coke or tea?

4. What is the most popular drink?

5. If there are 24 students in the class, how many students chose coke as their favourite drink?

8

Name _____ Date _____

Q8. Venn diagrams

Venn diagram is a method to sort data.

1.

Part	Square	Black
A	Yes	No
B	Yes	Yes
C	No	Yes
D	No	No

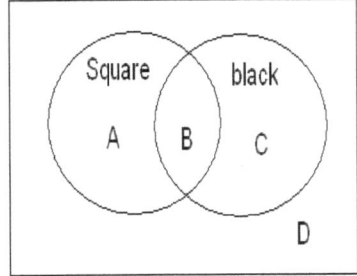

5. Below each object, write the part of the Venn diagram to which it belongs.

b. Find the number of each part.

A _____

B _____

C _____

D _____

2.

Tina	James	Melissa	Isabel
English	English	French	English
French			French

Kevin	Justin	Linda	Steven
English	English	French	English
French			

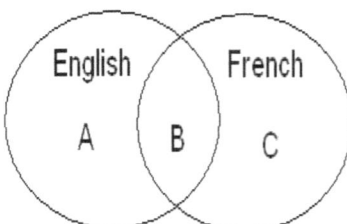

A ____ B ____ C ____

418

Name _____ Date _____

3.

Find the number in each part.

A _____

B _____

C _____

D _____

4.

Tina	James	Melissa	Isabel
glasses		glasses	

Kevin	Justin	Linda	Steven
glasses		glasses	

Jasmine	Sarah	Tom	Mathew
	glasses		glasses

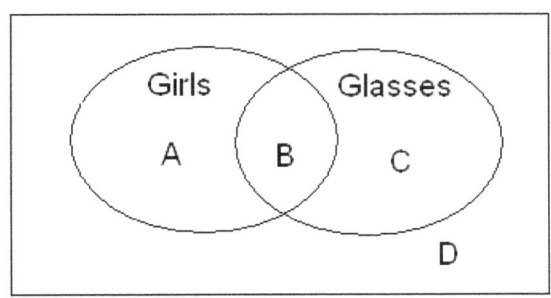

Answer the following questions.

6. How many girls wear glasses?

7. How many students wear glasses?

8. How many students are there?

9. How many boys do not wear glasses?

419

Name _____ Date _____

R. Probability

Make predictions whether each event is impossible, unlikely, likely, or certain.

1. Throw a dice, the probability of getting an even number is

2. Draw a card from a deck. The probability of getting a heart is

3. There are eight red marbles and one white marble. The probability of picking a white marble is

4. Throw a dice, the probability of getting a '7' is

5. There are three dimes and five quarters. The probability of picking a dime or a quarter is

6. Spin a spinner, the probability of getting a '2' is

7. There are five red marbles and five white marbles. The probability of picking a black marble is

8. Draw a card from a deck. The probability of getting a King is

9. Denny played chess against Benny. Benny won six times and lost two times. The probability for Denny winning the next game is

10. Spin a spinner, the probability of getting a '4' is

11. Throw a dice, the probability of getting an odd number is

12. Throw a dice, the probability of getting a number not less than 5 is

Name _____   Date _____

Make predictions whether each event is impossible, unlikely, likely, or certain.

1. A train is faster than a car. _____

2. A dog is heavier than a cat. _____

3. A cow eats mice. _____

4. Steve can eat twenty eggs each meal. _____

5. A tree turns green during spring. _____

6. The earth rotates around the sun. _____

7. Winter is warmer than summer. _____

8. A cat will catch a mouse. _____

9. A bird cannot fly. _____

10. A rabbit runs faster than a turtle. _____

11. You will go hiking during summer vacation. _____

12. You can write twenty words in a minute. _____

13. If Sam doesn't eat for a whole day, he will feel hungry. _____

14. If you run, your heart will beat slower. _____

15. A horse is heavier than an elephant. _____

16. A goldfish can live without water. _____

17. A snake has four legs. _____

18. A bicycle has two wheels. _____

19. A crow is white. _____

20. Stone is harder than mud. _____

Name _____ Date _____

Equally likely and unequally likely

1. There are four red marbles, and four green marbles in a box. Pick up a marble randomly without looking. The probability of choosing green marble and a red marble is:

   a. equally likely   b. unequally likely

2. There are three nickels, four dimes, and four quarters in a bag. Pick up a coin randomly without looking. The probability of choosing dime and a quarter is:

   a. equally likely   b. unequally likely

3. Throw a coin. The probability of getting a tail and getting a head is"

   a. equally likely   b. unequally likely

4. 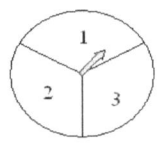 Spin a spinner. The probability of getting a '2' and getting a '3' is:

   a. equally likely   b. unequally likely

5. 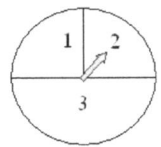 Spin a spinner. The probability of getting a '2' and getting a '3' is:

   a. equally likely   b. unequally likely

6. From the box to the left, choosing a triangle and a square is:

   a. equally likely   b. unequally likely

7. From the box to the left, choosing a circle and a square is:

   a. equally likely   b. unequally likely

8. From the box to the left, choosing a triangle and a circle is:

   a. equally likely   b. unequally likely

Find the probability of spinning each outcome.

1.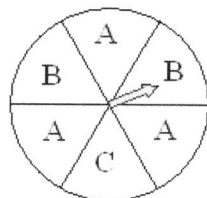
The letter B.
2 out of 6.

2.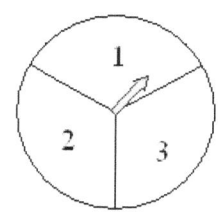
The number 1.
___ out of ___.

3.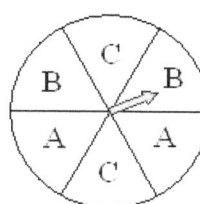
The letter B.
___ out of ___.

4.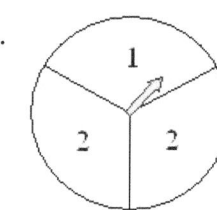
The number 2.
___ out of ___.

5.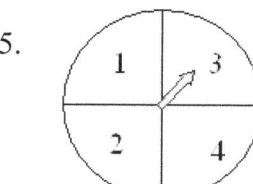
The number 3.
___ out of ___.

6.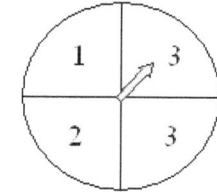
The number 3.
___ out of ___.

7.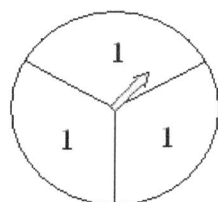
The number 2.
___ out of ___.

8.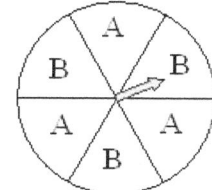
The letter B.
___ out of ___.

9.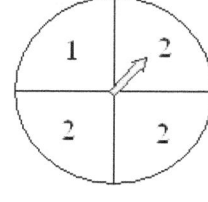
The number 2.
___ out of ___.

10.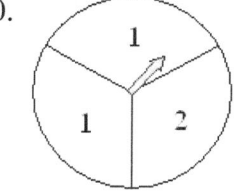
The number 2.
___ out of ___.

11.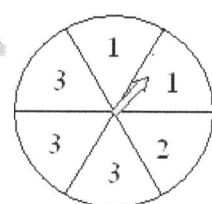
The number 1.
___ out of ___.

12.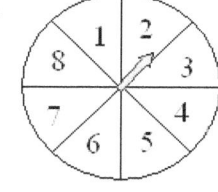
The number 3.
___ out of ___.

13.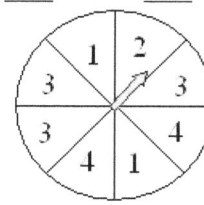
The number 4.
___ out of ___.

14.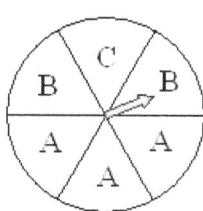
The letter A.
___ out of ___.

15.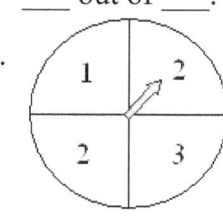
The number 2.
___ out of ___.

16.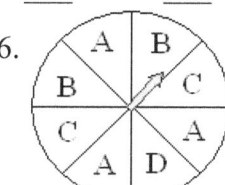
The letter B.
___ out of ___.

Name _____   Date _____

Find the probability of each outcome.

Example: Toss a coin. What is the probability of getting a head?

Total outcomes: head, tail

The probability of getting a head is: <u>1 out of 2</u>

1. Throw a dice. What is the probability of getting '3'?

2. One letter is randomly chosen from the word 'chess'. What is the probability of choosing the letter "s"?

3. There are 12 boys and fifteen girls in a classroom. If one student is randomly chosen, what is the probability of choosing a boy?

4. There are 5 red marbles, 3 white marbles, 4 green marbles, and 2 yellow marbles in a bag. Randomly choose a marble from the bag. What is the probability of choosing a white marble?

5. Throw a dice. What is the probability of getting an even number?

6. One letter is randomly chosen from the word 'butter'. What is the probability of choosing the letter "t"?

7. Throw a dice. What is the probability of getting a number not less than 5?

Name _____   Date _____

8. There are 6 red marbles, 2 white marbles, 7 green marbles, and 5 yellow marbles in a bag. Randomly choose a marble from the bag. What is the probability of choosing a red marble?

9. One letter is randomly chosen from the word 'singing'. What is the probability of choosing the letter 'I'?

10. A cube has 6 sides. The sides have the letters 'A', 'B', 'A', 'C', 'A', and 'B'. Throw the dice once. What is the probability of getting the letter 'B'?

11. There are 3 pennies, 5 nickels, 9 dimes, and 8 quarters. Pick a coin randomly without looking. What is the probability of picking a quarter?

12. There are 3 pennies, 6 nickels, 4 dimes, and 9 quarters. Pick a coin randomly. What is the probability of picking a penny or a dime?

13. There are 4 red marbles, 5 white marbles, 8 green marbles, and 3 blue marbles in a bag. Choose a marble from the bag randomly. What is the probability of choosing a red or a green marble?

14. One letter is randomly chosen from the word 'noon'. What is the probability of choosing the letter 'n' or 'o'?

Name _____ Date _____

Make predictions.

Example: There are 20 red marbles and blue marbles in a bag. Sam took out a marble, recorded the color and put it back.

Red	Blue

The result shows that there are three times as many blue marbles as red marbles. So, Sam predicts 5 red marbles and 15 blue marbles.

1. There are 50 dimes and quarters in a bag. Linda took a coin, made a record, and put it back. The record is shown as below. Make a prediction of the number of dimes and quarters.

Dimes	Quarters

2. There are 18 red and green tokens in a box. Linda took a token, made a record, and put it back. The record is shown as below. Make a prediction of the number of red and green tokens.

Red	Green

Name _____ Date _____

3. 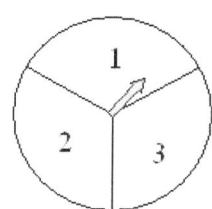 Spin the spinner 30 times. Prediction how many times the spinner will land on each number.

   1: _____   2: _____   3: _____

4. 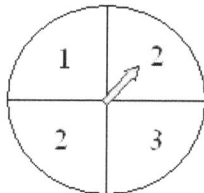 Spin the spinner 20 times. Prediction how many times the spinner will land on each number.

   1: _____   2: _____   3: _____

5. 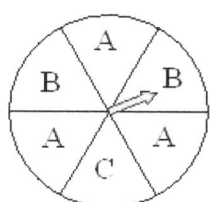 Spin the spinner 30 times. Prediction how many times the spinner will land on each letter.

   A: _____   B: _____   C: _____

6.  There are ten shapes in a box. Randomly pick a shape, make a record, and put it back. Repeat 50 times. Prediction how many times each shape will come up.

   Circle: ___   Square: ___   Triangle: ____

7.  There are 6 cards in a box. Choose a card randomly. Repeat 30 times. Prediction how many times each kind of card will show up.

   ▣: _____   ■: _____   □: _____

427

Name _____ Date _____

According to the experiment result, draw a spinner that matches.

1.

Red	||||| |||||
Blue	||||| |||||
Yellow	||||| |||||

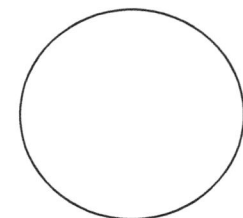

2.

Red	|||||
Blue	|||||
Yellow	||||| |||||
Black	||||| |||||

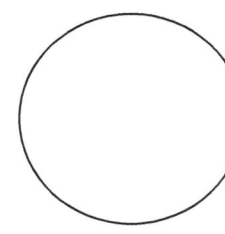

3.

A	10
B	20
C	30

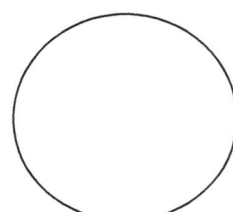

4.

1											
2																					

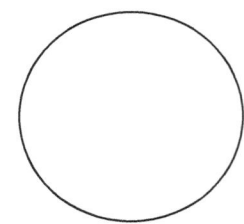

5.

A	||||| |||||
B	||||| |||||
C	||||| ||||| ||||| |||||

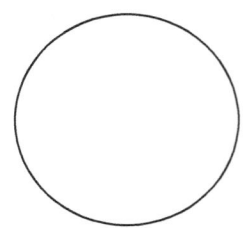

Test 1

30 questions for 30 minutes

1. Which of the following numbers represents three million sixty-two thousand five hundred nine?

(A) $30000 + 6000 + 200 + 50 + 9$
(B) $300000 + 60000 + 2000 + 50 + 9$
(C) $300000 + 60000 + 2000 + 500 + 9$
(D) $3000000 + 60000 + 2000 + 500 + 9$
(E) $3000000 + 600000 + 20000 + 500 + 9$

2. Charles surveyed his classmate about their favorite sports. How many people took the survey?

(A) 18
(B) 30
(C) 50
(D) 60
(E) 100

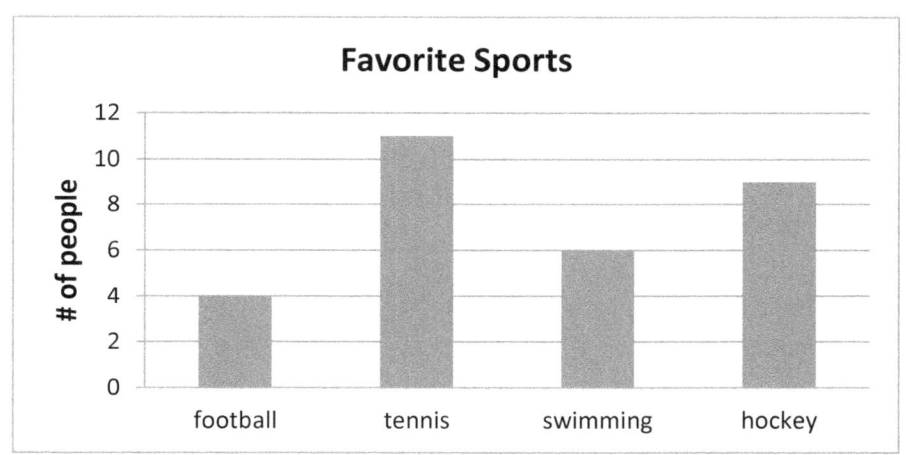

3. What is value of A?

$$A \xrightarrow{-3} \square \xrightarrow{\div 2} \square \xrightarrow{\times 3} \square \xrightarrow{+6} 90$$

(A) 59
(B) 61
(C) 67
(D) 129
(E) 141

4. Which number comes next?

$$2, 22, 242, 2662, \ldots$$

(A) 2882
(B) 28282
(C) 28482
(D) 28682
(E) 29282

5. How many grams does each pear weigh?

(A) 100 g
(B) 200 g
(C) 300 g
(D) 400 g
(E) 500 g

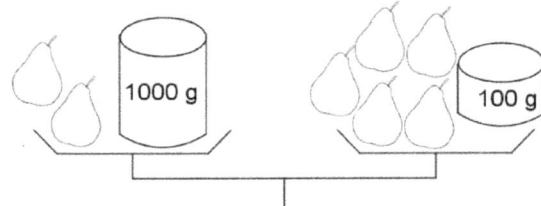

6. A rope is 6 feet 5 inches long. How many inches is this rope?

(A) 11 inches
(B) 23 inches
(C) 65 inches
(D) 66 inches
(E) 77 inches

7. How many triangles are there in the diagram?

(A) 3
(B) 4
(C) 5
(D) 6
(E) 7

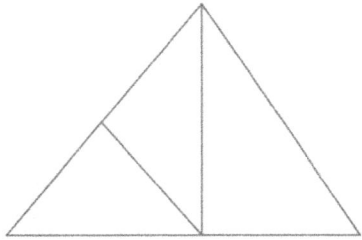

8. If 67A is a multiple of 4, what is the possible value of A?

(A) 0
(B) 1
(C) 2
(D) 3
(E) 4

9. Sophia started practicing piano at 9:40 a.m. She practiced for 1 h 25 min. At what time did she finish?

(A)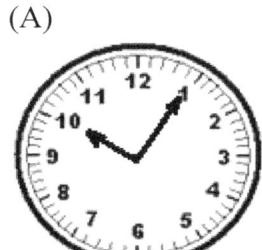

(B)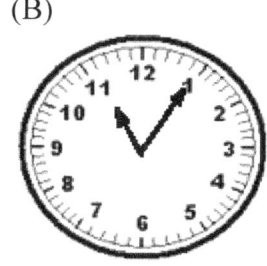

(C)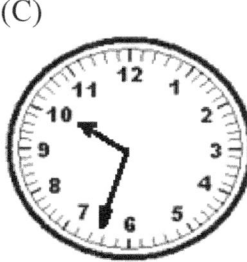

(D)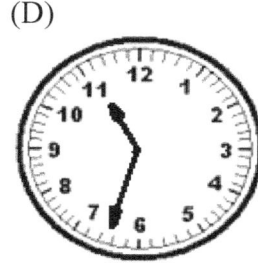

(E)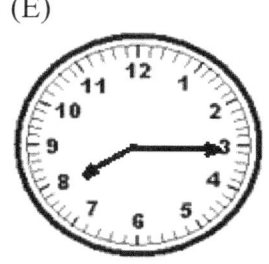

10. 86723 − 54672 is closest to

(A) 10000
(B) 20000
(C) 30000
(D) 40000
(E) 50000

11. John wants to put all 145 balls into boxes. If each box can hold 6 balls, how many boxes does he need to prepare?

(A) 6
(B) 18
(C) 25
(D) 139
(E) 151

12. Chris bought a hamburger. He paid with a $10 bill and got $2.45 change back. How much was the hamburger?

(A) $7.45
(B) $7.55
(C) $7.65
(D) $8.55
(E) $8.65

13. The width of a rectangular garden is 12 m. The length is 5 m longer than its width. Steven wants to fence the garden. How many meters of fence should he buy?

(A) 17 m
(B) 29 m
(C) 34 m
(D) 58 m
(E) 68 m

14. The area of a square is 9 cm². If three such squares put together to form a big rectangle, what is the perimeter of the rectangle?

(A) 3 cm
(B) 8
(C) 12 cm
(D) 18 cm
(E) 24 cm

15. Of the following, which results in a whole number solution?

I. $2 + 3$ II. $2 - 3$ III. 2×3 IV. $2 \div 3$

(A) I and II
(B) III and IV
(C) I and III
(D) II and IV
(E) All of them

16. The sum of three consecutive numbers is 51. What is the largest number?

(A) 5
(B) 17
(C) 18
(D) 19
(E) 51

17. Tom and Jerry are twins. Both are 9 years old. Their mom is 38 years old. How many years later will their mom's age be equal to the sum of Tom and Jerry's age?

(A) 9 years
(B) 10 years
(C) 15 years
(D) 20 years
(E) 29 years

18. The area of a rectangle is 24 cm². Both the width and length are whole numbers. Which of the following is the possible perimeter of the rectangle?

(A) 21 cm
(B) 22 cm
(C) 23 cm
(D) 24 cm
(E) 25 cm

19. Kenny goes to skating every three days. Danny goes to skating every five days. They both go to skating on Friday. When will be the next time they both go to skating again?

(A) Tuesday
(B) Thursday
(C) Friday
(D) Saturday
(E) Sunday

20. To prepare for the long-distance running, Benjamin ran every week for 9 weeks. He ran 5000 m the first week. Each week after that, he ran 200 m more than the week before. After 9 weeks, how many meters did he ran in total?

(A) 6.6 km
(B) 6.8 km
(C) 52.2 km
(D) 6600 km
(E) 52200 km

21. Annabelle has three more nickels than quarters, and two more dimes than nickels. If the total value of her coins is $1.85, how many coins does she have?

(A) 3
(B) 6
(C) 8
(D) 17
(E) 20

22. Cindy jogged a total of 70 miles for 5 days. Every day he jogged 4 miles more than the day before. How many miles did Cindy jog the last day?

(A) 6
(B) 10
(C) 14
(D) 22

(E) 28

23. Some friends want to share the cost of a basketball equally. Three more friends joined and thus reduce each share from $6 to $4. How many people are PRESENTLY in the group?

(A) 4 people
(B) 6 people
(C) 8 people
(D) 9 people
(E) 10 people

24. How many different rectangles are there in the following figure?

(A) 9
(B) 10
(C) 17
(D) 23
(E) 45

25. There are 2 red cars in every 9 cars in a parking lot. If there are 108 cars in total, how many red cars are there?

(A) 2
(B) 9
(C) 11
(D) 18
(E) 24

26. There are 2 pairs of white socks, 6 pairs of black socks, 4 pairs of red socks, and 8 pairs of striped socks. Take one sock from the drawer without looking; what is the probability of taking out a black sock?

(A) 6%
(B) 12%
(C) 30%
(D) 60%
(E) 120%

27. Tom can make a model car in two hours. Jerry can make a model car in six hours. How long will it take them to make a model car if they work together?

(A) 50 minutes
(B) 80 minutes
(C) 90 minutes
(D) 100 minutes
(E) 120 minutes

28. Melissa has x books. Caroline has 3 more than twice as many books as Melissa. How many books does Caroline have?

(A) $2x + 3$
(B) $x + 3$
(C) $2x$
(D) $2x - 3$
(E) $3x - 2$

29. If $m + n$ is an even number, which of the following must be an even number?

(A) $2m + n$
(B) $2m - n$
(C) $m + 2n$
(D) $m + 4n$
(E) $3m + 3n$

30. Spin the spinner once. What is the probability of NOT landing on "B"?

(A) $\frac{1}{6}$

(B) $\frac{2}{6}$

(C) $\frac{2}{3}$

(D) $\frac{1}{2}$

(E) $\frac{5}{6}$

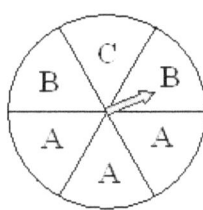

Name _____ Date _____

Test 2

30 questions for 30 minutes

1. Which one of the following numbers is three thousand five hundred one and four hundredth?

(A) 351.4
(B) 3501.4
(C) 351.04
(D) 3501.04
(E) 3501400

2. Which one of the following is not equal to a whole number?

(A) $6 \times \frac{1}{2}$

(B) $3 \div \frac{1}{2}$

(C) 5×0.36

(D) $\frac{2}{3} + \frac{4}{3}$

(E) 8×0.25

3. $5 \times 3 \times 4 \times 6$ is equal to the product of 10 and

(A) 36
(B) 24
(C) 20
(D) 15
(E) 12

4. $6 + 69 + 699 + 6999$

(A) 6663
(B) 6773
(C) 6673
(D) 7773
(E) 2689

5. If $568 + 124 + \square = 809$, then what is $\square$?

(A) 105
(B) 107
(C) 117
(D) 127
(E) 1501

6. How many triangles are there in the figure?

(A) 1
(B) 3
(C) 4
(D) 6
(E) 9

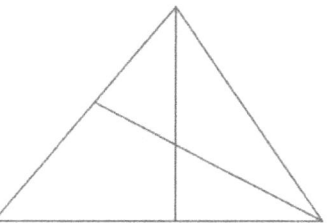

7. If Claire had three different skirts and four different sweaters, how many different outfits could she make?

(A) 6
(B) 7
(C) 8
(D) 10
(E) 12

8. Which of the following is NOT equal to a whole number?

(A) $4 \times \frac{1}{2}$

(B) $4 \div 2$

(C) $4 \div \frac{1}{2}$

(D) $2 \div \frac{1}{4}$

(E) $2 \times \frac{1}{4}$

9. If 5A2 is a multiple of 3, what is the possible value of A?

(A) 1
(B) 3
(C) 5
(D) 7
(E) 9

10. Which number comes next?

1, 3, 4, 7, 11, ...

(A) 16
(B) 17
(C) 18
(D) 20
(E) 24

11. How many plums will balance one pear?

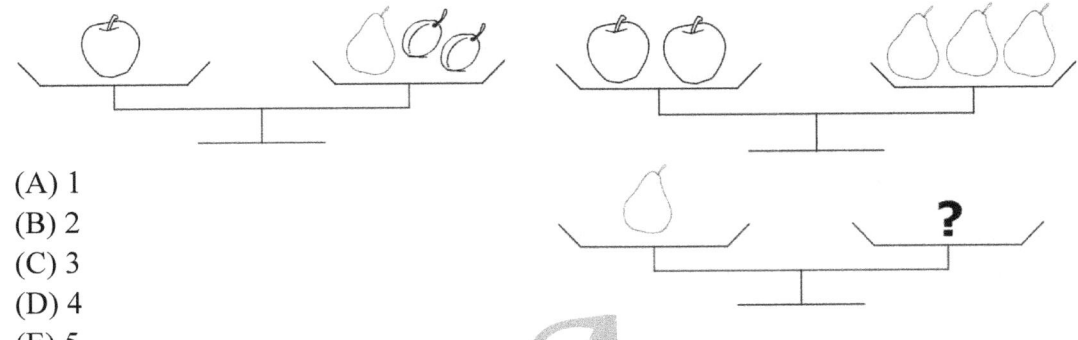

(A) 1
(B) 2
(C) 3
(D) 4
(E) 5

12. Henry's report card shows as follows. What is his average score?

Math	94
English	92
Science	88
Social Study	95
Physical Education	91

(A) 88
(B) 90
(C) 92
(D) 93
(E) 95

13. 286 × 623 is closest to

(A) 1200
(B) 18,000
(C) 120,000
(D) 180,000
(E) 280,000

14. There are five ropes with different length as follows. Which one is the longest rope?

(A) 150 cm
(B) 12 dm
(C) 1.8 m
(D) 188 mm
(E) 0.1 km

15. If $\frac{1}{3}$ of a number is 12, then $\frac{1}{2}$ of the same number is

(A) 4
(B) 8
(C) 18
(D) 24
(E) 36

16. In the diagram shown, which of the following is true?

(A) AB // AC
(B) AB // CD
(C) AB ⊥ CD
(D) AB ⊥ BC
(E) CD ⊥ BC

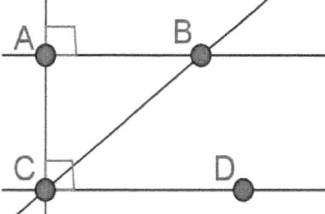

17. 6 is to 36 as 9 is to

(A) 33
(B) 39
(C) 45
(D) 54
(E) 81

18. Steve, Michael, Sandra, Lesley are standing in line to buy tickets for a movie. In how many ways can they stand in line to buy their tickets?

(A) 4
(B) 9
(C) 12
(D) 15
(E) 24

Name _____ Date _____

19. Which of the following point represents −2?

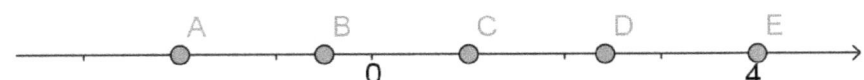

(A) A
(B) B
(C) C
(D) D
(E) E

20. Benno has 14 coins in his piggy bank. If he has 86¢ in his piggy bank with two quarters, then how many nickels does he have?

(A) 0
(B) 2
(C) 3
(D) 6
(E) 9

21. Kenny wants to buy paper cups for a party. Paper cups are sold in packages. Which one of the following is the best buy?

(A) 10 cups for $0.99
(B) 20 cups for $1.29
(C) 50 cups for $1.99
(D) 100 cups for $2.99
(E) 300 cups for $11.99

22. The perimeter of a rectangle is 32 cm. The length of the rectangle is l. What is the width in terms of l?

(A) $16 - \frac{l}{2}$
(B) $16 - l$
(C) $16 - 2l$
(D) $32 - l$
(E) $32 - 2l$

23. On a test with 60 questions, Chloe answered 9 questions wrong. What percent did she answer correctly?

(A) 85%
(B) 51%
(C) 18%
(D) 15%
(E) 9%

24. The sales in a department store, in thousand dollars, is shown. Find the percentage increase from March to April.

(A) 4%
(B) 15%
(C) 21%
(D) 29%
(E) 40%

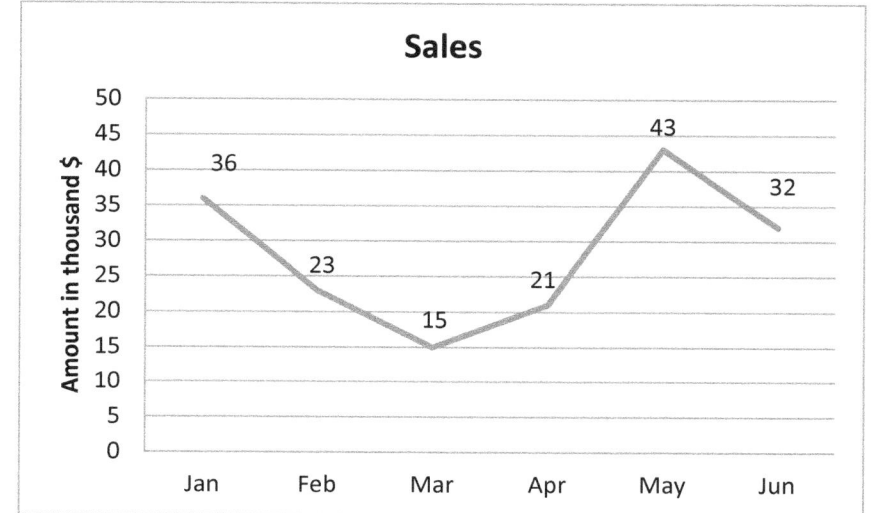

25. A ticket to a theatre is $10 for an adult and $6 for a student. There are 5 more students than adults. If the tickets cost $142 in a group, how many students are there?

(A) 7
(B) 9
(C) 11
(D) 12
(E) 16

26. $5^2 + 2(3 - 5) =$

(A) 21
(B) -24
(C) -100
(D) 29
(E) 6

27. Bradley got 51, 24, 39, and 42 points in four games separately. What was his average point of these four games?

(A) 24
(B) 39
(C) 42
(D) 51
(E) 156

28. Jason borrowed a book from the library. He read $\frac{1}{4}$ of the book on the first day. He read $\frac{1}{3}$ of what was left on the second day. He read half of what was left the third day. Then he had 32 pages left unread. How many pages were there in the book?

(A) 64
(B) 96
(C) 128
(D) 256
(E) 768

29. Given right triangle $\triangle ABC$, $\angle A = 58^0$, what is $\angle C$?

(A) 32^0
(B) 42^0
(C) 48^0
(D) 58^0
(E) 122^0

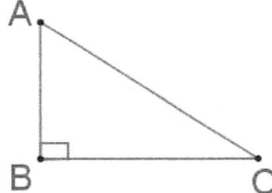

30. ABCD is a square. E, F, G, H are the middle points of DA, AB, BC, and CD separately. Throw a tiny ball into square ABCD. What is the probability the ball will land in square EFGH?

(A) $\frac{1}{2}$

(B) $\frac{2}{3}$

(C) $\frac{1}{3}$

(D) $\frac{1}{4}$

(E) $\frac{3}{4}$

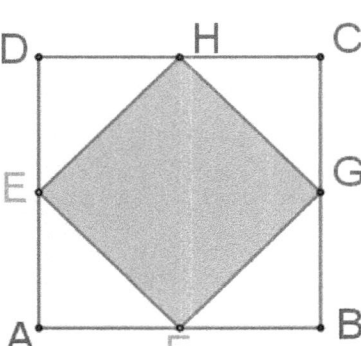

Name _____ Date _____

Test 3

30 questions for 30 minutes

1. Which digit is in the hundred's place?

$$41528$$

(A) 1
(B) 2
(C) 4
(D) 5
(E) 8

2. There are six bottles of juice in a box. How many bottles of juice are there in twelve boxes?

(A) 2
(B) 6
(C) 18
(D) 36
(E) 72

3. If $\frac{298}{6} = \frac{a \times 100}{6} + \frac{b \times 10}{6} + \frac{c \times 1}{6}$, then what is c?

(A) 2
(B) 6
(C) 8
(D) 9
(E) 29

4. $2 \times 5 \times 9 \times 7$ is equal to the product of 15 and what number?

(A) 10
(B) 14
(C) 35
(D) 42
(E) 63

5. If a dozen pencils cost $1.50, how much does 18 pencils cost?

(A) $1.50
(B) $1.80
(C) $2.25
(D) $3.00
(E) $3.60

6. There are 12 pens in each box, and three of them are red pens. If there are 156 pens in total, how many pens are red?

(A) 13
(B) 15
(C) 39
(D) 117
(E) 144

7. $12\frac{1}{4}\% =$

(A) 12.25
(B) 1.225
(C) 0.1225
(D) 0.1214
(E) 0.001225

8. How many squares are there in the diagram?

(A) 16
(B) 20
(C) 24
(D) 27
(E) 30

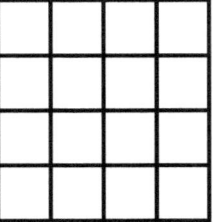

9. There are four kinds in a deck of 52 playing cards: heart, diamond, spade, and club. How many cards should you take to make sure you have at least two cards the same kind?

(A) 2
(B) 3
(C) 5
(D) 14
(E) 53

10. Which fractions below are ordered from the smallest to largest?

(A) $\frac{1}{2}, \frac{1}{3}, \frac{2}{3}, \frac{3}{2}$

(B) $\frac{3}{2}, \frac{2}{3}, \frac{1}{3}, \frac{1}{2}$

(C) $\frac{1}{2}, \frac{3}{2}, \frac{1}{3}, \frac{2}{3}$

(D) $\frac{1}{3}, \frac{1}{2}, \frac{2}{3}, \frac{3}{2}$

(E) $\frac{1}{3}, \frac{2}{3}, \frac{3}{2}, \frac{1}{2}$

11. Jackson wants to number his note book starting from 1. If there are 25 pages in his note book, how many digits will he write?

(A) 25
(B) 39
(C) 40
(D) 41
(E) 42

12. Which number comes next?

$$64, 55, 46, 37, \ldots$$

(A) 19
(B) 26
(C) 28
(D) 29
(E) 30

13. $54 \times 42 \times 23$ is closest to

(A) 40000
(B) 45000
(C) 50000
(D) 60000
(E) 70000

14. The temperature of a freezer was -8^0. Kylie opened the door and caused the temperature increase by 5^0. What temperature is the freezer now?

(A) -5^0
(B) -3^0
(C) 0^0
(D) 3^0
(E) 5^0

15. A quadrilateral has four equal sides and four equal angles. What kind of figure could it be?

(A) Triangle
(B) Square
(C) Rhombus
(D) right
(E) isosceles

16. All the following are equal EXCEPT:

(A) 0.3×0.4
(B) $10\% \times 12$
(C) $3 \times \frac{2}{5}$
(D) $2 - 0.8$
(E) $6 \div 5$

17. What is 8 ninths − 3 ninths?

(A) 5
(B) 5.9
(C) $\frac{5}{9}$
(D) 54
(E) none of above

18. Henry has 38 ¢ with 6 coins. How many nickels does he have?

(A) 0
(B) 1
(C) 2
(D) 3
(E) 4

19. Steven is three times as old as Jack. Steven will be twice as old as Jack six years

later. How old is Jack?

(A) 3 years old
(B) 5 years old
(C) 6 years old
(D) 12 years old
(E) 18 years old

20. If $a \times 6 = 54$, then what is $\frac{a}{3}$

(A) 3
(B) 6
(C) 9
(D) 18
(E) 27

Question 21 and 22 are based on the graph below.

Rides	Number of people
Drop Zone	12
Gladiator	7
Hell's gate	6
Revelation	15

21. Students were surveyed to find out their favorite rides on a play land. What percent of the students choose Drop Zone as their favorite ride?

(A) 3%
(B) 10%
(C) 12%
(D) 20%
(E) 30%

22. What is the range?

(A) 6
(B) 7
(C) 8
(D) 9
(E) 10

23. A big rabbit eats three carrots each time. A little rabbit eats two carrots each time. There are 8 more little rabbits than big rabbits. The number of carrots eaten by little rabbits is 2 more than big rabbits. How many little rabbits are there?

(A) 10 little rabbits
(B) 14 little rabbits
(C) 19 little rabbits
(D) 22 little rabbits
(E) 25 little rabbits

24. Given AB is perpendicular to BC, ∠DBC = 24^0, what is ∠ABD?

(A) 54^0
(B) 64^0
(C) 66^0
(D) 76^0
(E) 86^0

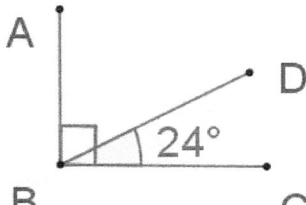

25. David was x years old last year. How old will he be next year?

(A) $x+2$
(B) $x+1$
(C) $x-2$
(D) $x-1$
(E) $2x$

26. If $15 + A = 32$, then what is A?

(A) 7
(B) 17
(C) 27
(D) 37
(E) 47

27. The area of the square ABCD is 36 cm². E is the midpoint of DC. What is the area of the triangle ABE?

(A) 6
(B) 12
(C) 18
(D) 24
(E) 36

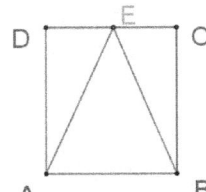

28. Aden has t stamps. Benjamin has three more stamps than Aden. Katelyn has twice as many stamps as Benjamin does. How many stamps does Katelyn have?

(A) $2t + 3$
(B) $2(t + 3)$
(C) $2(t - 3)$
(D) $2t - 3$
(E) $\frac{t-3}{2}$

29. If $x * y = x + 3y$, then what is $12 * 5$?

(A) 17
(B) 20
(C) 27
(D) 41
(E) 75

30. A fair die is rolled. Find the probability of getting a number greater than 1 and less than 4.

(A) $\frac{1}{6}$

(B) $\frac{1}{5}$

(C) $\frac{1}{4}$

(D) $\frac{1}{3}$

(E) $\frac{1}{2}$

Name _____ Date _____

Test 4

30 questions for 30 minutes

1. Which one of the following is one thousand thirty-five and nine tenth?

(A) 135.9
(B) 135.09
(C) 1035.9
(D) 1035.09
(E) 13509

2. If $5 + 10 + 15 + 20 + 25 = 5 \times \square$, then what number should be $\square$?

(A) 5
(B) 8
(C) 10
(D) 12
(E) 15

3. If $15 + 3 \times \square = 87$, then what is $\square$?

(A) 14
(B) 24
(C) 34
(D) 216
(E) 306

4. Which of the following is between $\frac{1}{5}$ and $\frac{2}{7}$?

(A) $\frac{1}{7}$

(B) $\frac{2}{5}$

(C) $\frac{9}{35}$

(D) $\frac{1}{2}$

(E) $\frac{2}{35}$

450

5. If the pattern continues, what is the 20th number?

$$5, 8, 11, 14, 17, \ldots$$

(A) 25
(B) 55
(C) 58
(D) 62
(E) 65

6. The following pie chart shows Sam's expense last month. If he spent $2400 last month, how much did he spend on transportation?

(A) 158
(B) 168
(C) 240
(D) 1580
(E) 16800

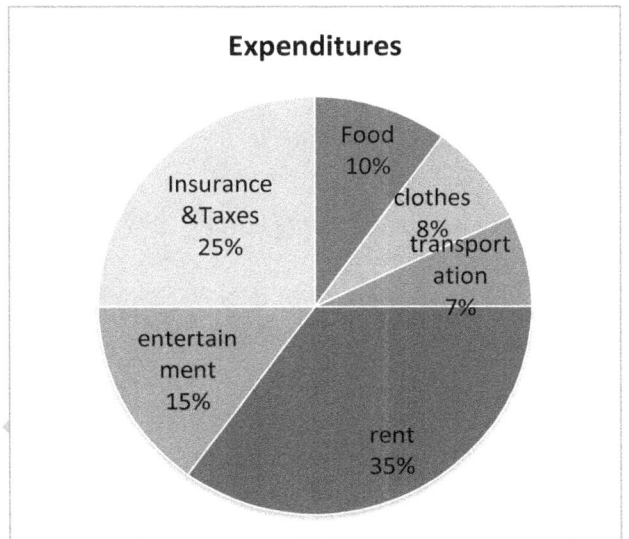

7. What time is it 135 minutes before 8:10?

(A) 5:55
(B) 6:05
(C) 6:15
(D) 6:45
(E) 6:85

8. Which of the following is the greatest?

(A) 2.05
(B) $2\frac{1}{5}$
(C) 25%
(D) $\frac{5}{2}$
(E) -2.5

9. Which one of the following figure CANNOT be drawn with one stroke without lifting your pencil from the page or going over any line twice?

(A)

(B)

(C)

(D)

(E)

10. How many line segments can be drawn between 9 different points?

(A) 8
(B) 9
(C) 25
(D) 36
(E) 45

11. Five friends met at a party. Each friend shook hands with each other. How many handshakes were there altogether?

(A) 4
(B) 5
(C) 7
(D) 8
(E) 10

12. There are 20 bicycles and tricycles. There are 45 wheels in total. How many bicycles are there?

(A) 5
(B) 8
(C) 10
(D) 12
(E) 15

13. Of the following, which results in an even number?

452

| | | | | Name | | Date | | |

I. $24 + 3$ II. $24 - 3$ III. 24×3 IV. $24 \div 3$

(A) I and II
(B) I and III
(C) II and III
(D) III and IV
(E) all the above

14. If each row and column contains the numbers from 1 to 5, what should be *k*?

(A) 1
(B) 2
(C) 3
(D) 4
(E) 5

				5
4		2		
		k	3	
	1			3
	2			

15. All the following are equal EXCEPT:

(A) $2 \div 5$
(B) $4\% \times 10$
(C) $1 - 0.6$
(D) $\frac{1}{10} + \frac{1}{5}$
(E) 2×0.2

16. 3 eighths + 2 eighths =

(A) 5
(B) 5.8
(C) 40
(D) $\frac{5}{8}$
(E) none of the above

17. I have equal number of nickels and dimes. The total value of the coins is $1.05. How many coins do I have?

(A) 7
(B) 9
(C) 10
(D) 12
(E) 14

18. Which is a multiple of 12 but not 15?

(A) 90
(B) 60
(C) 48
(D) 45
(E) 30

19. The temperature was 2^0 during the daytime. It dropped 6^0 at night. What was the temperature at night?

(A) 0^0
(B) -2^0
(C) -4^0
(D) -6^0
(E) -8^0

20. Jackson has 16 marbles and 27 stones. 12 of these items are red, the rest are blue. How many blue items does he have?

(A) 31
(B) 23
(C) 21
(D) 13
(E) 1

21. In the graph, given ∠BAE=62^0, find the value of *x*.

(A) 28^0
(B) 56^0
(C) 59^0
(D) 62^0
(E) 118^0

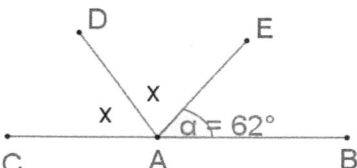

21. There were 24 people in a party. $\frac{2}{3}$ of the people were children. $\frac{1}{4}$ of the children were dancing on the floor. How many children were dancing on the floor?

(A) 2
(B) 4
(C) 5
(D) 6
(E) 8

22. Which net can be folded to the cube on the left?

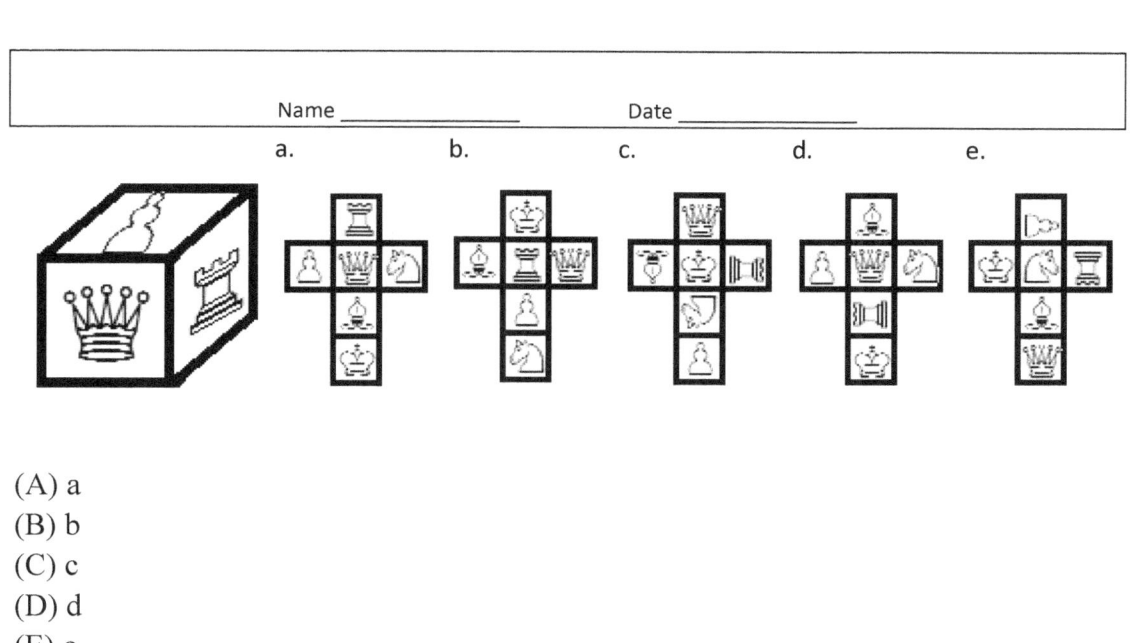

(A) a
(B) b
(C) c
(D) d
(E) e

24. A parking lot charges $2.50 for the first hour and $1.75 for each succeeding hour. If Selena parked her car for 3 hours, how much should she pay?

(A) $4.25
(B) $5.25
(C) $6.00
(D) $7.50
(E) $7.75

25. Four workers painted half of a building in five days. Since it would rain soon, they wanted to finish the job in two more days. How many friends should the workers call for help, if they do not want to bother more people than was necessary?

(A) 2
(B) 4
(C) 6
(D) 7
(E) 10

26. There are two distinct numbers. When they are divided by 5, both leave a remainder of 3. What is the possible difference of these two numbers?

(A) 15
(B) 24
(C) 28
(D) 42
(E) 44

27. Sam, Steven, Linda, Hanna, Candice, and Ann are divided into three groups of two. If the two boys cannot be in the same team, how many different teams can be formed?

(A) 3
(B) 6
(C) 12
(D) 18
(E) 24

28. If $31 - w = 12$, then what is w?

(A) 9
(B) 19
(C) 29
(D) 43
(E) 372

29. If $a \diamondsuit b = (2a - b) \div 3$, then what is $11 \diamondsuit 10$?

(A) 2
(B) 4
(C) $1\frac{1}{3}$
(D) 10
(E) 19

30. A number is selected randomly from 1 to 20. Find the probability of choosing a factor of 20.

(A) $\frac{1}{20}$

(B) $\frac{1}{10}$

(C) $\frac{1}{5}$

(D) $\frac{1}{4}$

(E) $\frac{3}{10}$

Test 5

30 questions for 30 minutes

1. If $2 \times 12 + 3 \times 12 = \Box \times 12$, then $\Box =$

   (A) 2
   (B) 3
   (C) 5
   (D) 6
   (E) 12

2. $3 \overline{)3\ 2\ 3\ 4} =$

   (A) $\frac{3}{3} + \frac{2}{3} + \frac{3}{3} + \frac{4}{3}$

   (B) $\frac{3000}{3} + \frac{200}{3} + \frac{30}{3} + \frac{4}{3}$

   (C) $\frac{3}{3000} + \frac{3}{200} + \frac{3}{30} + \frac{3}{4}$

   (D) $\frac{3}{3} + \frac{3}{2} + \frac{3}{3} + \frac{3}{4}$

   (E) none of above

3. $9 + 99 + 999 + 9999 =$

   (A) 10006
   (B) 10016
   (C) 11006
   (D) 11106
   (E) 11116

4. How many grams does each plum weigh?

   (A) 8 g
   (B) 10 g
   (C) 12 g
   (D) 40 g
   (E) 50 g

   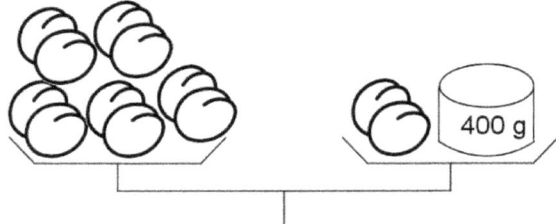

5. Which one of the following is the largest unit of measurement?

(A) meter
(B) millimeter
(C) kilometer
(D) centimeter
(E) decimeter

6. How many triangles are there in the figure?

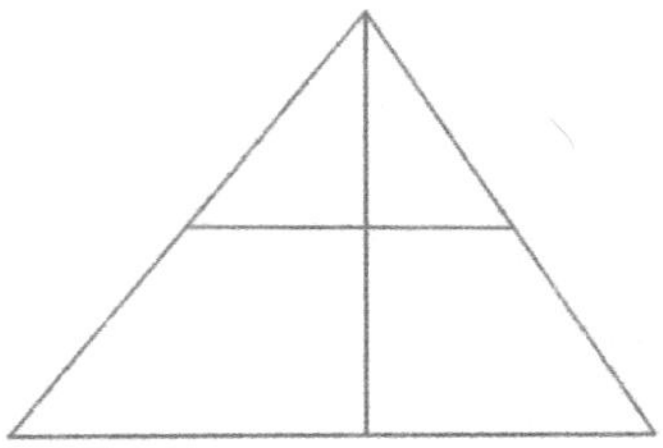

(A) 1
(B) 3
(C) 4
(D) 5
(E) 6

7. Which one of the following CANNOT be drawn with one stroke without lifting your pencil from the page or going over any line twice?

(A)

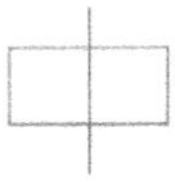

(B)

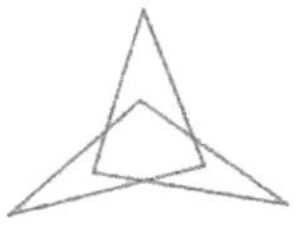

(C)

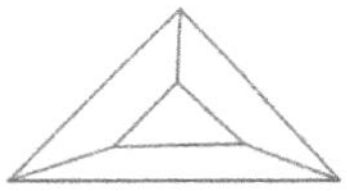

(D)

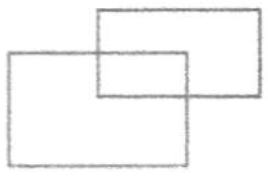

(E)

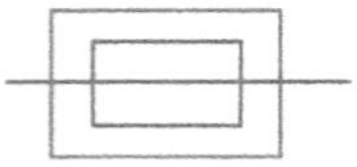

8. There are 5 people in a party. If everyone shakes hands with each other exactly once, how many handshakes will there be in total?

(A) 4
(B) 5
(C) 8
(D) 10
(E) 15

9. Victor collects baseball cards. He collects 5 cards for the first week, 10 cards for the second week, and 15 cards for the third week, and so on. If this pattern continues, how many cards will he collect for ten weeks in total?

(A) 50
(B) 100
(C) 250
(D) 275
(E) 500

10. What number comes next?

$$12, 29, 46, 63 \ldots$$

(A) 70
(B) 72
(C) 80
(D) 88
(E) 95

11. $12.5\ cm = $ _____m

(A) 0.125
(B) 1.25
(C) 125
(D) 1250
(E) 12500

12. If 52A is divisible by 6, what is the possible value of A?

(A) 4
(B) 6
(C) 7
(D) 8
(E) 9

13. 561×663 is closest to

(A) 42,000
(B) 300,000
(C) 330,000
(D) 360,000
(E) 420,000

14. At least how many people must be in the room to make sure two of them are born in the same month?

(A) 7
(B) 8
(C) 12
(D) 13
(E) 365

15. Which of the following is a prime number?

(A) 4
(B) 9
(C) 18
(D) 25
(E) 37

16. $\frac{1}{2} + \frac{1}{3} =$

(A) $\frac{1}{5}$

(B) $\frac{1}{6}$

(C) $\frac{2}{5}$

(D) $\frac{2}{6}$

(E) $\frac{5}{6}$

17. Which of the following represents parallel lines?

(A)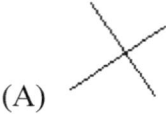

(B)

(C)

(D)

(E)

18. Danny's age this year is a multiple of 3. Next year, Danny's age will be a multiple of 5. He is below twenty years old. How old is Danny now?

(A) 3
(B) 5
(C) 9
(D) 15
(E) 19

19. I have twice as many dimes as nickels with a total of 75¢. How many coins do I have?

(A) 3
(B) 6
(C) 8
(D) 9
(E) 10

20. The area of the triangle is

(A) 20.5 cm²
(B) 24 cm²
(C) 39.36 cm²
(D) 41 cm²
(E) 48 cm²

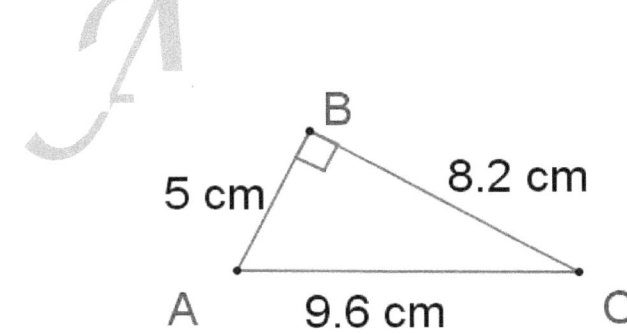

21. The sum of three consecutive numbers is 24. What is the middle number?

(A) 2
(B) 3
(C) 5
(D) 8
(E) 9

22. Isabella saved a total of $105 for 7 days. Every day she saved $3 more than the day before. How much did she save on the first day?

(A) 5
(B) 6
(C) 8
(D) 12

(E) 15

23. If $F \div 4 = 8$, what does $F \div 2$ equal?

(A) 2
(B) 4
(C) 8
(D) 16
(E) 32

24. Two rabbits eat 9 carrots in three days. How many carrots will three rabbits eat in four days?

(A) 12 carrots
(B) 15 carrots
(C) 18 carrots
(D) 20 carrots
(E) 24 carrots

25. An eraser costs 25¢ each and a ruler costs 32¢ each. Pauline bought 10 erasers and rulers with $2.99. How many erasers did she buy?

(A) 3
(B) 4
(C) 5
(D) 8
(E) 10

26. In 15 years, Jimmy will be four times as old as he is now. How old will he be three years later?

(A) 3
(B) 5
(C) 8
(D) 15
(E) 18

27. Claire spins the spinner once. What is the probability that she gets a prime number?

(A) $\frac{1}{8}$

(B) $\frac{1}{4}$

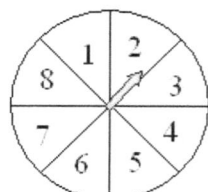

(C) $\frac{1}{2}$

(D) $\frac{5}{8}$

(E) $\frac{7}{8}$

28. I have 12 coins of nickels and dimes. The total value of dimes is 15 cents more than that of nickels. How many nickels do I have?

(A) 3 nickels
(B) 6 nickels
(C) 7 nickels
(D) 9 nickels
(E) 12 nickels

29. The perimeter of a rectangle is 28 cm. The area of the rectangle is 48 cm². What is the length of the rectangle?

(A) 5
(B) 8
(C) 12
(D) 14
(E) 24

30. Which of the following cubes can be made from the net below?

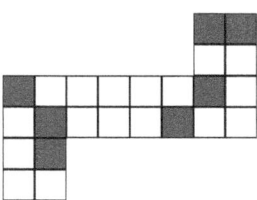

(A) (B) (C) (D) (E)

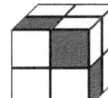 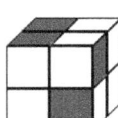 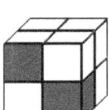  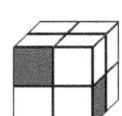

Name _____ Date _____

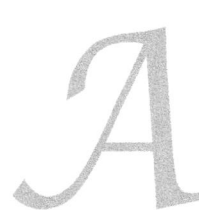

www.ingramcontent.com/pod-product-compliance
Lightning Source LLC
Chambersburg PA
CBHW080721300426
44114CB00019B/2451